COMPETITION AND COOPERATION IN JAPANESE LABOUR MARKETS

STUDIES IN THE MODERN JAPANESE ECONOMY

General Editors: Malcolm Falkus, *University of New England, Armidale, New South Wales, Australia*; and Kojiro Niino, *Kobe University, Japan*

An understanding of the modern Japanese economy remains both important and elusive. Its importance needs little stressing. Since the 1950s Japan's economy has grown at a rate unparalleled elsewhere and, despite predictions that such success could not last, the economy remains strong, dynamic and sustains full employment. Yet an understanding of the many unique features of Japan's economic and social life is essential if we are to appreciate the Japanese achievement, but on the other hand this very uniqueness makes communication difficult. Straightforward translations of Japanese works frequently mean little to Western readers because the underlying attitudes and assumptions are so unfamiliar.

This series has been planned in the belief that there is an urgent need for scholarly studies on the modern Japanese economy which are written by experts (both Japanese and Western) and aimed at Western readers. Accordingly, we have planned a series of books which will explore all the major areas of Japanese economic life. The books will present up-to-date material, and, where necessary, they will place Japan in its wider international context.

Published titles include:

Yujiro Hayami
JAPANESE AGRICULTURE UNDER SIEGE

Toru Iwami
JAPAN IN THE INTERNATIONAL FINANCIAL SYSTEM

Ryōshin Minami
THE ECONOMIC DEVELOPMENT OF JAPAN (2nd edn)

Ryōshin Minami. Kwan S. Kim, Fumio Makino and Joung-hae Seo (*editors*)
ACQUIRING, ADAPTING AND DEVELOPING TECHNOLOGIES

Carl Mosk
COMPETITION AND COOPERATION IN JAPANESE LABOUR MARKETS

Mitsuaki Okabe (*editor*)
THE STRUCTURE OF THE JAPANESE ECONOMY

Yoshitaka Suzuki
JAPANESE MANAGEMENT STRUCTURES, 1920–80

Competition and Cooperation in Japanese Labour Markets

Carl Mosk
Professor of Economics
University of Victoria
British Columbia, Canada

 First published in Great Britain 1995 by
MACMILLAN PRESS LTD
Houndmills, Basingstoke, Hampshire RG21 6XS
and London
Companies and representatives
throughout the world

A catalogue record for this book is available
from the British Library.

ISBN 0–333–63944–8

 First published in the United States of America 1995 by
ST. MARTIN'S PRESS, INC.,
Scholarly and Reference Division,
175 Fifth Avenue,
New York, N.Y. 10010

ISBN 0–312–12683–2

Library of Congress Cataloging-in-Publication Data
Mosk, Carl.
Competition and cooperation in Japanese labour markets / Carl
Mosk.
p.   cm. — (Studies in the modern Japanese economy)
Includes bibliographical references and index.
ISBN 0–312–12683–2
1. Labor market—Japan.   2. Industry and education—Japan.
3. Competition (Psychology)   I. Title.   II. Series.
HD5797.A6M67   1995
331.12'0952—dc20   95–4170
                                                          CIP

10   9   8   7   6   5   4   3   2   1
04   03   02   01   00   99   98   97   96   95

Printed in Great Britain by
The Ipswich Book Co Ltd
Ipswich, Suffolk

To Simon and Damon

Contents

List of Tables

List of Charts

Preface and Acknowledgements

The labour specialist trained in contemporary North American economics who becomes a serious student of the Japanese labour market is confronted with paradox. Trained in a discipline which is almost obsessively preoccupied with the forumalition of general theories centred around individualistic self-seeking behavior and efficiency, theories which are presumably applicable to all countries and all periods in human history, the specialist must grapple with a Japanese language literature which continually refers to 'Japanese' labour market practices, Japanese labour contracts, 'Japanese' work discipline, 'Japanese' skill formation and so forth. On the one hand, Japanese scholars continually stress how competitive their labour market and how wage and effort levels are the outcome of individual level optimizing behavior. And of course maximizing behavior of individuals channelled through trades in markets is the centrepiece of the efficiency-based economics taught in North America. On the other hand Japanese scholars refer to mutually felt altruistic attitudes held by both Japanese employers and employees which bind them together in a web of mutual cooperative dependency. And they refer to government regulations which constrain market outcomes. And they refer to the Japanese family system which shapes labour supply decision making. That serious thoughtful Japanese scholars feel there are special conditions in Japan must be taken seriously. But in so far as special Japanese constraints exist, do these generate conditions which run against the grain of generally accepted economic theory with its focus on self-seeking individualic behavior and efficiency in some fundamental way?

The essence of the present volume is an attempt by a Western scholar to pinpoint what he believes are the most salient special ('Japanese') features of the Japanese labour market, to explain how and why these features came into being, and to tie together the various features so highlighted into the simple general concept of integrated segmentation. In explaining how integrated segmentation operates I stress both market forces and extra market forces, for instance institutional constraints imposed by the government and by the family system. On the demand side I place special emphasis upon segmentation developed within the educational system and defined in terms of the credentials one secures immediately before entry into full-time employment. On the supply side I stress segmentation defined in terms of the nature of monitoring costs which, in my opinion, underlie labour contracts. I argue that three types of firms, sharply distinguished from one another by dint of the contracts they offer workers, are prominent in the modern Japanese labour market: small family-run firms, small commercially run firms, and large firms. Now using standard models Western economists have developed theories about, and have found evidence concerning the existence, of these types of segmentation in a myriad of countries. This being the case, what is peculiar to Japan? In my view what is peculiar to Japan is the way demand and supply segmentation overlap, and the way government institutions forge integration of market outcomes in these segmented markets, so that the difference in actual market outcomes between one submarket and another is relatively muted. Because it is segmented on both supply and demand sides the Japanese labour market is highly competitive; but because it is integrated, cooperation is deeply rooted within it as well. In short my emphasis in this volume is on segmentation which is integrated. It is this integrated segmentation which I believe distinguishes Japan's labour market from those in other modern industrial powers. And because the mechanisms of integration include variables which are typically excluded from most mainstream economic accounts, my account differs from accounts of labour markets offered by Western economists for Western economies.

Nevertheless the basic viewpoint developed here in this book is the creation of a Westerner schooled in Western social science. I recognize that many readers may feel that my background as a North American limits my ability to speak in an informed manner about things Japanese. That I have the confidence to present my views before the public is due to two circumstances. The first is my belief that an outsider sometimes has an awareness of the special nature of certain conditions, that is an awareness of how parochial certain things are, which a native lacks. And the second is the fact that I have benefited from the criticisms of many Japanese scholars who have been kind enought to comment on various facets of the present work at various stages of its completion. My greatest debt is to Professor Yoshi-fumi Nakata of Doshisha University in Kyoto with whom I have collaborated in the past. Over the last fifteen years, Professor Nakata and I have discussed issues concerning Japanese labour and I have always found his insights incisive and helpful to me in developing my own thinking. My second greatest debt is to Professor Yasukichi Yasuba, formerly of the Economics Department of Osaka University and presently associated with Osaka Gakuin University. Professor Yasuba was kind enough to read through several previous drafts of this book and to make detailed and cogent comments on those drafts. I am extremely grateful to him for his assistance in improving upon earlier versions of this work. Professor Kazuo Koike, now of Hosei University, and Horiyuki Fujimura now of Shiga Univesity, assisted me in my first field work project concerning Japanese labour (not reported on in this volume) and conversations with them helped me to better appreciate the nature of skill formation and skill acquisition in Japanese firms. Professor Koji Taira of the Economics Department at the University of Illinois, Urbana-Champaign, has encouraged me in the research effort reported on here and I have benefited greatly from his criticisms especially on Chapter 6. With Professor Yoko Sano of Keio University I discussed collective bargaining and the dynamics of the Spring Offensive and this of was immense help to me in the analysis undertaken in Chapter 6. Mr Tsuneharu Gonnami, head librarian of the Japanese collection at the University of British Columbia, was kind enough to read an early draft of the manuscript and offered helpful suggestions, especially regarding Chapter 4. In addition I have benefited from the suggestions of seminar participations at a number of Japanese universities and institutions. In particular during the spring of 1992 I presented earlier versions of most of the chapters which appear in this volume at various locales throughout Japan: at the Institute of Economic Research of Hitotsubashi University, at Osaka University, at Doshisha University, at the Japan Institute of Labour in Tokyo and at the Kansai Labour Seminar. I have no doubt that the criticisms I have received from these Japanese scholars have enriched my knowledge of the how the Japanese labour market operates and, I trust, have informed my conceptual thinking.

North American scholars have also offerred me useful comments and useful criticism. In particular Michael Reich, Lloyd Ulman, and Clair Brown of the Economics Department and the Institute of Industrial Relations of the University of California at Berkeley invited me to make a presentation on two chapters of an earlier version of this work at the Institute of Industrial Relations in Berkeley and I greatly benefitted from their remarks. And faculty members at the University of Victoria have, both on a one-to-one basis and in seminar, helped me refine my ideas and the presentation of my evidence. In particular Professors Malcolm Rutherford, Kenneth Avio and Donald Ferguson of the Economics Department and Joe Moore of the Department of Pacific and Asian Studies have been of help to me. Of course I, and I alone, bear full responsibility for any remaining errors of interpretation or of theorical analysis.

The preparation of a manuscript, especially one which contains as many tables as this volume does, is an arduous and unpleasant task. I wish here to acknowledge the invaluable assistance of the secretarial staff of the

Economics Department at the University of Victoria. At one time or another Michelle Armstrong, Pattie Eccleston, and Lynn Pattison all typed tables for this volume and I wish to thank them here for their effort on my behalf.

Finally, on a personal note, I wish to express my love and affection for Kumiko, who has shared my joys and frustrations during the period when I was writing this volume. Without Kumiko I doubt I could have completed this work. And I also wish to record my thanks to Stacey Boal of the Victoria Symphony Orchestra for encouraging me in my study of the recorder. Daily recorder practice sustained me and gave balance to my life, especially during periods when the research and writing flagged. Finally I wish to express my thanks to my sons, Simon and Damon, who encouraged me to invest in the computers upon which most of the research for this volume was completed and upon which the final version of the manuscript was typed. *Competition and Cooperation* is dedicated to them.

CARL MOSK

Part I

Origins

1 The Approach

1.1 INTEGRATED SEGMENTATION

The postwar Japanese labour market is simultaneously deeply segmented and deeply integrated. Grasping this seemingly paradoxical fact is basic to a proper understanding of how the Japanese labour market operates. Sharp differentiation of the labour market on both the supply and demand sides is an especially salient feature of the Japanese economy. Why Japanese labour is productive and efficiently allocated is intimately linked to how the aggregate supply for labour decomposes into an inactive market of persons staying with their employers and an active labour market supply pool of persons looking for employment which is segmented according to whether or not the job seekers are on the verge of becoming fresh school graduates and, if they are, what submarket of the educational system they are in and what type of signal about effort capacity, expected costs of being trained, and time horizons is conveying by being in that particular submarket of the educational system. But equally crucial to productivity of workers and the efficiency of the market in allocating labour resources is how, on the demand side, the aggregate demand for labour decomposes into submarkets differentiated by the types of contracts employers offer already employed workers and prospective hires, contracts which affect the degree of effort supply and the degree of training workers undergo once hired, and contracts which affect the incidence of job turnover and the steepness or flatness of age-wage profiles. In short sharp labour market segmentation is characteristic of Japan. But equally characteristic is integration. In part integration of sub markets is achieved through the mobility of workers which, although constrained by barriers built into the some of the contracts offered workers, works to equalize earnings across submarkets. In part integration of submarkets is achieved by contract arrangements which link companies offering different labour market contracts together on the production side, allowing inter-firm cooperation to blunt inter-firm competition. In part integration within firms is achieved through the linking of cooperative behaviour to internal competition for ranking, in part it is achieved through the system of collective bargaining, and in part again it has been achieved by a host of governmental regulations and institutions ranging from price setting in the rice market to the centralization of curriculum in the compulsory educational system. As a result of the collective force of these various forms of integration, the wages and amenities enjoyed by workers in the various submarkets of the labour market are far less differentiated than they might otherwise be. The Japanese labour market is sharply segmented in terms of the contracts which govern effort training. But by dint of the force of integration, the relative rewards associated with segmentation are not nearly so sharply differentiated.

In the course of this study of the postwar Japanese labour market I hope to achieve three methodological goals. These goals are to describe, to explain in theoretical terms, and to explain in historical terms. First I intend to describe how integrated segmentation works in Japan, both in qualitative and quantitative terms. Many of the statistics which I present throughout the course of this volume fall into this category of analytical description. Second I develop a theoretical framework for explaining how and why segmentation and integration occur in postwar Japan. This involves the elaboration of simple stylized models for labour contracts in the various submarkets on the demand side and for advancement in the school system on the supply side. These arguments are designed to show how constrained rational decision determines market-oriented behaviour of students, workers and employers. But what are, and what determines, the constraints? The constraints involved include legal, government regulatory, and social institutions. For this reason my theoretical argument is not simply restricted to the analysis of rational economic actors maximizing objectives subject to constraints but ranges over a discussion of the constraints themselves. Without an understanding of the constraints I, for one, doubt that one can give a satisfactory general explanation of how and why the Japanese labour market operates as it does. Demonstrating that optimizing behaviour occurs within the context of a set of constraints, that is demonstrating that behaviour has efficiency properties, is not equivalent to demonstrating that the behaviour is 'meta-efficient' in the sense that the outcomes resulting from optimization under the constraints are more efficient than outcomes under other constraints.[1] Constraints vary across regions and countries for historical reasons which can not be explained in terms of efficiency or rationality. For this reason a third goal of mine in this study is to demonstrate how and why the constraints came into being and how the constraints interact with actual market outcomes and market forces. This third task involves history. And the fact that there is a historical dimension to this study explains why the account offered here covers a long time horizon, ranging over the period from the close of World War I to the late 1980s. Hence, by the very nature of the goals set for the study, the resulting work is interdisciplinary, combining history, statistical analysis, and theory.

In achieving these goals I intend to offer explanations for a variety of questions which frequently crop up in academic and or popular accounts about the postwar Japanese labour market:

1. Why do large firms tend to restrict their hiring to fresh school graduates and, within the category of fresh school graduates, to those who graduate from certain schools? Why do small firms behave differently?

2. When filling a higher-level managerial or supervisory post, why are large firms (but not small firms) reluctant to hire at the mid-career level, preferring to promote internally?

3. Why do both large and small companies use a broad range of criteria in evaluating workers (e.g. assessing potential leadership capacity, general knowledge of the industry and the firm's position within it, willingness to work overtime, as well as productivity) instead of restricting their evaluation to a narrow range of criteria defined in occupational or professional terms?

4. Why is labour turnover far higher in small firms than in large firms and why, when separations take place, are they fairly evenly spread over age and seniority classes in the case of small firms, but heavily concentrated among young, low-seniority workers and older, high-seniority workers in the case of large firms?

5. Why has the differential in age-standardized wages between large and small firms persisted for so long, under many different aggregate labour market supply–demand balance situations, that is in both tight and loose labour markets?

6. Why are age-wage profiles steeper in large firms than they are in small firms? With the ageing of the population and the slowing down in aggregate growth, why have profiles flattened so dramatically, especially in large companies?

7. Why does unionization tend to restricted to large firms? Why has overall unionization been on the decline over the last several decades?

8. Why is the typical collective bargaining agreement settled in terms of the firm's total wage bill rather than in terms of specific wages for specific occupations?

9. Why is measured unemployment so low? Why do hours worked adjust with a far higher elasticity to fluctuations in aggregate demand than does the number of employed workers?

I trust the reader will become aware of some of my answers to these questions at the outset of this volume, in particular in the remaining two sections of this chapter where I develop the basic elements of my formal model and discuss the issue of constraints at a general level. However some of my answers will not be developed – or at least will not be developed in detail – at the beginning of the study but rather appear in the later chapters which cover specific topics. For instance the first question is addressed in Chapter 4, which deals with education and the market for fresh hires; the second, third, fourth, fifth and sixth questions are addressed in Chapter 5, which deals with wage profiles, job retention and dualism; and questions seven and eight are addressed in Chapter 6, which deals with unions and collective bargaining. Finally material in Chapters 5 and 6 addresses question nine.

In the next section of this chapter I present the basic elements of my stylized models of optimizing behaviour in the three submarkets of the labour market as seen from the demand side which I focus on: in small family-managed firms; in small commercially managed firms; and in large firms. The nature of the labour contract and the nature of recruitment of fresh hires varies across the firm types, as do the economic determinants of effort and training. Then in the third section I discuss how political and social constraints and the structure of aggregate demand help shape the relative shares of each submarket on the demand side of the aggregate labour market. This discussion is cast at a general level. Details concerning particular institutional constraints are presented later on in the book. And the historical forces shaping these constraints are discussed in the second chapter of the first part of this study, which focuses on the interwar period.

1.2   THE ELEMENTS OF THE FORMAL MODEL

In this section I lay out the basic stylized features of segmentation on both the supply and demand sides. On the supply side I discuss market signalling through educational certification. On the demand side I discuss contracting and optimizing behaviour subject to contracting terms for three types of firms: family-run small firms (whose entire staff of workers is made up of family members); commercially run small firms (which operate with hired labour), and large firms. Then I turn to the relationship between the aggregate supply/demand equilibrium for the entire labour market and the demand structure of aggregate output. Finally I turn to the issue of the relationship between stylized theory and concrete Japanese reality. Stylization requires extreme simplification. To some readers the costs of simplification may loom large. But the advantages secured through stylization are considerable. Stylization permits succinct discussion of theoretical concepts which correspond only imperfectly to real world analogues. For the reader uninterested in a mathematical formulation of the model, the presentation in this section should suffice. For those readers interested in the precision which one secures through mathematics, the discussion in the appendix to this chapter should prove helpful. In any event the purpose of the remainder of this chapter and the associated appendix is to provide the reader with a basic knowledge of the main theoretical concepts which occupy our attention here and their relationship to the empirical phenomena which I discuss in the remaining chapters of this volume.

The basic premise underlying this study is that both labour supply and labour demand are segmented, each breaking down into submarkets; that there is a close relationship between supply and demand segmentation; and that on the demand side the distinct submarkets differ from one another in terms of the labour market contracts accorded to employees. Because contracts vary from subsector to subsector, so do the level and type of training a worker receives; so do the incentives to give effort; and so does the relationship between internal and external market forces in determining wages and/or per worker income and productivity. In particular in small family run enterprises and large firms wages and/or incomes per worker are at least partially determined by internal firm forces, and therefore may differ from wages set on the market by the forces of supply and demand for new hires. By contrast, in small commercially operated firms the levels of worker productivity and earnings are strictly determined by external market conditions. In the model of the family run small firm the per worker unit effort level and marginal productivity is determined by a weighing of benefits to consumers against disutility of work for workers for the incremental hour of work. In the case of the large firm, effort and productivity are determined by market forces in the case of new hires, and for senior workers by either efficiency wage or insider–outsider rent-sharing arrangements, efficiency wage payments accorded to promoted workers, and insider-outsider rent sharing accorded to non-promoted workers.[2] Before I enter into a technical discussion of the various contracts and the optimizing behaviour associated with them it is useful to schematically contrast the three types: As the reader can see from the preceding discussion, firms offer quite different contracts depending on their type, and the behavioral outcomes associated with the different contract types also differ markedly from type to type. Now let us turn to a more detailed discussion of the contracts and associated behaviour.

Firm type	Contract features	Outcomes determined by Optimizing behaviour
Family managed small firm	(1) No firing – only family members employed. (2) Internal training; some skills transferable across firms. (3) Monitoring costless but not a factor in determining effort.	(1) Effort levels (as measured by hours worked by work unit). (2) Supply price of labour to other firms.
Commercially run small firms	(1) Firing is costless and regularly occurs. (2) Training is limited and is only in skills transferable across employers. (3) Monitoring costless and important in determining effort levels because of threat of firing.	(1) Workers pay for their own training with reduced wages. (2) Employers fire workers whose expected productivity falls below market determined reservation wage.
Large firms	(1) Firing is costly due to morale problems (social sense of fairness) and firm specific skills possessed by workers. (2) Training is extensive and some of the skills acquired are non-transferable. (3) Monitoring important for ranking employees and expensive, hence imperfect. (4) The firm promotes some of its junior workers on the basis of effort and productivity and pays promoted workers by efficiency wage principles; non-promoted workers are paid part of the rent accruing to workers and the firm from firing costs.	(1) Promotion rates, quit rates and firing rates. (2) Effort levels for promoted workers. (3) Age-wage and seniority-wage profiles.

1.2.1 Some Initial Considerations at the Aggregate Supply and Demand Level

Although my principal interest in this section is on developing theory applicable to submarkets of the labour market, it is necessary to first consider the initial clearing of the active labour for new hires. On the demand side I assume there are two types of firms considering hiring in the market: commercially run small businesses and large firms. By assumption, family run businesses rely only on family members and hence are not active in the market for hired workers. On the supply side I assume there are three types of individuals seeking employment: persons with previous work experience (the experienced); fresh school graduates with relatively good school performance records (high achievers); and fresh school graduates with relatively poor school performance records (low achievers). Note that the labour market breaks down into submarkets defined differently on the supply and demand side.

Educational achievement for fresh graduates sends a signal to prospective hiring agents: (a) on the basis of previous hiring experience firms know that the mean and variance in effort capacity; and (b) the speed with which a worker can be trained; and (c) the intrinsic rate of time discount (the individual rate of time preference) varies depending on which subgroup of the fresh graduate labour force one draws from. Specifically by comparing the high-achiever fresh graduate population to the low-achiever fresh graduate population firms can tell, without additional screening, that the mean for effort capacity is higher, the mean for training time lower, and the rate of time discount smaller for high than for low achievers. For the general labour market of experienced workers I assume that the firm must engage in screening if it wishes to secure information about the submarket of the general employee market (for instance some of the persons in this submarket are former high achievers who were not promoted in large firms (see below), some were fired from small firms, some come from family-run businesses, etc.).

In what follows I assume that the large firm cannot fire workers at zero cost but small firms can. Or in terms of the stylization adopted here the large firm offers a contract with a high probability of being (but not 100 per cent chance of being) a two-period contract to fresh hires which involves extensive training in the first period, while the small commercial firm offers a one-period contract with some probability of renewal of the contract in the second period without training. For this reason large firms are more risk-adverse than small firms about hiring workers who fail to supply effort and/or are slow to be trained and/or are likely to quit at the end of the first period. Hence large firms are willing to pay a premium to hire high-achiever fresh graduates, but the magnitude of this premium depends upon the balance of supply and demand in the markets for fresh graduates. For instance if in the submarket for high-achievers demand by large firms is in excess of supply and in the submarket for low achievers the reverse is the case, we would expect the premium paid to high achievers to be large. In any case because of the overlap between school achievement and the firm one is hired into, the wage premium for high achievement in the school system is close to the wage differential for reservation wages paid to fresh hires in large firms (called w_e) and small firms (called w_r). For general workers I assume that large firms will not hire from this pool but that small firms will, and that the small firms pay them the reservation wage w_r for inexperienced fresh school graduates and screen them as they monitor the behaviour of the workers in the first period.

With these preliminaries established let us turn to the different contracts and hence different relationships between effort and productivity and rewards offered by the three types of firms: family run small businesses, commercially operated small businesses, and large firms. Let us first consider family run small business.

1.2.2   Family-Operated Small Business

I assume that the family run small business does not 'fire' its members and that all separations take the form of voluntary quits. For simplicity of exposition I work with a two-period model, supposing the family run small firm offers employment to family members and only to family members for two periods over all states of nature. In explaining how effort is determined in this submarket of the labour market and how it is rewarded, I carry out the analysis with a framework in which effort is captured by the number of hours worked per worker unit $h = H/W$, where W stands for the number of worker units (where, for instance, a single worker unit represents the effort capacity of a prime-age male worker. In prewar Japanese agriculture a prime-age female was reckoned to be 0.8; a teenage boy 0.8; a teenage girl 0.6; and so forth); and the rewards of production are allocated to individuals in accordance with their consumption needs. Then we can write output per consumption unit q as $q = Q/C$, where Q is total family income (output at market prices net of intermediary costs, that is total market value added accruing to the household), and C stands for total household consumer units (for instance a prime-age male is one; a small child 0.2, etc). Furthermore, as is shown in Section A of the appendix, per-worker work effort in the household, as measured by the number of hours worked per worker, depends on the ratio of workers to consumers in the household and on the ratio of two psychological variables, namely the unpleasantness of an incremental unit of work to workers (which rises as the number of hours increases) and the satisfaction secured to consumers from the incremental consumption of an incremental unit of output (which declines as consumption per consumer unit increases). In short, in reaching a decision about the intensity of work effort imposed on workers, the household compares the benefits of extra work in the form of extra consumption for consumers with the costs associated with securing the extra consumption in terms of work effort; and in so doing it takes into account its own internal demographic structure, that is the number of mouths which must be fed and the number of able hands available to work. The 'optimal' level of welfare for the household is reached at the balance point at which extra costs and extra benefits are just equated: at the 'optimal' point the marginal product of an hour's worth of work for the household as a whole is equated with the ratio of disutility from incremental work to workers to incremental satisfaction from consumption to consumers. The household reaches a decision on work intensity through a consideration of its own internal capacity for work and its own internal demands for consumption. The relationship between the marginal product of labour determined within family run businesses like farms, which is set in terms of the family's demographic conditions, and the wage set in the 'spot' market for fresh hires in businesses, which mainly rely upon employees, is complex and is discussed at some length in Chapter 2.

1.2.3 Commercially Operated Small Business

I assume that since the owner/manager of a small business can typically observe his small labour force on a daily basis (monitoring), and since the smallness of the operation affords her or him a reasonably accurate idea of what each worker's separate contribution to firm value added is (assignment of productivity contribution), the owner/manager can accurately and evaluate effort and productivity for each worker at zero cost during the period of the contract. In a society in which individualism and the concept of individual rights are strongly entrenched this assumption is not necessarily valid. But it does seem to be a reasonable assumption for Japan, given the difficulty individuals face if they vigorously resist the intrusion of their fellow workers, friends, and family members in their private activities

The contract the commercially operated small business offers is as follows: the newly hired worker is guaranteed employment in the first period during which the worker works but no training occurs. During this period the owner/manager evaluates the worker according to both effort and productivity, realizing that a worker may be less productive than he or she might otherwise be because of the job into which he or she is placed. Thereby the manager takes into account the fact that the correlation between an employee's effort and marginal revenue productivity is less than unity. On the basis of the expected productivity which the owner/manager infers for each of his or her workers, he or she decides whether to retain the worker for a second period or not. Assuming that the decision is made on economic grounds and economic grounds alone, the logic of securing a positive (or at least not a negative) profit from each employee retained suggests that the owner/manager retains only those workers whose expected contribution to firm output exceeds the costs associated with securing the workers' services, namely wages determined in the market. In sum, the assumption is being made that owner/manager is constantly 'shopping around' for workers and has no particular vested economic interest in retaining workers from one period to the next. This is what is commonly meant by the term 'spot' market. In the appendix I provide a formal discussion of the 'spot' market for hires in commercially operated small business and I also consider the case where the firm trains workers.

1.2.4   Large Firm

Unlike the commercially run small business, the large firm (1) extensively trains its newly hired workers, thereby considerably enhancing the cluster of skills over which the worker has command, some of which are not readily transferable from the firm at which the worker is presently employed to any other firm; and (2) due to its scale of operation and the complexity of many of the tasks which its employees perform, it can not monitor at zero cost its workers and cannot perfectly evaluate the separate contribution which each employee makes to firm output. Because of the extensive firm specific training embodied in the worker and because a firm's reputation among both its incumbent labour force and among the labour pool it expects to hire from is degraded when the firm fires workers who are in fact productive and hard working, the costs of firing workers are substantial. For this reason the firm resists firing workers and only fires those whose expected productivity during the second period falls below the expected wage the firm expects to pay the worker during the second period minus expected firing costs. There is an implicit acknowledgement when a worker is hired into a large firm that the cost incurred by the firm of firing a worker during either the first or second period is high. Were these firing costs low, as they are for a small company, workers would be reluctant to be trained in firm-specific skills which are not easily transferred to other employers in the absence of some (rather complicated) contingent contracts governing the sharing of costs for the training. In short, in the case of large enterprises, high firing costs are built into the firm's training and recruitment strategy.

In the appendix it is shown in detail how the large firm operates in terms of the training and incentives it gives workers, and how quit and firing rates are determined. For our purposes here the following points suffice. During the first period the firm trains and imperfectly monitors workers, thereby arriving at a judgement about whom to promote to managerial status, whom to retain but not to promote, and whom to fire. Some disgruntled workers quit at this point. During the second period those promoted to managerial posts monitor the new hires and those who are not promoted but who are retained. Since managers can not be effectively monitored, and since keeping their judgement about subordinates honest is important to the firm, managers are paid according to efficiency wage principles, that is they are paid premium wages which induce honesty and hard work. Since the firm does not wish to lose money on these workers it sets a premium wage for managers which minimizes the unit cost of getting effort from this pool of promoted workers. And then, based on this wage and the expected productivity of managers in the second period, it promotes the optimal number of most highly ranked workers from its first-period internal labour supply pool. The 'optimal' number is formally determined by equating expected marginal revenue productivity with the efficiency wage which is paid to promoted workers. For workers who stay with the firm and who are not ranked highly enough to be promoted, wage determination involves rent sharing, the rents arising from the high cost of terminating workers, and is determined through a process of collective bargaining. In Chapter 6 the nature of the collective bargaining process is discussed at considerable length.

It should be noted that the firm undermines its reputation as a 'fair' employer if it goes outside of its internal ranks in securing managers, for instance if it hires mid-career workers from other large enterprises. For in this case it has effectively reneged on its implicit contract to promote as many entrant workers as it possibly can. And for this reason in the model promoted workers do not quit, since they do not expect to be hired at premium wages in another large firm.

1.2.4   Aggregate Labour Market Supply and Demand Outcomes

Using the arguments developed here in combination with some general observations about the Japanese economy, it is possible to derive some useful implications concerning the aggregate Japanese labour market. The first point is that the structure of demand is a major determinant of the distribution of firms according to size. For instance because the agricultural sector centred around the small family managed farm has been heavily protected throughout the period 1955–90 the number of family workers has been quite large. When income per capita was relatively low (as it was during the 1950s and early 1960s), the structure of demand was heavily weighted toward consumption of necessities like foodstuffs, in turn bolstering the economic basis for family run small businesses. As income per capita rose there was an associated drop in the relative importance of family employment in the overall labour market. The second point is that because of the job security commitment extended to prospective hires, many large firms are reluctant to expand production solely on an internal basis. They are likely to use a combination of subcontracting and securing of intermediate products from internal sources. The technology of production plays a role here, since this mix depends in part on the existence of indivisible factors of production and/or scale economies in the production process. For instance in vehicle assembly subcontracting is extensive, but it is much less common in petroleum refining or chemicals. In any case because subcontracting is fairly common in many industries, commercially operated small firms abound. Moreover restrictions on the size of department stores and other retailers have encouraged the flourishing of small commercially and family run small firms in retail. As a result the Japanese labour market is highly diverse in terms of the nature of labour contracts under which employees work. And in turn its aggregate level behaviour depends upon the distribution of employment in the various sub-markets.

For instance during a downturn in demand the greater is the proportion of workers employed in family run businesses and large firms, the less does employment suffer. By the same token hours worked (and effort) are likely to fluctuate with changes in the capacity utilization rate the more is employment concentrated in large firms and family run small businesses where effort levels are endogenous. That Japanese employment fluctuate relatively little but hours worked fluctuates a great deal is testimony to the concentration of employment in family run small business and large firms. Similar reasoning explains why measured unemployment is low in Japan.

The models also help us to understand why, within the private economy, unionization is almost exclusively limited to large companies. It is mainly in such companies that substantive bargaining between employers and employees over the distribution of rents can occur. The incentive for unionization to workers in small companies (and especially in family run businesses) is far less than it is in large businesses, mainly because of the contracts under which these workers are employed.

1.2.6 Reality and the Model

However useful models are to the clarification of reasoning, this writer is reluctant to base analysis solely on an abstract stylization, which does not exactly correspond to what he understands is the reality of Japanese labour contracting and labour–management relations. In particular I would like to close out this section by discussing a few of the points where I think the divergence between reality and the models are especially important.

First, private-sector commercial firms range from the very large with 5,000 employees or more down to the very small (5 employees or less). Most official Japanese publications classify firms in three not two categories: large (1,000 employees or more); medium-sized (100–999 employees); and small (0–99 employees). Many medium sized firms behave like large firms, but many do not. To develop a separate model for the medium sized firm seems fairly pointless to me, but as a matter of empirical reality the medium sized firm with a labour contract which is often intermediate between the small and the large firm is an important and distinctive organization. Moreover bankruptcy rates among small firms are relatively high in Japan, which is one reason workers do not assume they can be employed for more than one period.

Second, implicit labour contracts in large firms and some medium sized firms involve many periods, not just two. For instance collective bargaining usually occurs on an annual basis, and a typical male entrant into a large company enters in his or her early twenties and retires under compulsory retirement rules around the age of sixty. In effect one has nearly forty periods rather than two. The typical promotion in reality is very slow and occurs over many periods. A gradual weeding out takes place as one moves higher and higher up the managerial hierarchy. The model oversimplifies the process, although I believe it captures some of its most essential features.

Third, in large firms some workers are employed on a part-time basis, either as true part-time workers (*paato*) or as temporary workers who work fulltime but on a short-term terminal contract. Many of these workers have previous employment experience elsewhere and some are promoted up into the ranks of 'regular' (*jōyōrōdōsha*) ranks after their contracts expire. This can be conceptualized as a screening process for fresh hires who are not fresh school graduates, although in reality firms employ this strategy of hiring when they are expanding production and are unsure as to whether the expansion will prove transitory or permanent.

Fourth, the distinction between firing and quitting is much more difficult to make in reality than in theory. For instance many Japanese firms force their workers to quit by transferring them to remote locales, by assigning them to especially onerous and unpleasant jobs, by selecting them for early retirement, or by transferring them to subsidiaries or subcontractors or even to firms in other industries with which the employer has a contractual labour transfer arrangement. These issues are taken up in Chapter 5.

Fifth, many workers in the Japanese labour market work at several jobs and so it is unclear into which category they should be placed. For instance it was and is not uncommon for farmers to work during the week at a factory job and during the weekends on their farms. This fluidity between sectors helps to explain why unemployment is low even as structural change occurs and/or the capacity utilization rate fluctuates.

Sixth, the labour market is not only segmented by educational status but also by sex. Because of social norms there is a prevalent assumption in Japan that time horizons for males and females differ. Even in the case of large firms the assumption is that female employees will only work a few years until they get married. Thus the 'large-firm' contract does not apply to most women who are employed in large Japanese enterprises. This issue is discussed in Chapters 2, 4, and 5 in considerable detail.

Seventh, I have excluded the public sector and the bureaucracy from the formal model of sub-sectoral behaviour. In fact workers in the public sector constitute an important and distinct submarket of the Japanese labour market. I discuss it in Chapter 6.

Finally, Japanese unions do have some voice in the way managerial evaluations are used in the company and the way firing (and/or forced transfers, etc) are handled. The assumption of complete managerial discretion is not completely realistic.

Despite these stated reservations, however, I feel the stylization is appropriate for focusing the analysis which ensues. However, when I apply the logic of the model in the subsequent chapters of this volume, I will tailor the discussion to take into account the divergence between the stylized assumptions of the model and the actual institutional details governing labour contracts.

1.3 INSTITUTIONAL CONSIDERATIONS

One of the most interesting aspects of segmentation in postwar Japan is that it is strongly integrated. In particular the gap in earnings between promoted workers in large companies and workers in small firms is quite modest. There are a number of reasons for this integration, but one of the most important is the impact of political and regulatory constraints on market outcomes. For instance setting the price of rice at a level high enough to generate manufacturing workers' wage levels for farmers' labour input in farming was a major factor reducing earnings differentials between family run firms and small commercially operating firms. The dynamics of collective bargaining in Japan are shaped to some degree by governmental public bargaining with its public-sector unions. Governmental regulations concerning overtime work payments and work environment play a role in determining the total wage package associated with a worker, especially in large companies (many regulations do not apply to small companies).

But the institutional considerations considered important in this study are not limited to government policy constraints, important as these constraints are. For instance the institutions of the family system are important in shaping labour supply, training of family members in family run firms, and the rate of time discount for females. And social concepts of fairness are important in determining the distribution of wages between promoted and non-promoted workers in large firms. In short there are a host of social and political institutions which help shape the actual market outcomes of integrated segmentation in Japan.

In the next chapter I consider the origins of these postwar institutions during the interwar period. Then in the second part of this volume I take up particular topics concerning the operation of integrated segmentation in postwar Japan. Chapter 4 focuses on the educational system and supply-side segmentation; Chapter 5 deals with dualism and age-wage profiles; and Chapter 6 concentrates on collective bargaining. In each of these chapters attention is devoted to the institutional constraints; to the behavioral outcomes associated with optimizing behaviour subject to these constraints; and to the interaction of the specific institutional rules governing the constraints with market outcomes. In short I consider integrated segmentation in Japan to be a system in which constraints are important in determining the outcomes flowing from rational behaviour, and, over the long run, as market outcomes change so do the precise forms taken by the institutional constraints.

APPENDIX: MATHEMATICAL PRESENTATION OF THE FORMAL MODEL

In what follows I use the notation developed in Section 1.2 of the text as well as additional notation which is defined below.

A.   Family-Operated Small Business

Let $U(q)$ stand for utility of a consumer unit as a function of q, and $V(h)$ for the disutility of a worker unit as function of h (with both first and second derivatives positive). Thus total household welfare $WE(h)$ as a function of hours worked is:

$$WE(h) = C{\cdot}U(q) - W{\cdot}V(h). \tag{1.1}$$

If the household is to maximize welfare by selecting the optimal level of effort per worker unit it selects h^* such that at h^*:

$$dWE(h)/dh = C\,[(dU/dq)(dq/dh)] - W(dV/dh) = 0, \tag{1.2}$$

or

$$dq/dh = (W/C)\,[(dV/dh)/(dU/dq)]. \tag{1.3}$$

Effort $e(h^*)$ is endogenously determined in this model and it depends on the demographic composition of the household: on the basis of household level decision making, workers give effort up to the point at which the worker-to-consumer ratio times the ratio of incremental work unpleasantness to incremental utility (the cost in disutility terms of an incremental amount of output to the household consumer) is equated to the marginal payoff in consumption per consumer for the extra hours worked. Let $x = (dV/dh)/(dU/dq)$, which, on the margin, is the real cost of labour to the household. Then note that

$$dq/dh = (W/C)\,x \qquad \text{or} \qquad x = dQ/dH. \tag{1.4}$$

Effort is endogenously determined in this model by the balance between the disutility of work and the utility of consumption adjusted for the ratio of consumers to workers in the household.

B.   Commercially Operated Small Business

According to the discussion in Section 1.2, the contract which the commercially operated small business offers is as follows: the freshly hired worker is guaranteed employment in the first period, during which the worker works but no training occurs. During this period the owner/manager evaluates the worker according to both effort and productivity, realizing that a worker may be less productive than he or she might otherwise be because of the job into which he or she is placed and hence the fact that the correlation between effort and marginal-revenue productivity is less than unity. Combining the information about the individual i's effort e_i and contribution to firm product q_i the owner/manager predicts the expected productivity of the worker $e(q)_i$ for the next period. For instance with equal weighting the expected productivity $e(q)_i$ is

$$e(q)_i = (1/2)e_i + (1/2)q_i. \tag{1.5}$$

Then the firm commits itself to offering the worker a contract during the second period if and only if

$$e(q)_i \geq w_r. \tag{1.6}$$

It is possible to introduce training into this model. For instance if we assume all training is of a general nature (for instance the training is a substitute for training which could be secured at private expense through a course in a vocational school) and hence the skills can be transferred at zero cost from one firm to another, which is in fact not an unreasonable assumption in the world of small business in Japan, then the firms offering training and a wage for a new hire should offer a wage equal to

$$w_t = w_r - c_t, \tag{1.7}$$

where c_t is the marginal cost of training. Then assuming the training raises productivity by δ the firm will retain the worker in the second period at a wage $(1+\delta)w_r$ if and only if

$$(1+\delta)e(q)_i \geq (1+\delta)w_r, \tag{1.8}$$

which is simply a restatement of the earlier condition taking into account the fact that the training makes the worker hired in the base period potentially more productive in the second period.

C. Large Firm

Following Lindbeck and Snower (1988), I call newly hired workers in large firms 'entrants' and, as indicated in Section 1.2, the firm pays them w_e the competitively established market wage.

   As part of the implicit contract offered by large firms to its new hires during the course of the first period the firm (imperfectly) monitors entrants and on the basis of this monitoring for each worker i the firm arrives at an evaluation for effort e_i and productivity q_i. Combining its estimates of worker effort and productivity, the firm establishes a rank r_i for each of its entrants i, taking into account both factors. (It is natural for Japanese firms to proceed in this manner since the school system, which is where future workers first experience institutionalized monitoring and screening on a systematic scale, operates along ranking lines.) For example, using the scheme developed in equation (1.5) the firm might use simple equal weighting for the two factors in securing its ranking:

$$r_i = (1/2)e_i + (1/2)q_i. \tag{1.9}$$

On the basis of a hierarchical ranking defined in terms of r_i, the firm makes a decision about which category to place these entrants in the second period and who, if anybody, will be fired. The two categories of retained workers are promoted workers L_p and non-promoted workers L_{np}. A worker is promoted if his or her ranking is above the promotional cutoff defined in terms of r_i. The cut-off r^* is not known at the time when the entrant is hired, because, as will be demonstrated below, it depends on the expected cost curve for effort and the expected marginal revenue productivity for promoted workers for the second period, and these expectations are not developed before the end of the first period. It is at the end of the first period that entrants take into account the rankings established for them and decide whether or not they should leave the firm or not. Let us designate these individuals by Q. Assuming strict rational calculation these are individuals whose reservation wage, taking into account what they themselves know about their own effort levels and the transferability of skills learned in training, exceeds what they expect to get in the second period (options for quits include self-employment with or without family members as well as employment in another firm). For reasons to be discussed below, quits are drawn from the ranks of workers who are not slotted for promotion. At this point the firm also establishes a firing cutoff, that is it fires workers at the bottom of the list of ranked workers whose expected productivity falls below firing costs minus the wage the firm expects to pay to non-promoted workers who are not fired. Denote these individuals by F. The total separations S equal the sum of $Q + F$. Letting L_e stand for entrants hired at the beginning of period 1, and ignoring any loss due to mortality, in period 2 L_e breaks into three groups:

$$L_e = S + L_p + L_{np}. \tag{1.10}$$

Because I assume promoted and non-promoted workers are paid according to different principles it is useful to treat each category in a separate section.

C.1. Large Firm: Promoted Workers

Promoted workers function as a corps of managers within the firm which by dint of size and complexity of operation can not be efficiently managed by the owners or a small board of directors selected by shareholders. Among other tasks each manager directs the training of, and monitors and evaluates, a subgroup of subordinate workers drawn from the ranks of the current crop of entrants L_e and non-promoted workers L_{np}. Monitoring and evaluating managers is extremely costly so the firm prefers to pay these workers premium wages according to efficiency wage principles in order to discourage shirking and rent-seeking in the monitoring and evaluation of subordinates. Let $\phi(w_p)$ be the cost of a unit's worth of effort as a function of the wage paid to promoted workers w_p. For instance with effort $e(w_p)$ a function of the wage paid the unit costs of effort is

$$\phi(w_p) = w_p/e(w_p). \tag{1.11}$$

Assuming that the derivative of ϕ, $d\phi/dw_p$ is monotonic increasing from negative values to positive values, the firm minimizes costs per unit of effort by selecting w_p such that $d\phi/dw_p = 0$. This optimization is captured in Figure 1.1. It then selects a cutoff rank r^* from the pool of workers L_e such that the firm maximizes profits with respect to the selected level of L_p. Let firm nominal net value added pO (where p is the price of output and O is real value added) be a function of the three types of workers L_e, L_{np}, and L_p, $O(L_e, L_{np}, L_p)$. Then writing (expected) firm profits π as a function of the three types of labour inputs we have

$$\pi(L_e, L_{np}, L_p) = pO(L_e, L_{np}, L_p) - w_e L_e - w_{np} L_{np} - w_p L_p. \tag{1.12}$$

Then maximizing profits with respect to L_p we have

$$\partial\pi/\partial L_p = p[\partial O/\partial L_p] - w_p = 0, \tag{1.13}$$

or

$$w_p = p[\partial O/\partial L_p], \tag{1.14}$$

where the marginal revenue product of a manager should be thought of in terms of expectations. As the reader can see from the equations, the optimal choice of promoted workers (and hence the promotion rate out of the group L_e and the cut-off rank r^*) depends on how productive these workers are expected to be over the duration of the second period, which in turn depends upon the expected demand for firm output, the number of new entrants and their distribution according to effort capacity and costs of being trained and so forth.

C.2. Large Firm: Non-Promoted Workers

For non-promoted workers wages are determined by bargaining process, which may or may not be collective in nature. Following Lindbeck and Snower (1988) I assume that the non-promoted workers are insiders who can negotiate a share of the turnover rent. Lindbeck and Snower (1988) demonstrate that under the assumption of individualistic bargaining between workers and owners workers end up receiving a wage w_{np} which is the minimum of the marginal revenue product of labour for non-promoted workers net of firing costs (which in this case are zero, since no firing occurs) and the sum of the entrant wage w_e plus the sum of marginal turnover costs (which in this case consist of hiring and training costs). However, individualistic bargaining is not a reasonable assumption in the Japanese case. In Chapter 6 I discuss a more realistic scenario for rent sharing between non-promoted workers in large firms and owners of enterprises.

C.3. Large Firms: the Size of the Entrant Labor Force

The number of quits Q is determined by a comparison between (a) what an entrant who is about to become a non-promoted worker can expect to get if he or she stays with the firm and (b) the opportunity on the outside. Firms with relatively poor expected market potential presumably will suffer considerable defection, especially on the part of disgruntled hard-working and skilful workers who expected to be promoted and were not. Because of the rather extreme stylization adopted in the model the most likely destination for these workers is self-employment, because they themselves know that given the effort they are capable of giving (as opposed to the level of combined effort and/or the productivity which the managers assigned to them) they can expect to do better on their own. Of course in reality some of these quitting workers seek and find better opportunities in other large or small firms. Firings F are determined by a comparison between the expected wages for non-promoted workers and the sum of expected marginal revenue and firing costs for low-ranked employees. Through these opportunity cost calculations the firm's total retained labour force $L_p + L_{np}$ is determined. Now the size of this retained senior worker labour force is major factor in determining the expected marginal revenue productivity of new hires and hence the number of new-entrant hires. In order to maximize profits (cf. equation 1.13a) the firm hires new-entrants up to the point at which:

$$p(\partial O/\partial L_e) = w_e, \tag{1.14}$$

where it takes w_e as exogenously given by supply and demand on the market for high-achiever fresh graduates. Note that the expected marginal revenue productivity of an entrant will be larger, *ceteris parabis*, the greater is the number of quits Q; and *ceteris parabis* the greater is expected output expansion during the period.

2 Labour Segmentation in Interwar Japan

2.1 INTRODUCTION

The origins of the postwar subdivision of the labour market, into distinct submarkets, demarcated on the demand side in terms of specific contracts offered workers, and on the supply side in terms of distinctive signals about expected levels of effort capacity and costs of being trained, lie in the interwar period. To assert this is not to deny that economic and social institutions dating back to the Tokugawa period and even earlier are of no importance to an understanding of origins of postwar Japanese labour market practices. Indeed, to search for origins is to embark on a journey backward through history to which there is no obvious and predetermined final resting point. But in my view it is first and foremost during the interwar era that one comes upon institutions of labour market subdivision sufficiently similar to those of the postwar era, and sees labour market outcomes resulting from their operation of sufficient similarity to the outcomes of the postwar period, for us to refer to the interwar period as the formative era for the system dominating the four decades after 1950. In making this argument I emphasize the emergence of dualism between the combined sectors of agriculture and light industry on the one hand, and heavy industry on the other. In the former sector wages were relatively low, and archetypical labour market contracts tended to be either of either the family firm or the small-commercial-firm type. In the latter sector wages were significantly higher and archetypical labour market contracts tended to be the large firm type. For the relatively low costs of monitoring, however, I do not seek to define origins. I do discuss these costs in this chapter – especially in the context of interwar village life and textile factories – but I feel the origins of pervasive monitoring in Japanese economic affairs predate the interwar era.

That describing origins for labour contracts and labour market outcomes matters for the analysis in this book is a consequence of the view, now becoming increasingly common in the field of economic history, that path dependence exists. That is, in the presence of scale economies which allow one type of technology once chosen to drive out competitors, the historical path taken by firms in adopting competing technologies matters. Once firms have selected a path – which in the aftermath, may be viewed as inefficient from the viewpoint of long-run technological progress as a whole – switching over to the other competitor technology may simply be too costly. Thus we can say that 'path dependence' exists. Over time, organizational forms and technological progress tend to move in small increments along paths. Thus the fact the labour market contracts took a certain form during the nineteenth century is of significance to the labour market in the twentieth century. However, the further one goes back in time the more tenuous does the search for origins become: in the interim many choices have been made and these choices are not foreordained on the basis of what happened in the remote past, for the existence of path dependence does not rule out choice in the present. It simply constrains the nature of the choices made in any given point in time.

To be specific, in this chapter I show that the during the first fifty years of Meiji industrialization (1868–1918) labour market contracts of the large-firm type tended to be restricted to a small élite, many of whom were of samurai origin, and that for the overwhelming majority of firms contracts were of the small-family and commercial variety. We can speak of the Meiji period as being an era of balanced growth in which labour flowed back and forth from the dominant manufacturing subsector, light industry as exemplified by textiles and food processing, to agricultural households which were firms of the small family-run type and the differential between wages in the two sectors was minimal. With the rapid expansion of heavy industry – of shipbuilding, machinery manufacturing, chemicals and the like – during World War I and after a second major subsector emerged into prominence, and with this emergence a characteristic large firm contract became increasingly common, one which combined rules for training and promotion which had dominated Tokugawa merchant houses with principles governing the ranking and advancement of the samurai élite in the feudal fiefs. In the new type of contract the firm took far greater risks in recruiting workers than firms in the light manufacturing sector: risks associated with offers of job security, extensive training and payment of premium efficiency wages, and with the fact that it needed highly motivated workers with sufficient technical expertise to understand and adapt the foreign technology which these firms were importing from the West. For this reason firms were reluctant to offer these contracts to persons who lacked extensive screening in advance of hiring for effort capacity and for the expected costs of being trained. They limited efficiency wage payments to their white-collar élite, and attempted to limit their selection of future efficiency wage workers to graduates of institutions of higher learning who could be expected to have mastered the ability to learn foreign languages and/or the technical engineering and scientific literature, knowing that entry to these schools could be only secured after passing through a protracted hurdle of examinations and by successful competitive promotion up the rungs of the educational ladder. Therefore heavy industrial firms tended to exclude the pool of rank-and-file blue-collar workers from these contracts. In consequence interwar dualism engendered tensions: tensions between those agricultural households and communities who had the wherewithal to educate their children sufficiently for them to be able to profitably take advantage of the emerging high-wage opportunities in heavy industry, and those who could not do so and were constrained to continue selling labour to the light-industrial sector or into casual labour markets in construction and heavy industry at relatively low wages; and tensions between blue-collar workers in heavy industry who were committed to working exclusively in heavy industry but who were denied access to promotional ladders reaching up to efficiency wage positions and the educated élite expecting promotion to these premium wage posts. The unionization in both agriculture and industry which occurred during this period was strongly, although not exclusively, rooted in discontent fomented by this dualism.

Thus interwar Japan witnessed significant outbursts of political unrest directed at perceived inequities stemming from dualism. However, a combination of secular economic tendencies and government policies counteracted the inequities, and helped pave the way for reforms of the postwar period. In the aftermath of World War II a combination of land reform and protective tariffs and import restriction reduced disparities in economic opportunities and market rewards between hitherto marginal tenant producers, other small family-run firms in the countryside, and industrial-wage-earning households. Interwar legislation while not as dramatic was moving in this direction. And government promotion of a rapid expansion in the middle level of the educational system, and in particular of vocational schooling, coupled with compulsory military service for males found physically and mentally fit for service, increased the efficiency of labour market signalling as far as the hiring of blue-collar workers was concerned. As a result heavy industrial firms felt more secure in increasing the training afforded their blue-collar entrants. In turn this expansion in training on the shop floor refashioned the relative productivity of white- and blue-collar workers in favour of blue-collar workers, and hence diminished wage differentials between blue and white-collar employees in heavy industry. With a squeezing of the differential in training and payment, firms had an increasing incentive to extend downward promotional opportunities to workers on the shop floor. Again, as with the agricultural sector, wholesale reform was postponed until the period 1945–55, but the seeds for the reform were planted during the interwar period, especially during the decade leading up to the Pacific War. For these reasons I feel that the immediate origins of the postwar labour market system lie in the interwar period, and that an understanding of the economic factors shaping the system can best be found in analysis of this period. However, because an understanding of the institutions surrounding interwar segmentation into submarkets with differing implicit contracts, requires some knowledge of the pre-1918 situation I devote the next two sections of this chapter to a discussion of the most important features of Tokugawa and Meiji labour markets.

2.2 TOKUGAWA LABOUR MARKET SEGMENTATION

During the Tokugawa period (1603–1868) labour markets were sharply segmented along geographical, class and family lineage lines. From the standpoint of political organization, a divide-and-rule strategy which pitted the rulers *(daimyō)* of fiefs *(han)* against one another, created a stable balance of power between fiefs and staved off internal warfare. Social class distinctions were formalized, with different standards of behaviour and different economic functions expected of the four distinct classes: the *daimyō*, the samurai military retainer-bureaucrats of the *daimyō*, peasant farmers *(nōmin)*, and the mix of urban craftsmen, domestic servants, and merchants and their employees (known collectively as *chōnin*).

The Tokugawa political system was basically designed to provide a balance of power solution to the problem of civil war which had plagued the country for a number of centuries before 1600. After Tokugawa Ieyasu managed to assemble a powerful coalition of warlords and to defeat a rival coalition at the battle of Sekigahara in 1600, three years later being appointed military ruler *(shōgun)* of the country by the emperor, he claimed about a quarter of the land for himself and his heirs and permitted the remainder to be divided into roughly 250 fiefs, selecting *daimyō* from the ranks of both victorious and defeated warlords. The conundrum which the Tokugawa *bakufu* (literally 'tent government', the term referring to the Tokugawa family and its administration) faced was how to sufficiently emasculate the military prowess of the *daimyō* so that they could not successfully challenge the delicate balance of power which propped up the regime. To that end the *bakufu* took a variety of actions. First it forced all *daimyō* to withdraw from the countryside persons authorized to carry swords (the samurai class), requiring that this military class now reside within the castle town, the administrative centre of each fief. Over time as a result of the Pax Tokugawa the samurai ceased to perform military functions (although they continued their military training and tradition of discipline), and became an élite bureaucratic class, responsible for managing the finances of the fiefs, including the collection of taxes in volumes of rice from the peasant villages. In their dealings with villages they tended to work through the village headman. The samurai were ranked in an elabourate pecking order which determined the volume of rice each samurai family was allotted and which at least at the beginning of the period was largely based on family name. However, towards the end of the Tokugawa period, reform-minded fiefs, desirous of improving the efficiency with which they managed their resources, introduced competition into the ranking system, using achievement in the fief educational system run for the training of samurai as a criterion for promotion. Thus the focus on formal educational certification as a criterion for élite treatment in interwar companies has its distant origins in the late-Eighteenth and nineteenth-century promotional practices of the more progressive fiefs.

Another act taken by the *bakufu* to weaken the centripetal force of local fief rule was the introduction of the *sankin kōtai* system, whereby *daimyō* were obligated to reside in luxurious quarters in the *bakufu*'s capital, Edo (today Tokyo), during alternating years, and to leave their heirs behind when returning to their domains. This policy subjected the *daimyō* to considerable expense, depleting their resources and subjecting them to scrutiny (monitoring) by *bakufu* officials. An indirect consequence of the development of the *sankin kōtai* system was expansion in interregional trade, so that the rice taken by the fiefs could be efficiently exchanged for items of conspicuous consumption, and in the number of craftspeople and merchants satisfying the demand for the construction of lavish homes, beautiful art objects and clothing, and so forth. The explosive growth of Osaka and Edo during the Tokugawa period was partly a result of the *sankin kōtai* system. Again, after 1639, the *bakufu* announced a policy of national seclusion (*sakoku*). It effectively ended regular diplomatic relations with foreign powers other than China and Korea, permitting only one form of contact with Europe, that through the tiny island of Dejima in Nagasaki harbour, upon which only Dutch citizens were allowed to reside. By forcibly terminating relations with other powers and monopolizing any diplomatic interchange solely unto itself, the *bakufu* attempted to permanently squelch the forging of alliances between individual (or groups of) *daimyō* and foreign powers.

The organization of labour markets reflected the political divisions, the cutting up of the land area into autonomous fiefs, and the social divisions between the four formally distinct status ranking groups. In practice as opposed to theory there was mobility. Despite being tied to the land, individual peasants did move across fief boundaries. For instance, women moved to marry into households residing in distant locales, and young members of peasant families took up positions as domestic servants and/or apprentices in artisan or merchant households in big cities like Osaka, which because of their high mortality were in constant demand for fresh inflows of population. Moreover, some lower samurai disappeared into the ranks of the farming class or the merchant class. Still, as a whole, formal political and social segmentation was associated with labour market differentiation in the sense that implicit labour market contracts varied between the classes. Here I consider four types of submarkets: those for the samurai, those for the peasant *nōmin*, those for merchants and artisans, and those for common harbour. In discussing the organization of the labour markets for samurai and peasants I will take special note of the institution of the family in so far as it has a bearing on the way the labour markets for these distinct groups functioned because this has implications for the subsequent discussion in this chapter. To speak of the Japanese family system is to speak of a concept limited both by historical time and by economic and demographic constraints. For the purpose of the analysis here I shall refer to the Japanese family system (in Japanese the term ie denotes the family; I will refer to '*ie* system' on occasion in the ensuring text) as an *ideal* type formed in or before the eighteenth century. The ideal type is known as the classic stem family. In practice as opposed to theory families may have deviated from the ideal type because of economic or demographic constraints. But the ideal type was important because it provided an organizational model to which individual households aspired when they engaged in economic and demographic strategy-making. The specific organizational rules governing families have changed over time. But the stem family ideal has remained unchanged since the Eighteenth century.

What is a stem family system? It is a system characterized by the following rules: (a) a spouse is brought into the family for one and only one offspring in each generation; (b) succession of the family headship falls upon the offspring who has married within the family (or to the married couple); (c) inheritance, which is unequal, favours the single heir/successor; and (d) the family's organizational form passes through an alternating cycle of conjugal phase followed by stem phase (in which the junior and senior conjugal units coreside) followed by a conjugal phase

and so forth. The transition from the stem to the conjugal phase is marked
by the death of the last member of the senior couple; the transition from
the conjugal to the stem phase is marked by the marriage of the heir.

That demography conditions the concrete realization of a stem family
system is apparent from condition (d), for adult mortality and the timing of
marriage play a critical role in lengthening or shortening the two phases
of the alternating cycle. But demographic reality conditions the operation
of the family system in other ways. For instance what if the family is
unable to biologically produce an heir; or produces an heir who is too
young to assume the family headship at the time when the older couple
wishes to 'retire' and commence the stem phase of the cycle? Were there
no religious ideology buttressing the family system, families might have
been content to watch with equanimity while their lines died out. But
because of the practice of ancestor worship, during the Tokugawa period
concentrated in the Buddhist temple with which the family registered,
families had a strong aversion to the demise of lines. Under the ancestor
worship ideology family was conceived of as dynastic as well as stem,
that is as extending through past and future generations through the
worship of ones ancestors. For this reason, securing a successor to take
over the headship and attend to the family's relics and religious artifacts,
was a matter of paramount concern. Thus families resorted to a variety of
fictions to secure heirs. For instance, males not related to the family head
by blood ties were adopted as 'sons'. In this way family lines could be
perpetuated even when biology failed. But biology limited most families
simply because relying on the market for adoption was risky: risky
because in-adopted heirs might be less inclined to attend to the religious
rites of the ancestor cult; risky because the heir was not trained in the
customs of the family from an early age.

Still, families did employ in-adoption from time to time, even passing
over biologically produced heirs on occasion. Why? Part of the reason was
demographic and was tied up with the timing of the transition from
conjugal to stem phases of the cycle. But economics played a role as well.
For it must be kept in mind that the actual working of the system was
constrained by more than demographic probabilities. The family was both
a demographic unit and, in the case of the peasant and/or craft/merchant
households, a unit of economic production was well. If it seemed to the
household head that the biologically produced putative heir could not
shoulder the task of managing the household economy in a competitive
economy in which households vied with each other for land, rank and
other assets, the family head might well be inclined to pass over that
individual in favour of a more competent person unrelated by blood ties.

Thus economics and demography constrained the family system in practice as opposed to theory. But how actual adjustments were arrived at very much depended on the class status of the family. Here I contrast two stylized types: the peasant type and the samurai warrior/bureaucrat type. Adaptation to demographic constraints differed between the representative family in these two classes. The reasons were both economic and ideological: economic because the ways a family generated its income and type of labour market in operated in were fundamentally different in the two social spheres; and ideological because the code of behaviour which in principle applied to the representative samurai was at variance with the code of behaviour followed by the typical peasant.

The peasant family was a production unit in which all family members, excepting the very young or the very old, were expected to do the physical work which generated the basic output upon which the household subsisted. The family trained its own members as they grew to the age when they could begin working. There was sexual division of labour – women devoted more time to domestic chores and were more likely to engage in by-employments, especially if this side activity involved weaving or spinning – but this sexual division of labour was between the categories of potential income generating work, and did not demarcate those who restricted their activities solely to domestic tasks from those who engaged in market activities. The status of women heavily depended on the actual economic functions they performed in the family economy. If she possessed sufficient acumen or physical prowess, the mistress of the ie might well command greater authority than her husband. For this reason it is hardly surprising that the headship of the ie might devolve onto the mistress of the house or onto a daughter. Indeed, there is considerable evidence that male primogeniture, which is the form of inheritance typically associated with the stem family system in Japan, was not as common as was formerly believed. For instance, in some regions families employed ultimogeniture, and succession by the eldest child regardless of sex *(ane katoku)* occurred in some villages in the northeast. Thus in the life cycle of the peasant *ie* the headship might well pass back and forth between the sexes. Given the pragmatic orientation of the peasant household towards the markets it operated in this is hardly surprising.

In stark contrast functioned the samurai house. Only males could become samurai and the head of a samurai household was invariably male. And among members of the bureaucratic/warrior class the income enjoyed by the *ie* was a function of the rank of the male, of the head of the house, within the pecking order of the domain's bureaucracy. Yamamura (1974) shows that there were marked differences in family support income allotments (measured in terms of the number of *koku* of rice allotted to the house) according to the position of the head. Now in so far as performance on competitive examinations was a criterion for bureaucratic ranking, and towards the end of the Tokugawa period this was becoming increasingly true in at least some of the fiefs, rank was linked to effort capacity and costs of being trained. Thus samurai households in such a setting had a strong incentive to educate their male offspring in the domain schools. In addition, if they failed to produce a surviving male heir or if they felt their own male offspring was insufficiently competent, they had a strong incentive to in-adopt an able male heir . As a result the proportion of in-adopted *ie* heads (*yoshi*) was quite high. Yamamura (1974: 79ff.) demonstrates that among the bannerman, the military retainers of the *bakufu*, there were a significant proportion of *yoshi* successions to the headship. These were mainly triggered by the failure to give birth to male issue, and secondarily to the death of the son(s). In short in comparing peasant and samurai houses we see that nature of the family's interaction with labour and product markets conditioned the household's strategy for continuing the stem family system down through the generations and its attitudes towards formal educational training for children. Peasants had a pragmatic attitude towards training which they acquired on the job and a pragmatic attitude towards succession, while the samurai favoured formal education and a rigid adherence to the male headship.

Merchants and artisans occupied a middle ground as far as education and training is concerned. For instance merchant families did tend to send their children to *terakoya* (so-called 'temple') schools for commoners (and towards the close of the Tokugawa period even to the domain schools in some cases) for the training in the basics of numerical and linguistic skills. But according to Saito (1987) they also internalized their training within the merchant house itself, bringing in young teenage apprentices (*detchi*) whom they promoted only after a long trial period during which they were carefully and continually monitored (a period of up to ten years in some cases) to clerk (*tedai*) status. And Leupp (1992) shows that artisans, typically organized in craft guilds, also had a protracted and internalized promotion system. Thus it is fair to say that merchants and artisans combined both internal training, which was by far the dominant form of training in the peasant household (firm), with some use of formal external education outside the house, which was characteristic of the samurai. As for common labour Leupp (1992) shows that the most common organizational form was the *oyakata-kokata* type according to which experienced harbour with connections yielding work contracts, took on the role of the 'father' (the *oyakata* role), and recruited subordinates who took on the 'child' (*kokata*) role. The *oyabun* trained his/her subordinates and distributed wages to them on the basis on the contracts which he negotiated for the work group. Training was within the group but after it there was little barrier to mobility. Common labour often moved around from one group to another, unlike the typical merchant's trainee, reflecting the fact that merchants restricted the filling of higher level posts (for example clerk positions) to those they themselves had internally trained.

In short during the Tokugawa period there were a variety of labour markets which were segmented from one another by dint of geography (fief boundaries) and by formal social status. Education and training and the way the stem family system operated varied between these different submarkets. This segmentation according to class background, according to the training and education afforded children, and according to the degree of pragmatism the household exercised in passing down the headship, had important implications for the development of labour submarkets in Japan once the country began to industrialize using Western technology in a systematic fashion, that is once the Tokugawa regime collapsed and the Meiji period began. From the viewpoint of the model of labour contracts which we developed in Chapter 1, we can say that both the samurai labour submarket archetype and the merchant labour submarket archetype have features common to the model of large firms (i.e., both markets reveal evidence of formal screening, long-run job security, and promotion according to effort and productivity) while the operation of peasant households displays characteristics of the model of family-run small firms with internal mechanisms in place for determining training and effort.

2.3 LABOUR MARKETS UNDER MEIJI BALANCED GROWTH

During the early Meiji period government policy coalesced around a set of key programs and institutions which, taken together, I dub 'imperial nationalism'. While the institutions changed and evolved partly in response to modifications in the international economic and political environment, and partly in response to domestic social and political movements intentionally and unintentionally triggered by the original set of policies (the programme was not without its internal contradictions, partly because of factional disputes; and no governmental leader, even the most intelligent and forceful, can perfectly mould the populations they represent and/or control or foresee the long run consequences of their plans), the key institutions of Imperial Nationalism possessed remarkable survival value, persisting until 1945, when a Japan lying in ruins at the close of the Pacific War abandoned them under the direction of a conquering power.[1] To interpret Imperial Nationalism in economic terms, it is useful to begin with a modified version of the famous late-developer thesis pioneered in the field of European economic history by Gerschenkron (1966, 1968).[2]

The late-developer theory fashioned by Gerschenkron is first and foremost a critique of those stage-theories in economic history which presuppose that all countries move along the same path of development. Marx's famous set of stages – prefeudalism, feudalism, capitalism and socialism – is the most famous example of the stage-theoretic paradigm. Gerschenkron argues plausibly enough that when countries commence industrialization they take into account the international environment which they face at the moment, and, in doing so, attempt to skip stages which earlier industrializing countries passed through. They borrow from other economically advanced nations. And they do so in a selective fashion, tailoring the nature of this borrowing to the type of backwardness they find themselves in on the eve of industrialization. Moreover the related characteristics of their early industrialization (as measured in terms of the speed and jerkiness of growth, the emphasis on large-scale factories, the role played by large banks and the state in promoting capital accumulation and the creation of an entrepreneurial class, the role of ideology as a motivating tool, institutional innovation as a device for expanding the supply of skilled labour capable of working with foreign technology) vary depending on the degree of backwardness of the country relative to developed countries. Later-developing countries like Japan use the very constraints imposed by backwardness to develop a set of substitutes with which they can leapfrog development stages and achieve rapid growth, avoiding the long, slow gestation period of primitive accumulation of capital (in the Marxist stage-theoretic sense) which Western European countries like France and England experienced during the 1600–1780 period as they moved forward by dismantling feudalism and establishing the groundwork for industrialization. Gerschenkron (1968) himself concedes that one of the limitations of the degree-of-backwardness approach is its dearth of predictive power: for example he cites the case of Bulgaria's failure to industrialize as an example of the inability of the state and the banks to adequately overcome the hurdles of backwardness. So the theory perhaps lends itself more to analytical description than to prediction. In this chapter I use the framework in the descriptive sense; namely as a motivation for pursuing the interrelated ideas of the importance of ideology and state initiative in promoting growth, and of institutional innovation as a mechanism for coping with the bottlenecks imposed by a dearth of skilled labour. It is the burden of my argument that Imperial Nationalism served as a substitute for missing prerequisites in early Japanese industrial development.

Imperial Nationalism was a set of legal, political and social institutions buttressed by an ideology. Two-word Meiji phrases (each consisting of four Chinese characters) best capture the essence of ideology in so far as it bears on the development of new labour market institutions: *fukoku kyōhei* (wealthy country/strong military) and *ryōsai kenbo* (good wife/wise mother). Most of the Meiji oligarchy came from the ranks of the former samurai class with its neo-Confucian military orientation and a male-dominated version of the stem family system. In promoting the importation of foreign technology and industrialization they wished to build up Japan's military and political prowess so that she could join the ranks of the great imperial powers. To this end they fashioned an ideology centred on the cult of the emperor, one that would break down the regional exclusiveness of *han* (fief) loyalty, one that would motivate bureaucracy and military, one that would serve as the ideological basis for ancestor worship and the cult of the male-oriented family system upon which the welfare policy (or rather, the rejection of an ambitious state-managed welfare system) rested. To this end the government early on directly built up the social overhead capital of the country, especially in railroads, shipping and electrical generating capacity, hired foreign experts to train Japanese in technical, managerial and military matters, and selectively borrowed economic, political and social institutions (for instance the joint stock company with limited liability, chartered banking, a national parliament, French-style police organization and a German-inspired university and medical system) from various countries in the West, reworking the institutional details so that the new institutions could function more effectively in an environment still strongly imbrued with the Tokugawa heritage. Thus in the state managed companies, in the government-run mines and in the railroad system once it was nationalized – we see the development of labour contracts for élite white-collar workers recruited out of the few institutions of higher education operating in the first years of Meiji which combine a mix of the principles of screening and promotion common to the Tokugawa samurai and merchant submarkets together with a premium on effort which in pragmatic terms meant mastering the details of Western scientific and engineering and managerial knowledge so that it could be profitably applied in these newly developing sectors. In this sense we can say that the germ of the large-firm contract lies in the early Meiji military arsenals, railroads and shipping concerns, and mines. These companies, facing a small supply pool of potential employees capable of learning the basics of Western technology (i.e. workers capable of learning directly from Western experts or from reverse engineering or from reading Western manuals and articles) had an incentive to experiment with institutional rules which would minimize turnover among the ranks of their technical personnel. Tokugawa models for submarkets using hired labour with low turnover existed: namely the samurai and merchant models. Hence given the late-developer status of Japan and the Tokugawa tradition in merchant and bureaucratic submarkets, these companies found it especially attractive to combine historical models with selected Western practices in order to develop a recruitment policy based on screening in the educational system, job security, and promotion tied to productivity and effort capacity.

But in arguing that the programme of Imperial Nationalism contained within it many of the institutional large-firm labour market contracts, I do not wish to leave the reader with the impression that the large firm contract of the postwar period existed to any significant degree in the early Meiji labour market. For we must not exaggerate the discontinuity during the first three to four decades of the Meiji period. The fact is that most of the manufacturing concerns of early Meiji were in the fields of light industry – especially in textiles and food processing – and these firms employed a labour force dominated by females for whom rates of time discount were high, that is the bulk of these female workers were young women who expected to work for a few years before returning to their households of origin or to enter another household through marriage. They were usually sold into a factory job by their parental households on a short-term contract, the relevant opportunity cost determining the supply price of labour being marginal revenue productivity in agriculture. Because most agricultural households worked to a margin in which marginal productivities for additional hours worked fell below the wages at which agricultural workers were hired in (a point which I shall develop in greater detail in Section 2.5), wages in agriculture actually exceeded those in manufacturing. Consider Table 2.1. Note that for females throughout the prewar period and for males up until around the turn of the century when heavy industrialization began to take hold, the agricultural wage tended to exceed the manufacturing wage, and wages in manufacturing and agriculture tended to move together. Moreover, as late as 1930–4, after more than half a century of industrialization, the percentage of total manufacturing in three major subsectors of light industry – food products, textiles, and lumber and wood products – exceeded 45 per cent. Indeed it was only around World War I that heavy industry really emerged as a significant force in terms of the demand for labour. However, it is also

Table 2.1 Wage differentials in prewar Japan; males and females, 1889–1939

*Panel A Nominal daily wages: quinquennial
average (yen per day), 1880–1939*

Year	Agriculture		Manufacturing	
1880–84	0.212	0.133	0.21	0.11
1885–89	0.151	0.099	0.18	0.08
1890–94	0.206	0.141	0.19	0.10
1895–99	0.323	0.238	0.28	0.14
1900–04	0.382	0.294	0.38	0.17
1905–09	0.416	0.334	0.46	0.21
1910–14	0.517	0.395	0.53	0.26
1915–19	0.859	0.624	0.93	0.44
1920–24	1.521	1.160	2.04	0.92
1925–29	1.386	1.108	2.14	0.87
1930–34	0.882	0.658	1.98	0.64
1935–39	1.116	0.886	2.09	0.68

Panel B Wage differentials

Year	Female/male		Agriculture/manufacturing	
	Agriculture	Manufacturing	Males	Females
1880–84	0.63	0.52	1.01	1.21
1885–89	0.66	0.44	0.84	1.24
1890–94	0.69	0.53	1.08	1.41
1895–99	0.74	0.50	1.15	1.70
1900–04	0.77	0.45	1.01	1.73
1905–09	0.80	0.46	0.90	1.59
1910–14	0.76	0.49	0.98	1.52
1915–19	0.73	0.47	0.92	1.42
1920–24	0.76	0.45	0.75	1.26
1925–29	0.80	0.41	0.65	1.27
1930–34	0.75	0.32	0.45	1.03
1935–39	0.79	0.33	0.53	1.30

Source:
Ohkawa and Shinohara (1979: Table A52, pp. 389–91).

apparent from Table 2.1 that the discontinuity is much more characteristic of the interwar period than it is for the Meiji period. In this context, note that manufacturing/agriculture wage differentials for males sharply widen during the interwar period. This is something new. Associated with this is a widening of the male–female wage differential in agriculture but not in manufacturing. Thus we can characterize the Meiji period as one of balanced growth, balanced in the sense that the agricultural and manufacturing sectors appear to have been closely linked through the transfer of labour back and forth at roughly comparable wages. But in the early decades of the twentieth century, and especially with the explosive growth of heavy industry during the interwar period, balanced growth ended and sharp labour market dualism emerged, at least as far as male workers are concerned. But for the submarket of females we can say that balanced growth continued into the interwar period.

In highlighting the contrast between males and females we are implicitly touching on the issue of signalling. Consider the élite *ie* model of the former samurai: according to that model it was a sign of low status for a wife or daughter to take on factory employment. And in the case of the agricultural household the prevailing assumption was that wives worked in agriculture and daughters could be sent to work in factories for short periods prior to marriage. Thus it is reasonable to suppose that the time horizon expected for a typical female Japanese factory recruit was short, or, to put it differently, the intrinsic internal rate-of-time discount for such a worker was high, and therefore companies hired them under the assumption that they would leave after a brief employment stint. Thus a characteristic of balanced growth was overwhelming reliance on short term labour, that is on labour which tended to flow back and forth from rural households to factories. This being the case – and because on the demand side the training periods required to bring a worker up to a relatively high rate of productivity was short – light-industrial factories, regardless of scale of operation, had little incentive to develop large firm contracts for the bulk of their workers. Which was a more important consideration: market supply or market demand? That the characteristics of the supply side may have been more weighty than the characteristics of the demand side is suggested by the reluctance of the tiny group of heavy industrial firms during early Meiji to extend long-term contracts to blue-collar workers. It is reported that factory owners felt that Meiji craft workers were guilty of drinking and gambling, indifferent to the needs of their families, and unwilling to save for the future. It is said that wives of workers waited by the factory gates in order to secure their husbands' wages before they drank them up or consumed them in brothels (Gordon, 1991: 28–9). Turnover of workers was high. In part this was because workers moved around on their own. In part because many attached themselves to labour bosses (*oyakata*) who then negotiated with factories for their work group as a whole and moved the work group around depending on the terms that could extract from potential employers. Recall that the *oyakata-kokata* organizational form was characteristic of common harbour during the Tokugawa period. For instance among the workers at the famed Shibaura and Ishikawajima engineering works in 1902, a very large proportion of the workers had been on the job less than one year (Gordon, 1985: 87):

	0–6 months	7 months–1 year	6 years or more
Shibaura	24.7%	14%	16.8%
Ishikawajima	12.7%	10.1%	18.3%

Recognizing this, employers treated the typical blue-collar male worker as they did the typical female worker: as a worker with a short time horizon and therefore one upon whom lavish training was likely to be wasted. In practice there were exceptions even among female workers: in some textile firms for instance women who signalled through their unwillingness to quit a firm that they had a long time horizon were 'promoted' along the lines of the large-firm model as were some blue-collar male workers during the Meiji period. But as a rule these were exceptions.

In short the dominant labour contract of the Meiji economy was – to characterize it in terms of the lingua franca of the model in Chapter 1 – either of the small family firm or commercial small firm variety. This is consistent with the idea of balanced growth in which wage differentials are small and labour constantly turns over, flowing between industrial firms or between the agricultural sector and the industrial sector on a regular basis. Only among a small élite of highly educated male workers and among merchants can we speak of a different type of labour market contracting, one which in the changing structural circumstances of the interwar era was to grow rapidly to prominence and to serve as the model for the postwar large firm contract.

2.4 IMPROVEMENTS IN EFFORT CAPACITY, TRAINING, AND SIGNALLING: THE ROLE OF THE FAMILY, THE EDUCATIONAL SYSTEM AND THE MILITARY

Imperial Nationalism was the brainchild of former samurai. From its inception military considerations were wedded to social and economic considerations in a way which the former warrior – bureaucrats found sensible and congenial. Hence it is not surprising that the model for the family system promoted by the new government was that of the samurai type; that great stress was placed on educational qualification in hiring and promoting influential bureaucrats; that the government was aggressive in expanding the educational system which was fashioned by the Meiji oligarchy was centralized and severely hierarchical, promoting nationalism and the cult of the emperor at its lower compulsory levels, technical learning crucial to the importing and adapting of foreign technology at its higher levels, and practical knowledge for commerce and agriculture at the intermediate level; and that a programme of extending militarism down into the villages and into the school system seemed natural and reasonable to the political élite. A perhaps unintended consequence of this programme was a secular reduction in the expected costs of training for workers, especially male workers, and a secular improvement in the efficacy of labour market signalling. Diffusion of the samurai family ideal increased the demand for education among the general population, raising the income elasticity of demand for education. In turn, bureaucratically driven supply shifts in the scope and diversity of the school system accommodated the demand expansion, increasing the degree to which fresh school graduates could signal their expected training costs and effort capacity through certification. The more finely differentiated the educational system was in terms of specialization and hierarchical ranking, the more readily could an individual signal through his or her certification the expected level of training costs (within a specific set of industries) and effort capacity he or she was likely to possess upon hiring. These secular trends on the supply side of the labour market were instrumental in the refashioning of labour markets which was taking place as heavy industrialization gained momentum during the interwar period.

One of the most contentious issues in early Meiji governmental policy was the hammering out of a Civil Code which governed family (*ie*) affairs and the legal organization of households. Use of Western European models for household legislation – especially the French – was much debated and opposed in many quarters. In matters as fundamental to everyday social life as the family system, the argument for using Tokugawa precedence was strong. But if Tokugawa precedence was to be relied on, what precedence was it to be? For while the stem family system had become firmly entrenched throughout rural and urban Japan by the mid-eighteenth century, there were at least two quite different ideal types forms which the stem family system took (and in reality consideration variation within each ideal type): that of the peasant household and that of the samurai household.

In fashioning a Civil Code which would serve the interests of the Imperial Nationalist philosophy the Meiji oligarchy, seeking to enhance the standing of the Japanese people in the ranks of the imperial powers who were either European or of European origin, found themselves caught between the desire to formulate a code modelled on Western institutions and the realization that in matters so fundamental to the daily lives of the populace, a sharp break with the past could create havoc. This explains the long delay in promulgating the Civil Code. In fact the code was not issued until 1898 after three long decades of Meiji rule during which countless fundamental reforms had transpired including revision of the land tax, creation of joint stock banking, creation of a draft army, and the establishment of the basis for an elabourate school system. In purporting to find a model in the family system confined to the French family code, the Meiji oligarchy borrowed from abroad the barest trappings of the stem family system of the West; what they mainly did was to resuscitate the samurai form of the Tokugawa stem family system.

To the end of promoting the samurai ideal the government invested substantial resources. Compulsory elementary-school textbooks made a great virtue of the idea of *ryōsoi kenbo* (good wife/wise mother) and the writings of the Tokugawa philosopher Kaibara in support of this ideal were made assigned reading in the schools. The impact of this campaign was perhaps not immediate, but as generation after generation of girls passed through the compulsory school system, and as magazines written specifically for females promoted the concept, the ideal diffused down to even the most remote villages. For instance Embree (1939) and Smith and Wiswell (1982) give fascinating accounts of family life in a small relatively isolated village in Kyushu, *Suye mura* during the interwar period. According to these accounts older women in the village were quite loose in their morals. They were observed openly displaying their genitals at festivals and rituals; they give birth to illegitimate offspring; they drank and sang lewd songs at parties and gatherings. Several had married and divorced a number of husbands. But the younger women were far more chaste and circumspect in their relations with the other sex. Smith (1983) attributes this change to the influence of women's magazines and to the school system, to which one can add the diffusion of the *ryōsai kenbo* ideal through these vehicles. This can be taken as a partial indicator of the diffusion of the other norms associated with the samurai, for instance the high value placed on education. No quantitative proof exists, but from a qualitative point of view it is quite likely that the diffusion of the Imperial Nationalist ideology did have the impact of increasing the income elasticity of demand for education in a secular sense. That is, preferences regarding the merits and demerits of schooling above and beyond the compulsory elementary school level were to some extent shaped by ideology.

In my discussion I have made repeated reference to the educational system in terms of demand. But in fact supply-side constraints on the expansion of the system were as important as demand, if not more so in determining the speed at which enrolments could and did increase and the amount of differentiation within the system. This leads me to consider one extreme model of the Japanese educational system: the 'bureaucratic-supply-of-slots model'. By this I mean the notion that the national educational bureaucracy, the Ministry of Education, determines through its regulations, administrative actions and expenditures in the market, the availability of slots in educational institutions of various sorts. In principle, as long as there is excess demand for slots at each level of schooling, given any cohort of new elementary school entrants, the number of slots available to them as they progress upwards through the successive layers of the educational system determines the advancement rate. The flow of graduates into the market is determined by the number of slots allocated to entrants n years before, where n is the length of time from entrance to graduation. Control of slots and control of the quality and characteristics of the graduates are closely related. Other things equal, the greater is the resource input into each student then the greater is the potential for training that student. Thus a restrictive supply of slots policy may sacrifice quantity of graduates for average quality. For this reason a bureaucratic supply of slots policy may attempt to effectively utilize scarce resources by accomplishing different aims at different levels of schooling: for example inculcating discipline and basic literacy into the masses at the elementary school level at relatively low cost per pupil, meeting the demand for training in practical skills in agriculture and manufacturing at the middle level, and meeting the demand for theoretical skills and the capacity to understand, and work with, documents written in other languages at the highest level at relatively expensive costs per student.

It is not difficult to find a theoretical rationale justifying the bureaucratic supply of slots model in Japan. For instance Dore (1976) uses a variant of the late-developer model in explaining how the Meiji educational system emerged and evolved. Bent of importing foreign technology and foreign institutions in both the public and private sectors, the Meiji government had a strong incentive to produce a flow of high-quality, technically oriented graduates with knowledge of foreign languages. Constrained by relatively low tax intake per-capita because income per capita was not high, the per capita resources it could marshall for higher education were severely limited. Moreover it had to trade off the public supplying of slots in the higher and middle reaches of the system against the goal of providing every young person with a basic education, for successful promotion of the Imperial Nationalist programme of development required that a nationally oriented ideology centred around reverence for imperial institutions be developed for the masses; and there was no more efficient means of inculcating this ideology than a compulsory education system with a curriculum which included heavy doses of 'moral' education promoting the imperial system. In accomplishing this aim the national government showed considerable resourcefulness in economizing on the scarce resources which it could secure from the population: it required that localities assume the financial responsibility for a programme of compulsory elementary education (first 4 years in length, later extended to 6 years) whose curriculum was completely determined by the Ministry of Education, that is by the central authorities in Tokyo. It should be noted however that the Ministry of Education allowed for, and in practice did provide, subsidies to local districts for the maintenance of their programs.

In short the Imperial Nationalist theory of prewar Japanese development provides a convenient rationale for the bureaucratic-supply-of-slots interpretation of the development of Japanese education. And in many ways the rationale and the model are compelling: for the educational system which gradually emerged and vigorously expanded during the 1880–1940 period was centralized, hierarchical, and at higher echelons specialized and characterized by chronic excess demand. Thus it served both to train and to signal: the more hierarchical the ranking within grades, and the greater the excess demand at the higher levels of the system, and the more specialized the certification, the more clearly could employers gauge in advance of hiring the type of workers they were likely to take in.

But surely demand matters as well. For example, signalling at the upper end of the hierarchy is most effective if there is excess demand. Incorporating both supply and demand permits us to give a convincing account of the expansion in the prewar educational system. We now take up the task of analysing the prewar system, commencing with a discussion of the layers in the system itself; and then turning to the discussion of the three layers of the system: the lower-elementary, middle, and higher levels.[3]

That the system would be hierarchical was determined at the very inception of the Meiji experiments in higher education. Various alternative plans were legislated, tried and scrapped, so that no single system was in place for very long, but within the first three decades the basic framework was laid out: (a) elementary school was compulsory (in Japanese the term *gimu kyōiku* is the phrase used to designate compulsory education) and both males and females attended the same schools which were funded from local sources. At first four years of schooling was mandatory; this was subsequently changed to six years, with the final two years designated as higher elementary school. For instance in 1919 children entered into elementary school aged 6 (perhaps after attending a kindergarten which was non-compulsory) and graduated aged 12. (b) At the middle-school level education became voluntary, somewhat specialized, and tracking took over. First male and female tracks separated at this point. Consider males for a moment. In the year 1919 male graduates of elementary school could apply for entry into three basic types of educational institutions (in actual practice there were additional routes but these were the dominant ones): (a) middle schools with academic programs which prepared them to take the examinations for entry into high schools (which, in turn, were preparatory for entrance into universities) or into technical colleges (*senmonggakō*). Students who successfully passed the examinations for these schools could expect to graduate at age 16; (b) vocational schools (*jitsugyō gakkō*) or vocational continuation schools (*hoshū jitsugyō gakkō*). Graduates of these schools were typically aged 15. Some of these schools offered night courses so that students could combine work and study. Now consider the graduate of a male middle school. If he wished to apply for admission into a higher-level educational institution (this is the 1919 system I am describing) he could apply to a high school preparatory to university (typically entering it aged 17 and graduating at 19; if successful in entering a university he could expect to enter the labour market aged 23; Imperial university admission slots were especially demanded), or a technical college (entering aged 17 and graduating at 20 or 21), or a higher normal school (*kōtō shihan gakkō*) from which he would expect to graduate at 21. In short a myriad of paths, all leading up along specialized tracks and all designed to feed graduates into different submarkets of the active market for new hires, confronted the graduating elementary school boy. For instance those wishing to teach aspired to normal schools, those wishing to work in the national bureaucracy attempted to enter an Imperial university, and those wishing to work as technical personnel tended to select the *senmongakkō* route. Moreover with each category of schools a pecking order was established in terms of the degree of difficulty associated with passing the entrance examinations. Thus the system worked to separate out the population of graduates into distinct groups differentiated by expected training costs in specific areas (e.g., according to the type of school) and according to the expected speed with which one could be readily trained, that is in terms of the trained capacity to supply effort (as signalled by the ability to enter schools according to their rank).

For females a similar hierarchical structure existed in middle and higher education: one that was distinctly separate from that for males, one that did *not* permit entry into Imperial universities (however entry into some private colleges and universities was possible), and one that directed girls towards a domestic career (the *ryōsoi kenbo* policy), or into teaching or into the acquisition of vocational skills. As above I will describe the state of affairs in 1919. After graduation from compulsory middle school a girl could seek admission to: (a) a *kōtō jogakkō* (higher girl's school), from which after entering aged 12 she could expect to graduate at either 16 or 17; (b) a higher elementary school (*kōtō shōgakkō*), from which she could expect to graduate at age 15; or (c) a vocational school from which she would expect to graduate at either 15 or 17, depending on the exact track and programme she was admitted to. Graduates of *kōtō jogakkō* could apply for admission to higher normal schools for women (*joshi kōtō shihan gakkō*) or speciality normal schools (either graduating aged 18 or 20); and graduates of *kōtō shōgakkō* could enter regular normal school aged 15 and expect to graduate at 19. Note that the tracking and specialization characteristic of the male system also applies to the female system, although the options were more limited in practice. The limited range of options is consistent with the view that women were expected to have short time horizons as far as post-graduation employment was concerned, and therefore the anticipated social pay off to differentiation and specialization was far less.

Before we consider in greater detail how each level of the school system expanded, the constraints on growth and the interaction of supply and demand for slots at each level, let us consider some data in order to get a general sense of which sectors were expanding the most rapidly during which periods. Consider Table 2.2. In panel A.1 I give student/teacher ratios (growth rates in these ratios are given in panels A.2 and A.3). The following points are evident. (a) Student/teacher ratios tend to be higher at lower levels of education and vica versa. That is, resources per student were economized on at the lowest level of education, and at higher levels supply constraints on the number of entrants allowed in bolstered input per pupil. The one exception to this proposition is the continuation vocational school. (b) With the exception of vocational continuation schools, the growth rates for teachers and the growth rates for students are roughly the same, so that student/faculty ratios remained fairly stable over the course of the prewar period. (c) School attendance rates went up over time, since population growth rates fell far short of enrolment growth rates. This tendency was particularly evident at the middle and higher levels. However, once mandatory education was introduced, for the age

TABLE 2.2 Expansion of the prewar educational system, 1880–1940

[A] Annual growth rates for students and teachers [a]

| Period | | Middle level: non-vocational | | | High school: non-vocational | | | | Vocational | |
	Elementary schools	Middle school (males)	Higher schools (females)	High school (males)	Senmon-gakkō	University	Normal schools and related	Regular	Continuation
				A1 Student/teacher ratio						
1926–30	42.5	25.4	24.9	14.4	13.1	11.9	14.9	20.0	69.9
				A2 Teachers						
1873–85	11.8	45.8	n.e.	n.e.	3.4	n.e.	13.9	584.1	n.e.
1886–1900	0.1	12.7	19.4	28.7	5.4	2.9	2.2	23.3	n.e.
1901–1920	4.0	6.0	20.2	1.3	8.1	9.9	4.4	13.4	24.5
1921–1940	2.4	4.3	7.3	8.7	5.7	13.5	2.2	8.0	24.5

TABLE 2.2   (continued)

[A] Annual growth rates for students and teachers[a]

		Middle level: non-vocational		High school: non-nocational				Vocational	
Period	Elementary schools	Middle school (males)	Higher schools (females)	High school (males)	Senmon-gakkō	University	Normal schools and related	Regular	Continuation
				A3 Students					
1873–85	7.1	50.7	n.e.	n.e.	2.5	n.e.	6.2	597.0	n.e.
1886–1900	2.4	17.5	40.7	18.1	4.1	6.9	6.0	31.0	n.e.
1901–1920	3.6	5.8	21.1	2.2	8.5	9.0	5.4	15.0	59.9
1921–1940	2.0	5.3	8.9	6.2	4.9	15.0	2.2	9.2	6.3

[B] Annual population growth rates[b]

	Total, aged 6–12	Males, aged 12–17	Females, aged 12–16
1888–1903	0.6	1.0	0.7
1903–1918	2.3	1.7	1.7
1920–1940	1.4	1.8	2.0

TABLE 2.2   (*continued*)

[C] log–log regressions on the acceptance rate, selected types of schools[c]

School type period	Dependent variable	Constant	Year	Log of real consumption per capita	Log of percentage of labor force in non-primary activity	AR (1)	Adjusted R^2	Durbin–Watson statistic
Male middle school, 1906–1936	Acceptance rate, log	−51.64* (−2.89)	0.03* (3.10)	−1.53** (−2.61)	−0.03 (−0.26)	n.e.	0.43	0.48
Ditto.	ditto.	−24.77 (−0.83)	0.01 (0.96)	0.03 (0.08)	0.01 (0.13)	0.90* (10.20)	0.85	0.84
Female higher school, 1906–1936	ditto.	−41.02* (−2.60)	0.03* (2.86)	−1.33** (−2.56)	0.02 (0.24)	n.e	0.31	0.73
Ditto.		−13.03 (−0.73)	0.01 (1.02)	−0.57 (−1.09)	−0.05 (−0.46)	0.71* (4.38)	0.61	1.65
Male high school, 1906–34	ditto.	−28.55* (−2.01)	0.02* (2.76)	−2.57* (−5.55)	−0.11 (−1.22)	n.e.	0.86	1.48
Ditto.	ditto.	−25.81 (−1.59)	0.02* (2.24)	−2.47* (−4.67)	−0.11 (−1.03)	0.27 (1.29)	0.85	1.86

TABLE 2.2 [C]   (continued)

School type period	Dependent variable	Constant	Year	Log of real consumption per capita	Log of percentage of labor force in non-primary activity	AR (1)	Adjusted R^2	Durbin–Watson statistic
Vocational and commercial, schools selected 1882–93 and 1898–1940 (d)	ditto.	25.50*** (1.70)	−0.01 (−1.13)	0.01 (0.85)	−0.51* (−3.08)	n.e.	0.40	1.84
Normal schools, selected	ditto.	171.91* (8.30)	−0.09* (−7.62)	2.59* (6.25)	−0.06 (−0.41)	n.e.	0.91	0.84
Ditto.	ditto.	126.95* (4.02)	−0.07* (−3.75)	0.96 (1.22)	0.01 (0.08)	0.77* (4.21)	0.94	1.23

Notes:

(a)   Based on growth rates calculated between 5 year moving averages for the periods 1873–75, 1876–80, ..., 1936–40.

(b)   Based on growth rates for *koseki* (household registration) data for every 5 years after 1888, until 1918. In 1920 and after based on census data.

(c)   The costant term and the year are not entered as logarithms; the other variables are.

(d)   Based on combined figures for Tokyo *Kōtō Shōgyō Gakkō* (Tokyo Higher Commercial School), Tokyo *Kōtō Kōgyō Gakkō* (Tokyo Higher Industrial School), Yokohama *Kōtō Shōgyō Gakkō* (Yokohama Higher Commercial School), and Yamaguchi *Kōyō Shōgyō Gakkō* (Yamaguchi Higher Commercial School).

Sources:

Karasawa (1955: various tables); Ohkawa and M. Shinohara (1979: various tables); and Japan Statistical Association (1987, 1988: various tables).

group 6 to 12, population growth rates and student growth rates are virtually identical; after 1920 the rates are identical. (d) During the 1873–85 expansion of the educational system, increases in both students and teachers occurred across the board at all levels. During the period 1886–1900 elementary schools, having become well established during the earlier period, expanded at modest levels but middle schools expanded rapidly. During the phase 1901–20 the momentum of growth shifted towards higher schools for females and vocational continuation schools. Finally, in the interwar period growth was very strong in the university education sector. That is to say, in the early Meiji period the emphasis was on expansion in all sectors, but especially in the compulsory sector which offered the least social benefits in terms of signalling potential ability to supply effort in each assignment. Once the lowest level of the system was established, growth shifted towards the middle levels, which was consistent with an era of balanced growth when productivity was increasing in both agricultural and light-industrial sectors and thus the demand for agricultural vocational schooling was an important factor driving overall growth at the middle-school level. But in the interwar period, under the new demand conditions associated with the rapid increase in heavy industrial production, the tempo of growth shifted towards the highest level of the system where technical training had the highest expected payoff. In short these data suggest that slot expansion was strongly tempered by shifts in demand.

Now let us consider each level of the system commencing with elementary schooling. The Fundamental Code of Education of 1872, subsequently modified and developed into the Imperial Rescript on Education of 1890, required that local areas fund a programme whose content was virtually completely determined by the central authorities in Tokyo. From 1883 on, moreover, the Ministry of Education determined the number of future teachers to be trained at prefectural normal schools in accordance with its

	Percentage of elementary school personnel who were		
	Teachers	Assistant teachers	Instructors
1880	27.6	—	72.4
1900	55.5	21.4	23.3
1920	76.6	9.0	14.4
1935	89.1	2.1	8.8

estimates of the expected number of school age children (cf. Japan. Ministry of Education, 1963: 44ff.). That the Ministry was able to rapidly generate an increase in the number of normal school graduates sufficient to satisfy burgeoning demand is indicated by the figures in page 50 on teachers (subordinate and less trained), assistant teachers, and instructors.

Moreover as can be seen from Table 2.2, with the exception of the period 1886–1900, the growth in teacher stock exceeded the growth in the number of students. In short, working through prefectural governments the national Ministry of Education was effective in channelling resources into a system whose quality, as measured in terms of inputs per pupil, was increasing. What was taught and learned in the elementary schools? Students became literate and numerate. Estimates of the inability to write one's one name, specifically on the percentage unable to do so on marriage registers, in three non-industrial prefectures – Shiga, Kagoshima, and Okayama – provide interesting clues as to the success of the elementary schools (figures from Umemura *et al.*, 1988: 29 ff.): M = male and F = female):

Year	Shiga		Kagoshima		Okayama	
	M	F	M	F	M	F
1877	10.8	60.7	—	—	—	—
1885	9.9	41.5	63.2	95.9	—	—
1889	11.0	34.8	54.7	92.1	31.4	54.9
1892	11.6	35.4	—	—	26.4	49.3

Note that in Shiga, lying with the immediate reaches of the economically advanced prefectures of Kyoto and Osaka, male literacy was high from early Meiji on, and the dramatic change in this district was the decline in female illiteracy. By contrast in remote Kagoshima, in southern Kyushu, both male and female illiteracy rates were high, even in 1889. Still, trends towards improvements in literacy are evident for all three districts. And along with literacy came a heavy dosage of indoctrination in the Imperial system and nationalism. In early Meiji the level of indoctrination was muted; but after 1910 the intensity picked up considerably. In short, elementary-school education was aimed at teaching basic skills and at indoctrinating the young population in the institutions of Imperial Nationalism. It was differentiated by geographic region – schools in the agricultural villages often lagged behind their counterparts in the metropolitan areas – but the emphasis was on uniform homogeneous education, not on specialization and differentiation which signalled capacity for giving effort and being effectively trained at low cost.

Post-compulsory education was a totally different matter. It was highly specialized and differentiated. For females the high schools, which in terms of student age range were roughly comparable to male middle schools, were principally places where the domestic arts were taught and the *ryosai kenbo* ideology promoted (cf. Amano, 1991: 96ff). However the Meiji government observed that in Europe and North America females were extensively employed in teachers, especially at the elementary school level. Needing a large number of additional teachers in order to expand the compulsory school system, the Ministry of Education came down in favour of training women as well as men for the profession. Therefore special normal schools for women were established during Meiji; and this became one of the few wage labour markets which girls from 'polite' society could hope to enter. These remarks suggest that the demand for higher education for women, in particular the demand for the girl's high school, was mainly a function of family income. The better off a family was, the more readily it could afford to pay the fees for a female high school where a daughter could perfect the domestic arts, thereby enhancing her prospects on the marriage market. Now as real income per capita increased over the course of the prewar period, the acceptance rate of female high schools fell, and then subsequently rose. Since slots were expanding while income was going up, relieving pressure on the competition rate and working to increase the acceptance rate (which *ceteris paribis* reduced the acceptance rate), it is not clear whether the income effect was in fact working. But regressions reported in panel C of Table 2.2 do show that the elasticity of the acceptance rate with respect to income was negative; the regressions also show a positive elasticity on the 'year' variable, indicating that a positive time trend in the number of slots did increase the acceptance rate. In short the regressions show that income-related demand was interacting with supply to produce trends in overall female enrolments at the middle-school level. By inference, differentiation and specialization for females was strongly determined by the distribution of, and levels of income of, income in the population.

For males the situation is more complex. In general we would expect that improvements in the capacity to pay, that is increments in real income per head, would reduce the acceptance rate by shifting outward the demand for slots, and we would expect outward shifts in the demand for certain professions to which a specialized type of schooling led to reduce the acceptance rate in the institutions offering that type of schooling; we would also expect an outward shift in the number of slots, for instance resulting from time trend, to increase the acceptance rate. But for normal schools and military schools special government subsidies obviated the income requirement. Therefore we would expect the income effect on the acceptance rate to have been positive, since increases in income encourage males to pursue other non-subsidized lines of higher education. In light of these remarks consider the fluctuations in acceptance rates for vocational and commercial schools, for male middle and high schools, and for normal schools. For normal schools the income elasticity was positive but for the other types of schools it was negative. Again with the exception of normal schools the coefficient on the variable which measures the degree to which jobs were found outside of family employment (that is the variable measuring the degree to which employment is *outside* agriculture, fishing and forestry) was negative, suggesting that an increase in the demand for workers requiring a certain specific type of schooling did increase the demand for that schooling. Research by Karasawa (1955) which shows the demand for normal school slots moved inversely to the demand for vocational and commercial school slots during the prewar period – economic booms promoting vocational and commercial school enrolment and economic slumps promoting normal school enrolment – is consistent with my results indicating that demand was important in shaping acceptance rates. But it should be kept in mind that my regression results reported in Table 2.2 are not strong viewed from a narrow statistical viewpoint. In particular the Durbin–Watson statistics are poor, and adjusting for first-order serial correlation tends to render variables statistically insignificant.

What about the demand and supply for slots in the highest echelon of the systems: universities and technical colleges (*senmongakko*)? During the early Meiji period the government developed the imperial university system as the apex of the entire national educational structure, and made the imperial university the place where research would be carried out to acquire the knowledge needed to cope with Western technology; this would be imparted to the most academically competent, who, it was expected, would join the ranks of high-level government officialdom, government-managed companies, and large private industrial concerns, for instance the newly established *zaibatsu* (financial cliques). The imperial university system was officially inaugurated in 1886 at the University of Tokyo, created in 1877 out of an amalgam of the *Shoheiko*, the Tokugawa government's university, the *Kaiseijo* (Institute of Western Learning), and the *Igakusho* (Institute of Western Medicine). In recognition of the importance of learning from the West, teaching at the University of Tokyo was initially done exclusively in Western languages and not in Japanese. By 1906 there were two imperial universities, by 1916 four and by the 1930s seven. Growth in the imperial university system was slow, and because only graduates of the most prestigious high schools could apply for admission; slow because for many years the emphasis was almost exclusively on turning out graduates to staff the relatively small number of posts in the upper levels of the Imperial ministries. Thus during the Meiji period when there were relatively few high schools which had standing sufficiently high to guarantee admission into the imperial universities, actual acceptance rates into the imperial universities were high, since the weeding out had already occurred at the level of admission into the élite high schools. With the expansion of large heavy industrial firms with the need for technical expertise in Western science and engineering the supply and demand situation began to change significantly: for instance by 1935, 46 per cent of imperial university graduates found their way into industrial employment, many entering the *zaibatsu*. The point is that gaining entrance into imperial universities sent very strong signals to heavy industrial firms – about one's capacity to master English and/or German as well as technical information (the capacity to be trained in specific areas of interest to companies importing foreign technology), about one's individual willingness to study hard for many years in the pursuit of a long-term goal (implicit rate-of-time discount), and about one's intrinsic level of capacity to give effort and be trained. Is it surprising that companies in the new heavy industrial field overcame their general aversion to excessively committing to individual blue-collar workers drawn from a pool which was very heterogeneous with respect to time horizon, and capacity to be trained, and were willing to extend to graduates from the élite universities contracts based on job security, extensive training, and, eventually, after promotion, responsibility for training and monitoring blue- and white-collar subordinates? For among the pool of graduates who had passed through such a long competitive tournament heterogeneity was relatively muted, and the probability of taking on potential failures minuscule.

What was the composition of the student population at the university level? As befitted their élite status and their connections with the national government, and reflecting the fact that few commoners had advanced far in the educational system during the late Tokugawa period, the vast majority of students at Tokyo Imperial University during early Meiji were former samurai. For instance Kikuchi (1984: 9) shows that approximately three quarters of the students in the period 1878–80 were ex-samurai. However as the scale of enrolments increased the ex-samurai pool declined relative to the student intake. Moreover as the number of commoners successfully passing through the ranks of the high schools increased as cohorts born after 1874 worked their way through the post-Meiji Restoration educational apparatus, the proportion of former samurai dropped precipitously. By 1885 the percentage of former samurai was a mere 51.7 per cent. Still, it is clear that in its early phase, Tokyo Imperial University was elitist not just in the sense of drawing upon the cream of the crop of academically tracked middle school graduates, but socially elitist as well.

Important as the imperial university system was, however, as the educational system expanded in scale the bulk of graduates flowed through private and public institutions of lower prestige, institutions offering curricula more closely attuned to commercial and industrial pursuits. Consider the following figures on institutions of higher learning (Amano, 1979: 14 ff):

Year	Universities			*Senmongakkō*		
	Imperial	Public	Private	Imperial	Public	Private
1915	4	—	—	29	7	56
1925	5	10	19	59	5	79
1935	6	14	25	58	11	114

Notable in comparison with the halting increase in imperial facilities is the brisk expansion of private universities and *senmongakkō*. Ever since early Meiji the government had promoted the *senmongakkō* as a lower-level technologically oriented track for middle-school graduates. For instance, in 1935, 65 per cent of state *senmongakkō* graduates went into private industry upon graduation. And in 1918 an extraordinary conference on education recommended the establishment of a system of public and private single- and multiple-faculty universities to supplement the imperial university system, the University Ordinance of 1918 was issued permitting the term *daigaku* (university) to be applied to institutions accredited by the Ministry of Education that were outside the imperial university system (cf. Amano, 1983). As a result, a number of the *senmongakkō* were upgraded into universities, and, as can be seen from the figures above, the private sector grew more rapidly than the public. Overall, as the number of private universities grew, the proportion of *senmongakkō* graduates in the pool of higher education graduates declined,

from 81 per cent in 1905 to 65 per cent in 1935. In allowing the private
university sector to expand in response to a post-World-War-I surge in the
job opportunities in the heavy industrial sector, the Ministry of Education
displayed a market-oriented pragmatism which was characteristic of the
imperial nationalist programme: be efficient in the use of national
resources by permitting the private sector to participate on a regulated and
accredited basis, in a system designed to supply technically trainable individuals to the industrial sector.

In short, the educational system adopted by the imperial nationalist state
was centralized, hierarchical and specialized with manifold career-oriented
tracks. Centralization served the ideological needs of the state, which
increasingly turned the elementary school textbooks into tools for the
veneration of the imperial line and the national will. In these schools all
children learned discipline and respect for the nation's military-oriented
development programme. Hierarchy served the strategic labour recruitment interests of heavy industrial concerns in a relatively low-income
nation whose government aimed at efficiently allocating the limited tax
resources available to it. The system was steeply graded by prestige of
institution. As soon as it became evident from the success of a school's
graduates on the job market that considerable expected career benefits
were attached to graduating from a particular school, the status of a school
was enhanced (a good example is the experience of the two private
schools Keio and Waseda), and students failing the examinations for entry
into these high-status institutions often eschewed entrance into less highly
ranked institutions, electing rather to become *rōnin* (the term literally
means 'masterless samurai' and is jokingly used to describe those students
who are not currently enrolled in a regular educational institution but are
devoting their time to cramming for the entrance examinations into the
one or several institutions they are committed to entering), bent on gaining
admission in the next year or if necessary in subsequent years. That the
rōnin system developed in the prewar period testifies to the fact an excess
demand on the part of students for the slots offered by the higher echelons
of the educational system had developed. It also testifies to the fact that
because employers were interested in hiring technically trained workers
who were diligent and loyal – that is had a low rate-of-time discount –
attending a cram school for a year or two before securing acceptance to a
prestigious was not viewed as detriment to securing well paid employment
after graduation.

In sum the centralization of the system at the lowest level and the hierarchy and technical orientation at the higher levels that were characteristic
of the educational system at the beginning of the Meiji period continued to

be characteristic of the system as it evolved over the course of the interwar years. What changed was the relative balance between the various levels of the system. During the era of balanced growth the focus was on the lower and middle levels of the system, and the development of vocational schools aimed at farmers was an important aspect of the expansion. But under post World-War-I dualism as the demand for workers, whom employers in the heavy industries wished to hire under long-term labour contracts, increased the tempo of expansion in the educational system shifted towards the upper echelons of the system. In short, while the bureaucratic-supply-of-slots model is indispensable in understanding how the Japanese educational system operates, private-sector labour market demand has also been critical in shaping the actual structure of the system. Pragmatic compromise between the goals of the bureaucracy in Tokyo and the exigencies of the market was a definite hallmark of the system throughout the prewar period.

The diffusion of the samurai ideal for the stem family system, which was directly linked to the development of compulsory elementary school education, along with the expansion of the higher echelons of the educational system, which was fairly closely linked to the evolving structure of labour market demand, undoubtedly played a role in shaping preferences for education and the characteristics signalled by achievement in the system: effort and training capacity and a low rate-of-time discount. Militarization of society was also instrumental in shaping preferences. As with the writing of textbooks inculcating the imperial doctrine and nationalism, the militarization of society did not occur overnight once the new Meiji government took over. For instance until the turn of the century most young men from upper-income families managed to avoid serving in the military. And in spite of the success enjoyed by Japan in two major conflicts, one against China and the other against Russia, morale among the top military leaders was not high in the early years of the twentieth century. For instance owing to budgetary constraints military budgets were pinched and equipment was often out of date. But between 1910 and 1945 officers like General Giichi Tanaka managed not only to reverse the financial fortunes of the army and navy, but also to build up a network of military 'cells' throughout rural hamlets and schools supportive of the military and the *fukoku kyōhei* ideology. As a result society both male and female was militarized. Or, as Smethurst (1974) argues, the social basis of militarism was firmly established.

Smethurst (1974) focuses on several specific organizations in accounting for the diffusion of military consciousness throughout the rural and urban populations of Japan. First, the Imperial Military Reserve

Association, which by 1936 had 3 million volunteers within its ranks, was established in 1910. This organized men aged 20 to 40. Second, beginning in 1915 Tanaka and other officers promoted the development of a Greater Japan Youth Association with youth training centres. Third, women were brought into the network of militarization through the creation of a National Defence Women's Association. In developing this programme of comprehensive military service, Tanaka and his colleagues attempted to kill two birds with one stone: they built a solid base for support of the army and navy and for the Imperial Nationalist ideology at the community level, and they erected a political bulwark against the diffusion of radical left-wing European ideologies (i.e. Marxism-Leninism, syndicalism, anarchism) which, mainly through the agency of intellectuals, were being imported into Japan along with the technology sought after by industrial concerns and the bureaucracy. For in promoting education and the cultivation of things Western, the Imperial Nationalist programme unleashed political forces that could undermine it. Institutionalization of military discipline helped stem the tide. And an indirect consequence of this was a slow but inexorable reshaping of preferences in the general preference. In particular there was a growing acceptance of training.

In sum, in understanding how labour market submarkets evolved and the efficacy of signalling improved during the interwar period and before, the role of the governmental policy must not be denigrated. Government impact on the differentiation of the labour market on the supply side and on the expected levels of training capacity and of time preferences of workers in each of the distinct submarkets was felt through a variety of avenues: through the promotion of the samurai ideal for the stem family system, through the development of a centralized, hierarchical and specialized school system which was sufficiently flexible to respond to changing labour market demand, and through the militarization of society.

Now let us turn to a examination of the interrelationship of demand and supply for workers in the various submarkets of the prewar labour market.

2.5   THE FEMALE LABOUR MARKET IN LIGHT INDUSTRY: SUPPLY CONDITIONS

The overwhelming majority of textile workers in later Meiji and interwar Japan were young women, recruited from agricultural villages under contracts typically running between two and five years in duration, and signed by their household heads and representatives of the company. (Shindo, 1961; Tsurumi, 1990). Some were willing volunteers and some were not. But the contract was generally not an arrangement between the individual hired and the corporate entity. Rather it was an arrangement between a rural *ie* and a firm. It was common for the *ie* selling its labour to receive an advance payment at the time the contract was signed and in some cases a portion of the wages earned during the course of a year were remitted directly to the *ie* by the contracting firm. Thus calculations concerning the attractiveness or non-attractiveness of the remuneration stipulated in the contract were first and foremost calculations made by the patriarchal head of the *ie*, and the opportunity cost of a girl's daily labour as far as the head was concerned was what she was likely to contribute to the *ie* with a day's worth of labour input on the farm.[4] Thus there was an important linkage between labour productivity in agriculture and wages in light manufacturing in so far as light manufacturing was heavily dependent on the supply of female labour for rural households. In particular a rising level of hourly productivity in agriculture should be mirrored in a rising level of wages in light industry. This is the basic logic of balanced growth during the first four decades of Japanese industrialization.

As the Japanese population grew from around 37 million in 1880 to about 72 million in 1940, the composition of the employed labour force shifted away from agriculture, fishing and forestry towards manufacturing and service sector employment, but overall labour supply to agriculture did not change a great deal. Indeed between 1880 and 1940 the number of farm households remained virtually unchanged, fluctuating ever so slightly around a figure of 5.5 million. However since the number of resident workers per agricultural household did decline somewhat over time there was a slow decline in the overall stock of workers working in agriculture. For example consider the following figures on resident workers per household (data from various tables in Umemura *et al.*, 1988):

Period	Males	Females	Total
1880–89	1.42	1.23	2.65
1910–19	1.37	1.15	2.52
1930–39	1.25	1.21	2.46

Thus there was a small but steady decline in worker stock in agriculture; during the 1880–1919 period the number of females declined substantially and the number of males remained fairly unchanged; then during the interwar period the number of males dropped dramatically but the number of females increased, partially offsetting the drop in male input. But it is essential that we differentiate between worker stock and labour flow in analysing supply conditions. This is the message of the model of the family-run small firm discussed in Chapter 1. As can be seen from Table 2.3, total work days in agriculture increased tremendously over the period, in fact by almost 50 per cent since work days per worker went up from 113 to 163 and the number of workers declined at a relatively slow rate. This increase in days worked was partly a result of changes on the supply of labour side: to improved health and physical vigour and to electrification.[5] But the principal causes were demand-side changes: the introduction of more robust seed varieties which could be planted earlier in the year and/or harvested later in the year; more fertilizer (whose usage was complementary to the introduction of new seed varieties); more generous irrigation; and an expansion in sideline activities like raising silk cocoons. Hence there was a natural tendency for the supply price of short-term labour from agriculture to industry to rise. But why was the supply/demand situation for labour, most prominently represented by the balance of consumers to workers in farm households, so crucial to the industrial sector? The answer lies in the demographic imbalance between the rural and urban sectors. As can be seen from panel B of Table 2.3, the natural rate of population increase, the birth rate minus the death rate, was far higher in the rural sector (*gun*) of Japan than it was in the urban sector (*shi*). Indeed the natural rate of increase in 1920 was 14.1 per thousand population in *gun* and −3.3 per thousand in *shi* (cf. Mosk, 1983).[6]

That labour productivity in the agricultural sector rose at quite a high rate during the Meiji period is a basic feature of balanced growth. In effect investing in agricultural technological improvements and capital earned expected returns which were not too dissimilar from those earned by investments in light manufacturing. This is one reason landlords were quite actively involved in agricultural activities during the Meiji period and helps explain why absentee landlordism (commonly referred to as parasitic landlordism in the Japanese literature) was not much of a social issue during the Meiji period. However as dualism developed there was a growing disparity between the opportunities available to well-off landlords and those available to poorer tenant farmers. But it is not correct to conclude, as some scholars do, that agricultural-sector labour productivity growth completely stagnated: for instance during the 1930s labour productivity rose in real terms (deflating the nominal net value added figures per worker by a agricultural price index) at over 2 per cent per annum, and if we take into account the terms of trade between agricultural goods and manufacturing goods it rose at a rate of over 6 per cent per annum (deflating by nominal net value added figures per worker by the general

TABLE 2.3   Selected supply conditions governing female labour supply to manufacturing: 1880–1940

| | Year | | | | | | | |
Variable	1880	1900	1910	1920	1925	1930	1935	1940
[A] Agricultural sector								
Workers in agriculture: (1,000s)								
1. males	8,332	8,475	8,527	7,626	7,386	7,631	7,458	6,263
2. females	7,256	7,355	7,348	6,375	6,150	6,340	6,318	7,122
Workdays per:								
1. worker	113	131	139	163	159	151	160	163
2. male equivalent worker	131	150	160	187	183	173	183	192
Index of labour productivity (per workday) in agriculture, 1880 = 100.	100	119	137	159	171	187	190	191
Relative level of price index of agricultural goods to price index of manufactured goods[a]	75.3	76.6	73.7	74.6	100.8	77.8	102.3	113.9
Fertilizer value (1934–36 yen) per 100 workdays in agriculture	1.6	1.9	4.6	6.8	10.1	12.6	13.3	15.7

TABLE 2.3   (continued)

Variable	Year							
	1880	1900	1910	1920	1925	1930	1935	1940
[A] Agricultural sector								
Machinery per 100 workdays in agriculture (1934–36 yen)	31.6	31.7	36.1	42.4	48.9	55.1	57.7	60.6
Number of landlordtenant disputes[b]	n.a.	n.a.	n.a.	1,917	2,206	2,478	6,824	3,165
Percentage of landlordtenant disputes involving continuation of tenancy or compensation [b]	n.a.	n.a.	n.a.	0.8	7.8	41.6	44.8	44.6
[B] Demographic								
Standardized vital rates:								
1. birth rate, *gun*	n.a.	n.a.	n.a.	39.1	38.4	35.9	36.0	33.3
2. death rate, *gun*	n.a.	n.a.	n.a.	24.9	19.9	18.0	17.0	16.8
3. natural increase rate, *gun*	n.a.	n.a.	n.a.	14.1	18.5	17.9	19.0	16.5
4. birth rate, *shi*	n.a.	n.a.	n.a.	25.0	25.8	23.1	22.5	21.6
5. death rate, *shi*	n.a.	n.a.	n.a.	28.3	21.8	18.8	17.0	16.2
6. natural increase rate, *shi*	n.a.	n.a.	n.a.	−3.3	3.9	4.3	5.5	5.4

TABLE 2.3   (*continued*]

| | Years | | | | | | | |
Variable	1880	1900	1910	1920	1925	1930	1935	1940
[C] Education								
Percentage of female labor force who completed:								
1. primary education	n.a.	7.1	23.3	38.6	46.1	52.2	57.6	61.8
2. beyond primary education	n.a.	0.1	0.7	2.1	3.2	5.1	4.2	9.9

Notes:
(a)   Ratio of price indices, each index based at 1934–36 prices = 100. 1880 value is actually for 1885.
(b)   Value is for 1923 rather than 1920.
n.a. = not available.

Sources:
Japan. Ministry of Health and Welfare. Institute of Population Problems (1968: various tables); Hayami with Akino, Shintani and Yamada (1975: various tables); Ohkawa (1986: various tables); and Waswo (1977: various tables).

consumer price index).[7] For this reason the opportunity cost of a daughter's labour services continued to rise throughout the interwar period. The doubling of real female wages in manufacturing between 1885–9 and 1935–9 evident from Table 2.4 gives a rough measure of the upward shift in opportunity costs. But several factors conspired to keep fairly low the level of wages which competitive firms had to pay in the light-industrial sector.

First let us consider the issue from the viewpoint of our theory of the family-run small firm. From the analysis in Chapter 1 (in particular from the appendix to Chapter 1) we conclude that the each worker unit W within the household works a number of hours h such that the total marginal product of the total endogenously determined effort as represented by the optimal number of hours worked, $H^* = h^*W$, $dQ/dH(H^*)$, is equal to the ratio of the marginal disutility of an extra hour's worked per worker unit dV/dh divided by the marginal utility of an extra unit of consumption per consumer unit dU/dq. Alternatively, on a per-work-unit basis, the marginal product per consumer unit of an extra hour's worth of work is $dq/dh = (W/C) [(dV/dh)/(dU/dq)]$ at the optimal value of h^*. Now it is theoretically possible that if a worker departs, the remaining household members so reorganize their work effort that total hours remain unchanged. This depends on the functions dV/dh and dU/dq in the range relevant to the household as it makes its adjustment. In this case the remaining household members do have to work harder because there are less hands to work but consumption is bolstered because output is shared among less people. For instance consider a household consisting of the aged mother of the household head who consumes at a level of 0.6C of her adult male son who consumes one unit C, and contributes 0.5 units of work with her son contributing one unit W; suppose the son's wife consumes 0.8C and works 0.8W; that there are two small children generating a total child consumption demand of one unit C but no work; and finally there is an teenage daughter contributing 0.6W and consuming 0.6C. Then the total number of consumption units in the household is 4 and the total number of worker units is 2.9. The ratio of W to C on a percentage basis is 72.5 per cent. If the household sells the labour of its daughter to a factory it reduces its consumption demand by 0.6, dropping total C to 3.4, and its total worker units to 2.3. Now the ratio of W to C is 67.7 per cent on a percentage basis. We would expect dq/dh to fall through an increase in hours worked when the daughter leaves the household (since W/C falls), but we would not necessarily expect the remaining workers in the household to compensate fully for the loss of the daughter's work effort. They might compensate fully for the loss of the daughter's

TABLE 2.4   Daily real wages deflated by the consumer price index and by sectoral price indices
for broad sectors, Japan: quinquennial averages, 1885–1939

[A] Deflated by the consumer price index (1934–36 = 100)

Period	Agriculture			Service	Manufacturing		
	Total	Males	Females	Total[a]	Total	Males	Females
1885–89	0.61	0.73	0.48	n.a.	0.53	0.86	0.39
1890–94	0.73	0.87	0.59	n.a.	0.51	0.80	0.40
1895–99	0.84	0.96	0.71	n.a.	0.53	0.82	0.40
1900–04	0.81	0.91	0.70	n.a.	0.58	0.91	0.42
1905–09	0.74	0.82	0.66	0.60	0.58	0.89	0.41
1910–14	0.78	0.88	0.67	0.62	0.62	0.90	0.44
1915–19	0.86	0.99	0.73	0.74	0.78	1.09	0.51
1920–24	1.08	1.23	0.94	1.08	1.17	1.65	0.74
1925–29	1.08	1.20	0.96	1.13	1.25	1.85	0.75
1930–34	0.83	0.95	0.71	0.88	1.40	2.14	0.69
1935–39	0.87	0.97	0.77	0.82	1.32	1.84	0.60

TABLE 2.4   (*continued*)

[B] Deflated by price indices for sector

Period	Agricultural wages deflated by agricultural price index			Service sector wages deflated by price index for services	Manufacturing wages deflated by inde manufacturing price index		
	Total	Males	Females	Total	Total	Males	Female
1885–89	0.54	0.65	0.42	n.a.	0.32	0.51	0.23
1890–94	0.56	0.67	0.45	n.a.	0.32	0.50	0.25
1895–99	0.65	0.75	0.55	n.a.	0.35	0.54	0.26
1900–04	0.68	0.77	0.59	n.a.	0.39	0.62	0.28
1905–09	0.65	0.72	0.58	1.99	0.39	0.60	0.28
1910–14	0.68	0.77	0.59	2.21	0.46	0.67	0.33
1915–19	0.73	0.84	0.62	2.80	0.49	0.69	0.32
1920–24	0.96	1.08	0.83	4.50	0.91	1.29	0.58
1925–29	1.00	1.11	0.89	3.55	1.13	1.67	0.68
1930–34	0.98	1.12	0.83	1.91	1.40	2.14	0.69
1935–39	0.80	0.89	0.70	1.72	1.22	1.71	0.56

Source:
Ohkawa and Shinohara (1979: various tables)

effort contribution, but only under certain circumstances. If they do exactly compensate surplus labour exists in the sense of workers but not in the sense of an hour's worth of work (i.e. the marginal product of an hour's worth of work is positive, but losing a worker does not reduce output). Cross-sectional regression analysis of the farm household budget data for the year 1929 reported on in Table 2.5 is consistent with a surplus labour hypothesis of this form: for instance on fitting a Cobb–Douglas production function for agricultural output one finds that the worker variable is not statistically significant but the hours-worked variable is. However 1929 is not really an ideal year for testing this hypothesis, because the agricultural economy was in recession.[8] However even if we do not accept the labour surplus thesis it is still possible to take the position that the growth in the opportunity cost to the agricultural household of a loss in female labour was fairly slow even if labour was not in absolute abundance.

In my view what muted increases in real opportunity costs to rural households was the feedback effect of increases in real consumption per capita (ie per household member) on labour productivity in the future. Using the farm household budgets for the period 1931–40 Mosk (1993) shows that (a) the elasticity of expenditures on food, health and education in year $t–1$ on per worker productivity in year t is positive and significant (the estimated elasticities vary across the farm size/tenancy groups but are typically between 1 and 2 in value); (b) the elasticity of per-worker real productivity i year $t–1$ on real expenditures on food, health and education expenditures in year t is positive and significant (estimates vary across the tenancy/farm size groups, falling into the range 0.4 to 0.6); and (c) there is a positive correlation between fertilizer expenditures per hour worked in year t and real expenditures on food, health and education in year t. In short there appears to be a strong feedback process at work in agricultural households which caused rising income to feed back onto itself, generating future income increases. For this reason productivity continued to rise, partly because of better skills, partly owing to better education, and partly owing to improvements in physical capacity. As a result the marginal disutility of an hour's work, dV/dh, declined. The household was freed up to expand its sale of household labour into other activities, including work in factories and by-employments and other sideline activities. An important consequence of this is that during the interwar period the farm household was able to substitute female for male labour in response to the widening differential between male and female wages in manufacturing. In general females worked shorter hours than men and probably exerted less physical energy per hour. But as a result of the feedback running from productivity improvements to future productivity improvements, there was less tightening felt in the labour market than might otherwise have been the case.

The estimates in Table 2.5 on the difference between the wages which farm households paid out for hired labour and the estimated marginal products of labour for the three tenancy groups also help us to understand the nature of the supply curve facing the light-industrial sector. Note that the difference is not significant for owners but is significant for part-owners and tenants, with in-hire labour commanding higher wages than measured household productivity. The fact is that tenants almost never hired in outside labour, except in the periods of peak labour demand such as the spring transplanting and fall harvest. On the other hand owners hired in labour on a more regular basis. Owners also enjoyed higher per-consumer unit levels of income than tenants or part-tenant/part-owners. In effect owners operated close to the margin where their real cost of labour (the ratio of the additional disutility of an extra hours work to an extra unit of consumption per consumer unit) was equal to the wage they paid. Since they could either rent out land and/or hire in labour they operated at a margin where they were roughly indifferent between renting and hiring in labour. But the asset position of tenants was completely different: up to 40 per cent of their rice harvests went to pay rent, depressing their per-worker incomes net of rent, and as a result they tended to work to a lower margin than owners (since the incremental utility flowing from smaller incremental outputs was greater for them than for owners). For example, per-worker income in small-scale tenant farm families fell short of per-worker income in large scale farm owner households by a factor of over 30 per cent and fell short of income per worker in small-scale owner households by a factor in excess of 20 per cent (cf. Mosk, 1993). So workers in tenant households, especially in households operating with a minuscule amount of land (per-person incomes for tenants farming relatively large land areas were not nearly as depressed as were those for marginal tenant families) worked more hours per worker and drew more of the income from sidelines than owner or part-owner/part-tenant families. Under these circumstances a significant number of textile workers were recruited from tenant farm families with limited amounts of land under cultivation. Thus it is not surprising that manufacturing wages fell short of agricultural wages for females: there was little or no seasonality in the payment of the manufacturing wage, and the opportunity cost to tenants of extra labour input fell short of the prevailing (and highly seasonal) agricultural wage which was typically paid by landowners.[9]

Now as the productivity of family labour increased during the 1930s the use of hired in labour declined for all three tenancy groups. But the

TABLE 2.5   Labour input in prewar Japanese agriculture

Panel A   Estimates of the elasticities of labour, capital (value of feed and fertilizer inputs), and land (paddy equivalents) with a Cobb–Douglas specification for gross agricultural output: 219 farm families and three subgroups (owners, part-owners, and tenants) for 1929.

Group	Elasticities			Adjusted R_2
	Land (α_{Ld})	*Capital* (α_K)	*Labour* (α_{LT})	
(A) Worker units (W) for labour input				
Owners	0.13 (0.12)	0.52* (0.09)	0.20 (0.18)	0.31
Part-owners	0.34* (0.06)	0.49* (0.04)	−0.06 (0.09)	0.78
Tenants	0.22* (0.07)	0.44* (0.05)	0.08 (0.08)	0.67
All families	0.21* (0.05)	0.49* (0.04)	0.11 (0.07)	0.51
(B) Hours worked (H) for labour input				
Owners	0.13 (0.12)	0.50* (0.10)	0.21 (0.16)	0.31
Part-owners	0.28* (0.06)	0.43* (0.05)	0.17*** (0.09)	0.78
Tenants	0.22* (0.06)	0.39* (0.05)	0.25* (0.10)	0.70
All families	0.19* (0.05)	0.46* (0.04)	0.22* (0.08)	0.53

Notes:
(a)   Standard errors are below the coefficient estimates.
*   Significant at the 1% level (two-tailed test).
**   Significant at the 5% level (two-tailed test).
***   Significant at the 10% level (two-tailed test).

TABLE 2.5   (*continued*)

Panel B   Means and standard deviations for estimated hourly marginal revenue
product (MRP), wages paid per hour to non-household members
(WNH), and the difference between MRP and WNH for 219 Japanese
farm families in 1929 and three subgroups.

Yen figures

Group	*Estimated hourly marginal revenue product (MRP)*	*Wages paid per hour to non-household members (WNH)*	*MRP-WNH*
Owners	0.086	0.094	–0.008
	(0.260)	(0.086)	(0.273)
Part-owners	0.045	0.083	–0.037*
	(0.014)	(0.079)	(0.077)
Tenants	0.064	0.127	–0.063**
	(0.020)	(0.201)	(0.198)
All families	0.072	0.099	–0.027***
	(0.178)	(0.126)	(0.217)

Notes:
(a)   Significance test is for whether MRP-WNH is significantly different from 0.
It is a two-tailed test.
*   Significant at the 1% level.
**   Significant at the 5% level.
***   Significant at the 10% level.

wide differentials in relative per-capita incomes and per-capita consumption between the three tenancy groups did not shrink to any appreciable degree (Mosk, 1993). The typical landowning household had, in comparison with the smaller tenant household, considerable per-capita disposable resources available for educating its children (especially the sons who were not likely to take over the farm family headship), who by dint of the advantage which certification in middle or higher echelons of the educational system conferred, had a good chance of taking advantage the new labour market opportunities opening up with the expansion of heavy industry. This is one reason tension between landlords and tenants increased during the interwar period as evidenced by the fact that the number of unions formed by tenants to collectively deal with landlords soared during the post-World-War-I period, as did the number of landlord–tenant disputes. During the period of balanced Meiji growth tenants were the principal beneficiaries of the expansion of industrial employment. Moreover returns to material investment in agriculture (and/or vocational education in agriculture) did not markedly differ from those in industry during early Meiji. Hence landlords tended to be actively engaged in productivity enhancing activities – in the introduction of new seed varieties, the building of roads and irrigation systems, the promotion of vocational schools for agriculture and so forth – and had not yet become 'parasitic'. With the emergence of dualism there was divergence in the relative level of opportunity facing the various social groups in the countryside, a divergence which galled marginal tenants despite productivity growth, and a divergence which was eventually dealt with in the postwar period through government policy, especially land reform and rice price stabilization.

Finally let me close this discussion of the supply pool drawn on by light industry by noting that residents in Japanese villages were accustomed to being monitored. For the residential structures of hamlets were usually crammed together near the rice fields and/or dry fields farmed by the villagers, and during spring transplanting and the fall harvest everyone in the village from the very young to the very old was likely to be out working in the fields, so the holdings of any one family which, due to their small size and to their distribution here and there, tended to be visible to many other households. In short, light industry drew from a supply pool of workers who were willing to subject themselves to monitoring and to supply labour at daily wages which exceeded or were equal to the marginal productivity of daily labour in tenant and part-tenant/part-owner farms. In this way a low wage floor was set for the light-industrial sector.

2.6   THE DEMAND FOR FEMALE LABOUR IN LIGHT INDUSTRY: TEXTILES

Most accounts of conditions in the mills suggest that once recruited, the girls could be quickly trained in the techniques required for running looms and spinning machines (cf. Shindo, 1961; Tsurumi, 1990). Basic competency seems to have grown quickly – in a matter of months if descriptive accounts are to be credited. Monitoring was extensive: mills often tested girls on a weekly basis and some employed piece rate pay schemes.[10] And turnover was high and remained high despite the efforts of mill owners to introduce various paternalistic benefits: dormitories, tea ceremony and flower arranging classes, promises of donations for wedding ceremonies upon retirement, and so forth. Thus regardless of actual scale of operation, the typical textile firm operated with what I have called in Chapter 1 a small-commercial-firm labour market contract.

However there was a select subgroup of workers in the mills, both male and female, who were treated differently, more like the promoted workers in large firms from the viewpoint of the model than like workers in small-commercial-firms. These workers signalled the firm that they differed from most of their colleagues, either by their rate-of-time preference (i.e. the fact that they did not quit within the first few years) or by their productivity or by the speed with which they learned new tasks. Saxonhouse (1976) argues that the longer a girl stayed and worked in the industry the more productive she became, although it is likely there were rapidly diminishing returns to experience despite learning-by-doing and on-the-job training.[11] The interviews of Kiyokawa with former and/or still-employed silk reeling instructors indicates that the skill needed in order to become a competent silk instructor could be mastered in two or three years, because of the 'unique and strict management system, despite the fact that the job required very delicate finger-work' (Kiyokawa, 1991): 60), but that on average it took a worker of average ability 4.8 years to attain mature proficiency. Thus from most cohorts of new hires there were a tiny proportion who stayed with their employers long enough to gain high levels of skill and/or long enough to be promoted to the rank of manager. These workers monitored the rank and file (note Kiyokawa's phrase 'strict management system'), and were paid premium wages. Thus these workers should be thought of as an efficiency wage élite operating in firms in which the great mass of workers were operated with contracts of the small-commercial-firm type.

Now the index of labour productivity, set at a base of 100 in 1929, for large and medium-sized textile firms reached a level of 245.7 in 1935–9 (data from Shinohara, 1972). This productivity gain was associated with a variety of technical innovations including scientific cotton blending which reduced the dependence on expensive staples of cotton for the production of thread which would readily break on the spindles; the introduction of new looms as exemplified by the switch from flying-shuttle looms to wooden – iron narrow power looms, from wooden – iron narrow power looms to iron narrow power looms, and from this stage through broad power looms to automatic looms (cf. Minami and Makino, 1986); and electrification which Minami shows was of immense consequence to the development of spinning (cf. Minami, 1980, 1987). But real and nominal productivity growth are two different matters since the movement in nominal productivity growth reflects changes in output price was well as real product throughput per labour hour or per worker. For example in

Table 2.6 I trace the path of nominal labour productivity and nominal wages for cotton spinning and cotton weaving. Now there was a major decline in cotton weaving prices after 1925, a price fall which depressed sectoral nominal labour productivity in weaving. In the context of this drop in weaving output price, consider labour's share in value added per worker. For cotton spinning the share fluctuates but shows no trend or discontinuous break over time. But for cotton weaving a very sharp discontinuity is evident. After 1920 labour's share increases dramatically, peaking at almost 90 per cent in the 1935–6 period. By contrast in the 1895–9 period labour's share was a mere 9.8 per cent. The association between wages and productivity is tenuous, perhaps non-existent, in this sector. In fact wages in spinning and weaving are approximately identical, which is not surprising in light of the fact that fresh hires were being drawn from the same rural labour supply pools – or virtually the same labour supply pools: in fact some individual villages specialized in selling labour to cotton weaving and others to cotton spinning and others to silk spinning firms. Thus with the dramatic drop in the price of woven goods, labour's share in weaving soared, leading to a 'profit squeeze' in this sector.

Over time, what were the forces stimulating adjustments in nominal textile worker wages? If the wage was basically set by the productivity of labour in smaller and/or tenant farms (which only gradually drifted up as labour productivity in farming improved) then we would expect the wage floor for light industry to have been highly responsive to changes in the consumer price index but not to changes in average labour productivity. In Table 2.7 I present evidence consistent with this interpretation. Note that, in the case of females, the sum of the three elasticities – those for current prices, prices lagged one year, and prices lagged two years – exceeded 0.70. Also note that there is little evidence of a significant response to productivity increase. The results are consistent with the idea of a wage floor. And the parallel movements in agricultural and manufacturing wages for females documented in Table 2.1 are consistent with the idea that the wage floor gradually shifted upward as daily labour productivity in farming improved.

To reiterate, the salient characteristics of prewar employment in light industry are: (a) reliance on a female labour supply recruited with short-term wage contracts negotiated between rural *ie*, especially tenant and part-tenant/part-owner *ie*, and the factory representative at daily wages which were roughly in line with the opportunity cost associated with a day's work in agriculture; (b) short training periods and continual monitoring and evaluating of labour by a small élite group of workers who were

TABLE 2.6   Nominal wages, labour productivity and labour's share in the cotton spinning and cotton weaving sectors of the Japanese textile industry, 1895–1936. Quinquennial averages for three year moving averages (in yen on a daily basis)[a]

| Period | Cotton spinning | | | | | Cotton weaving | | | | |
| | WAGES | | | | | WAGES | | | | |
	Male	Female	Total	Labour productivity	Labour's share (%)	Males	Female	Total	Labour productivity	Labour's share (%)
1895–99	0.22	0.14	0.16	0.63	25.7	0.24	0.13	0.15	1.53	9.8
1900–04	0.34	0.21	0.24	0.51	46.6	0.37	0.22	0.22	1.32	18.2
1905–09	0.43	0.26	0.26	0.92	32.1	0.44	0.27	0.29	1.06	27.6
1910–14	0.49	0.31	0.35	0.88	39.8	0.53	0.34	0.37	1.90	19.2
1915–19	0.73	0.52	0.57	3.83	14.8	0.77	0.56	0.59	5.11	11.6
1920–24	1.61	1.24	1.34	3.93	34.0	1.70	1.24	1.29	3.72	34.8
1925–29	1.74	1.31	1.40	3.77	37.2	1.74	1.36	1.43	1.83	78.0
1930–34	1.57	0.92	1.03	3.50	29.4	1.58	0.97	1.08	1.52	70.7
1935–36	1.45	0.76	0.84	2.65	31.8	1.46	0.80	0.88	0.98	89.6

Note:

(a)   Calculated from wage and productivity figures carried out to more decimal lengths than reported in this table.

Source:
Fujino, Fujino and Ono (1979: various tables); and Ohkawa and Shinohara (1979: various tables).

TABLE 2.7   Textile worker wages, the consumer price index, and nominal labor productivity in Japan, 1892–1936[a]

Dependent variable: wages	Constant		Consumer price index				Labour productivity					Adj.
		Same year	Lagged one year	Lagged two years	Lagged three years	same year	Lagged one year	Lagged two years	Lagged three years	ar(1)	R^2
Female cotton spinner wages	−0.01 (−0.46)	0.44* (2.95)	0.42* (3.19)	0.24** (1.98)	0.23** (2.12)	0.08* (1.98)	0.01 (0.29)	0.05 (1.47)	0.04 (0.94)	0.40*** (1.98)	0.86
Male cotton spinner wages	0.01 (0.89)	3.2* (2.70)	−0.36* (−3.36)	0.17 (1.73)	0.16 (1.75)	0.05 (1.59)	0.01 (0.33)	0.04 (1.21)	0.05 (1.44)	0.40*** (1.95)	0.85
Female cotton weavers wages	0.02 (0.40)	0.41* (3.26)	0.41* (3.20)	0.17 (1.37)	0.17 (1.37)	0.06** (1.74)	0.02 (0.53)	0.01 (0.20)	0.08 (1.95)	0.57** (2.50)	0.84
Male cotton weavers wages	0.02 (1.34)	0.39* (4.50)	0.34 (3.79)	0.20 (2.21)	0.10* (1.20)	0.03 (1.05)	0.02 (1.12)	0.04 (0.179)	0.03 (1.03)	0.53*** (2.53)	0.88

Note:
(a)   Regression of the change in the logarithm of nominal daily wages as dependent variable on changes in the logarithm of nominal labour productivity and changes in the logarithm of the consumer price index (3-year moving averages for wages and labour productivity) using the Cochrance–Orcutt method for first-order autoregressive correction.

*   Significant at the 1% level (two-tailed test).
**   Significant at the 5% level (two-tailed test).
***   Significant at the 10% level (two-tailed test).

Source:
See sources to Table 2.6

treated like efficiency wage workers; and (c) direct control of the workers by the factory management. This state of affairs can be profitably contrasted with the nineteenth-century English situation discussed by Lazonik (1990: 80–104). In the English textile factory system which gradually emerged from a decentralized putting-out industry with production concentrated in rural households who specialized in either spinning or weaving, indirect management through a subcontracting system became the prevailing organizational form. Recruitment and supervision of rank-and-file workers was done by an aristocracy of labour. For instance in spinning the minders hired and directed the piecers who worked under their charge. The minders effectively operated like labour bosses, contracting with factory management and directly paying their assistants. In many cases male patriarchs brought their own children and/or wives into the mills to work under their direction. Thus wages were set through a bargaining process between the labour boss subcontractors and the firms. Rent sharing between firm and subcontractor characterized wage setting, and the junior operatives hoped to eventually become minders themselves. For example the famous Oldham and Bolton lists which resulted from a series of strikes in the latter half of the nineteenth century set the wages paid to minders. By contrast the Japanese industry almost exclusively employed short-term workers who were under direct factory control and who were paid wages set at the opportunity cost of labour in rural villages. In the case of the small group of élite managerial workers wages were paid on a different basis, but this only applied to a small portion of the light-industrial labour force. For this reason in light industry we can say that conditions of elastically supplied 'cheap' labour prevailed throughout the prewar period and especially during Meiji balanced growth.

2.7   THE MALE LABOUR MARKET IN HEAVY INDUSTRY, UTILITIES, AND TRANSPORTATION: SUPPLY CONDITIONS

Because the Japanese textile industry was able to readily import and adapt a foreign technology which could be combined with labour selected from a labour supply pool of inexpensive, elastically supplied rural girls, management was able to directly control workers from the outset and wages were by and large determined exogenously by the supply price set by productivity in agriculture. But in heavy industry the technology was far more sophisticated, the skill formation period was longer, monitoring costs were higher, and interrelationships between the output of one worker and his/her colleagues were extensive, rendering difficult evaluation of individual worker contributions. Initially corporations in iron and steel production and shipbuilding and the like relied on their contacts with labour bosses to indirectly recruit and manage workers. But this was unsatisfactory as a long-run solution to managing production workers. First there was always the danger that the labour bosses would extract rents from the firms they did business with. Perhaps a strike-prone system of industrial relations with strong craft unions might develop. Moreover labour bosses might move their workers over to a competitor at any time. Since many of these companies desired to train their workers in the use of machines and technologies which they had acquired through direct licensing agreements and the like with specific foreign companies, they wished to reduce turnover in order to keep secret the technical knowledge which they had acquired, and because trained workers possessed valuable skills.

To simplify a complicated story, most of the highly successful firms took three major steps in reaching these goals over the course of the late Meiji and interwar periods. First, they coopted labour bosses into the ranks of lower management; second, they recruited a new breed of technically trainable workers out of institutions of higher learning and gradually promoted these workers up into the highest managerial ranks of the company, including seating a few especially competent managers on boards of directors; and third, they gradually increased the amount of training they gave to shop-floor blue-collar workers. What emerged was a two-track system of recruitment and contracting: a white-collar élite consisting of former labour bosses and graduates of higher educational institutions were granted *shain* (literally 'company member') status, which involved payment according to age and performance (*nenko*), job security until compulsory retirement (*shūshin koyō*) set at age 55, and the opportunity to compete for promotion to the very highest levels of the company; and a subordinate group of blue-collar workers who were known as *koin* (literally 'employed members') and to whom no special job security or promotional opportunities were offered (basically a 'small-commercial-firm labour contract'). In fact this new form of firm contracting, which placed a strong emphasis on recruiting highly educated and technically sophisticated personnel for the ranks of the *shain*, was not adopted by all major large firms in heavy industry before World War II. For instance some adhered to a model based on the Tokugawa merchant house concept of early recruitment and internal education and training (the *detchi/tedai* model of promotion). But in industries where there was a high potential return to a detailed knowledge of Western technology, and where tie-up arrangements with Western companies were of great import, the two-track system with higher-education graduate *shain* and *koin* blue-collar workers became the dominant form.[12]

It is useful to look at the emergence and growing dominance of the two-track system from two viewpoints: from the viewpoint of the contracting characteristic of submarkets during the Tokugawa period, and from the viewpoint of the model in Chapter 1. As for the Tokugawa legacy, it can be seen that in the contracts for the élite *shain* are elements derivative from the samurai and merchant submarkets: for instance the elitist samurai submarket placed strong weight on formal education and on rank; and the merchant submarket emphasized internal training and promotion segmented off from other submarkets. The suggestion here is that the growing demand for technically proficient managers who would not quit encouraged companies to develop contracts which would both make them feel as if they were a privileged élite and would also give them a strong, purely economic incentive to stay with the firm. And the most logical models for this type of contract lay not in the West but rather in Japan's immediate past. That many graduates of universities during the first decades of the Meiji period were former samurai was probably a factor in turning innovative companies in the direction of the fief bureaucracies in searching for models. There is a social aspect to path dependence in contracts. But we can also look at the emergence and refinement of the system in terms of the economic model laid out in Chapter 1: in particular in terms of the efficacy of labour market screening. We have seen that during the first half-century or so hierarchical differentiation and specialization in the educational system were incomplete. There was a sharp distinction between the highest levels of schooling and the lowest, but gradations in between were not so clearly marked. Hence companies searching for workers with a high probability of possessing long time horizons, the capacity to give effort, and the capacity to be rapidly trained in sophisticated technical details, were naturally attracted to higher-education graduates. And they were willing to offer them contracts which guaranteed job security and subjected them to extensive training because by their achievement in the educational system they had demonstrated they were highly likely to have the desired background characteristics. But because differentiation below this level was far less complete – at least before the interwar period when the school system did become increasingly differentiated (owing partly due to an income-driven expansion in demand) – companies were reluctant to devise similar contracts for blue-collar workers, and/or some subgroup of blue-collar workers. As a result a two-track system emerged.

The key to the success of heavy industrial companies in managing to meet their expanding labour demand with this two-track contract system lay in two labour supply factors: a rapid expansion in the supply of techni-cal graduates from institutions of higher learning who could be trained to be managers, and the failure of the labour movement to grow to a position of strength in the labour market, thereby retaining at least partial control over training and evaluation of blue-collar workers and weakening the power of professional managerial élite to monitor and evaluate blue-collar workers in an unconstrained manner. Let us first consider the labour movement.

Much has been written about the failure of the Japanese labour move-ment to gain a strong foothold over the industrial labour force in the prewar period (cf. *inter alia* Gordon, 1985, 1991; Harada, 1928; International Labour Office, 1933; Large, 1972, 1981; Okochi, 1958; and Smith, 1984). Space precludes a extensive account of the development of the prewar labour movement. Here I restrict my remarks to a schematic periodization which serves as an overview. (a) *1868–97*. From the Meiji Restoration until approximately 1905, the labour movement was mainly disorganized and ideologically primitive, being mainly characterized by scattered strikes in textiles, mining, stone work, and so forth. With the exception of textiles and mining most of the organizing and strike activity was restricted to artisan associations which in some cases were descendants of Tokugawa guild organizational forms. (b) *1897–1911*. During this period a labour movement emerged with a clear ideological and political edge. For instance 1897 marks the founding of *Kiseikai* (standing for the Association for the Promotion of Labour Unions), which was almost exclusively the brainchild of progressive intellectuals influenced by Western radical movements. Partly in reaction to the step-ping up of left-wing activity and partly to head off the development of a strong labour movement, the government passed the Peace Preservation Law (*Chian Keisatsu Hō*, literally meaning 'Public Peace and Order Police Act') in 1900. Articles 17 and 30 of this law empowered the police to break up demonstrations it deemed subversive, including the calling of strikes and meetings in which radical unionizing activities were advocated. Organizations came and went during this epoch which ended with the passage of the Factory Act, the first major piece of legislation restricting hours of work and unsanitary conditions in factories of large and medium size (the law was not actually implemented until 1916). (c) *1912–36*. From the founding of the *Yuaikai* (Friendly Society) in 1912, until 1936, with fits and starts, union membership grew despite the Peace Preservation Law, whose articles 17 and 30 were repealed in 1926 to be replaced by more lenient regulations. 1936 is the prewar date for peak union membership. The hallmark of this period is the political fragmentation of the labour movement into three opposing factions: a right wing represented by the *Sōdōmei* which was a continuation of the *Yuaikai* (*Sōdōmei* standing for Grand Federation of Labour Unions Fraternity Association); a leftwing, the *Hyōgikai* (standing for Japanese Council of Labour Unions) which had originally formed out the merger of unions expelled from the *Sōdōmei* because of their leftist ideological stances; and a centrist wing associated with the *Nihon Rōnō Tō* (Japan Labour–Farmer Party), whose constituent unions had also been expelled by the *Sōdōmei*. (d) *1937–45*. During this period unions either declined in strength or were absorbed into right-wing fascist organizations. In 1940 the Diet outlawed labour unions altogether and promoted in their stead the *Sangyō Hōkokukai* (*Sanpo* for short), which was a patriotic front dedicated to 'service for the country,' *Sōdōmei* was dissolved in 1940 and joined the ranks of *Sanpo*.

Why did the Japanese labour movement fail to make more vigorous progress during the prewar period? Looking at the matter in terms of the costs and benefits of unionizing to potential members it is clear that under the ideology of imperial nationalism the costs of organizing were high, and, until the interwar period, the benefits were low. Specifically consider the following five points. First, owing to extensive reliance on short-contract female labour in light industry most industrial workers during the period of balanced growth had short time horizons and were not interested in long-term organizations representing labour's view. Second, Japanese industry did not make a pronounced shift towards male labour using heavy industry until the late 1920s and early 1930s, a period during which demand for blue-collar labour fluctuated considerably, owing in part to the impact of the international depression (cf. Blumenthal, 1987). As a result labour's bargaining position was weakened at precisely the time when unionization might have gained momentum owing to the increase in male blue-collar employment. Third, Imperial Nationalist policy was overtly hostile to the development of a radical Western European style socialistic labour movement, a hostility exemplified by the passage and implementation of articles 17 and 30 of the Peace Preservation Law. After these articles were rescinded in 1926, the government, acting in concert with major industrialists, set up a mediation authority, the *Kyōchōkai*, as a vehicle for peacefully arbitrating and settling industrial disputes. Fourth, Western ideologies were inherently foreign to the Japanese whether they were intellectuals or rank-and-file workers. Since the concepts did not emerge out of domestic tradition, organizers and workers alike found selecting and sticking to one view difficult. Thus the labour movement tended to fragment along doctrinal and nationalistic lines. And when a union did secure a foothold in a large enterprise, it tended to strongly favour an enterprise-specific, vertically oriented representation agreement, because through such arrangements it could bar competitor factions from organizing within its 'territory'. This played into the hands of those firms who were experimenting with worker training programs for shop-floor blue-collar workers and who resisted industrial or craft-specific unions which might constrain their plans for training workers. Fifth, the Ministry of Education gradually shaped and developed a system of specialized vocational and commercial schools (*jitsugyō gakkō*) tailored to providing technical training to future lower white-collar clerical staff and blue-collar personnel. That is, training of blue-collar workers fell either into the hands of a pro-business government or into the hands of the firms themselves.

Now at no time during the prewar period did unionization exceed 10 per cent of the industrial labour force. In fact most unions were in small and medium-sized companies which were themselves inherently unstable. For this reason the death rate for unions was high and Taira (1970) convincingly demonstrates that most unions were short-lived. As a result relatively little training occurred in union-controlled centres and schools. Simultaneously post-compulsory education in government-run and/or controlled institutions which had a strong orientation towards developing the skills required by industrialists was expanding in response to the demands of the business and military communities.

As for the supplying of professionally competent school graduates, I have already considered in the context of the discussion of Table 2.2 the increase in the middle, vocational, and higher schools. It is useful to go a bit further with this issue in order to get a better gauge on the degree to which supply kept up with demand expansion. To that end I have approximated growth rates for the demand and supply of engineers and scientists for the 1906–40 period working under the following assumptions. First, I have restricted my attention to the two sectors of manufacturing and of utilities, transportation and communications. This is reasonable since most technically trained professionals tended to go into these two sectors during the period in question. Second, I have assumed that the growth rate in demand for engineers and scientists within each sector can be approximated by adding half the growth rate in sectoral employment to half the growth rate in capital stock (actually mechanical horsepower in the case of manufacturing). The idea is that the demand for technical personnel in the sector, D, is a function of the number of employees requiring supervision and of the machinery requiring adjustments, maintenance, repair and the like.[13] That is:

$$D = f(L, K), \tag{2.1}$$

where L = employment and K = capital stock. Assuming this demand function is of the Cobb–Douglas form, with equal elasticities on K and K, the growth in demand is equal to the sum of the growth of each component separately weighted by one half. Third, I assume the combined sum of demand from manufacturing *plus* transportation, utilities and communications is the weighted sum of demand growth in each sector taken separately, where the weights are the proportions of employment in manufacturing and in transportation, utilities and communications in combined employment in both sectors. Supply growth is measured in several different ways: as the growth rate of technical graduates from universities and technical colleges only; and as the growth rate of technical graduates from technical colleges *and* vocational (*jitsugyō gakkō*) schools.

Demand and supply growth estimates appear in Table 2.8. As can be seen from columns 9 and 10 of the table, in most periods supply growth exceeded demand growth. With the war-related expansion of heavy industry after 1935 (and the war-related redirecting of young males away from higher schooling and towards military activity) demand outstrips supply. This is not surprising. But the most interesting point to emerge from perusal of the estimates is that in most periods the opposite is the case: supply growth exceeds demand growth. The expansion of the education system was so rapid that there was a tendency for the wages of higher-educated technical personnel to be driven down.

In short, supply conditions related to the vigorous development of the educational system and to the anaemic development of the union movement encouraged large companies to adopt a two-track recruitment/contracting system: white-collar workers recruited from higher-education institutions worked under conditions which are captured in my formal model of large-firm contracts; and blue-collar workers were employed on terms closer to those captured in the rubric of my small-commercial-firm contract model than to under the large-firm-contract model. But there was a inherent instability built into the two-track system. It made invidious distinctions between the élite *shain* and the subordinate *koin*, thereby stirring up discontent among the ranks of blue-collar workers. Also, firms themselves were ambivalent about the logic of the distinction, since they *were* interested in training their blue-collar workers in skills which were both transferable and non-transferable to other employers. After all, the textile mills on occasion did promote girls up to the ranks of managers and monitors. Indeed, several heavy industrial firms had themselves started, and received Ministry of Education, sanction and certification for schools aimed at improving the technical and theoretical knowledge of shop-floor workers before the interwar period. Thus the growing differentiation and

TABLE 2.8   Demand for, and supply of, engineers in prewar Japan, 1891–1940

| Years | Students of higher education in science and engineering | | Demand growth[a] | | | | Demand growth minus supply growth | |
| | Percentage of all higher education' students[a] | Estimated growth rate of graduates | Growth rate of employees in railroads and public utilities | Growth rate of prime mover horsesepower in manufacturing | Combined growth rate | Combined growth rate minus graduate growth rate | Growth rate of employees in railroads and utilities minus graduate growth rate |
	[1]	[2]	[3]	[4]	[5]	[5]–[2]	[3]–[2]
1891–95	15.8%	−13.7%	20.5%	31.7%	20.5%	+43.2%	+34.2
1896–1900	10.9	3.1	13.6	2.1	4.3	+1.3	+10.5
1900–05	7.7	12.1	6.4	16.4	14.4	+2.4	−5.7
1906–10	7.8	17.6	8.8	18.9	16.9	−0.7	−8.8
1911–15	10.2	11.5	7.1	14.7	13.3	+1.7	−4.5
1916–20	13.1	10.1	8.4	17.9	16.1	+6.0	−1.7
1921–25	14.2	17.3	6.1	12.6	11.4	−5.9	−11.2
1926–30	15.7	2.1	2.1	8.5	7.1	+5.0	−0.1
1931–35	11.8	8.3	0.2	7.5	6.1	+2.2	−8.1
1936–40	14.3	3.7	7.9	15.4	13.9	+10.3	+4.3

Notes:
(a) Column [1] data is for benchmark years 1890, 1900, 1905, 1915, 1920, 1925, 1930, and 1935 only.
(b) The growth rates in columns 3 and 4 are weighted by the share of support and utilities employment, and the share of manufacturing employment, respectively, out of the sum of employment in support and utilities and manufacturing combined.

Source:
Ohkawa and Shinohara (1979: various tables); M. Umemura, Akasaka, Minami, Takamatsu, Arai and Itoh (1988: various tables); Minami (1965: various tables); and Japan Statistical Association (1988: various tables).

specialization in the school system which was associated with and to a large extent caused by the income-driven expansion in demand for post-compulsory education enhanced the attractiveness of an already existing interest on the part of large firms in the heavy industries: an interest in bringing blue-collar workers under the type of contracts already extended to graduates of the universities and *senmongakkō*.

2.8   THE MALE LABOUR MARKET IN HEAVY INDUSTRY, UTILITIES, AND TRANSPORTATION: DEMAND CONDITIONS

In this section I use data on wages and productivity in the national railroads and utilities over the interwar period to demonstrate three points: (a) that the relationship between wages and the consumer price index was far weaker for (male) workers in capital-intensive industries than it was for (female) workers in the labour-intensive light industries, particularly in textiles; (b) wages were more sensitive to productivity gain in the capital-intensive industries than in textiles; and (c) the relative wages of white-collar workers were falling in comparison to those for blue-collar workers throughout the interwar period. I use this data rather than figures on heavy industrial subsectors because it is impossible to construct a systematic and consistent time series for the heavy industrial subsectors.[14] Thus when I refer to 'heavy industries' in the statistical analysis which follows I am specifically referring to railroads and utilities.

The first point to keep in mind about the development of nominal wages and labour productivity in the national railroads during the interwar period is that during an era when nominal labour productivity increased by about three times, manual wages increased almost five-fold and non-manual wages increased by a bit more than a factor of three. That is, the ratio of manual to non-manual wages declined from a ratio of 2.65 to one of 1.87. In short, non-manual wages increased at about the same rate as overall labour pro-ductivity, but manual wages increased at a much more rapid pace. A similar pattern is evident for private railroads and utilities, as can be seen from the data in Table 2.9. Note that paralleling a lower rate of increase in overall nominal labour productivity in private electric railroads (by 'lower' I mean lower than the other sector covered in the table, namely utilities), nominal non-manual wages in private railroads increased at a slower pace (than did non-manual worker wages in utilities). But note that the relative erosion of non-manual to manual wages was virtually identical in the two sectors.

How do time series wage increase equations for these industries stack up against those estimated for textiles? In Tables 2.10 I address this issue.

TABLE 2.9   Nominal and real wages and nominal labour productivity in the national railroads of Japan, 1896–1938. (quinquennial averages of five year moving averages).

A Nominal wages (monthly, in yen)

Period	Private street railroads	Private electric railroads			Utilities		
		Manual	Non-manual	Non-manual/ manual ratio[a]	Manual	Non-manual	Non-manual/ manual ratio[a]
1910–14	24.2	15.9	31.7	1.99	20.7	40.3	1.94
1915–19	33.6	23.4	45.8	1.96	30.8	59.6	1.93
1920–24	71.2	43.4	73.2	1.69	57.4	97.3	1.70
1925–29	87.8	54.2	84.3	1.56	73.4	112.6	1.53
1930–34	83.8	53.0	75.4	1.42	71.3	101.7	1.43
1935–38	86.2	47.8	72.3	1.51	67.1	101.9	1.52

TABLE 2.9   (*continued*)

B Real wages (in 1934–36 prices)[b]

C Nominal labour productivity

| Period | Manual workers | | Non-manual workers | | | Period | Private railroads | Electric utilities |
	Private electric railroads	*Electric utilities*	*Private electric railroads*	*Electric utilities*				
1910–14	27.5	35.7	54.6	69.4		1915–19	1375.2	1831.0
1915–19	30.5	40.2	59.6	77.4		1920–24	1695.4	2210.8
1920–24	34.7	46.1	58.7	77.7		1925–29	1783.0	4074.4
1925–29	46.5	62.6	71.1	95.9		1930–34	1656.0	4920.0
1930–34	56.9	77.1	82.2	111.0		1935–39	1909.6	5321.8
1935–39	44.5	62.4	66.5	92.7				

Notes:
(a) Manual worker wages = 100.
(b) Deflated by consumer price index with 1934–36 = 100.

Sources:
Minami (1965: various tables); and Ohkawa and Shinohara (1979: various tables).

TABLE 2.10   Wages for workers on the private railroads and in electric utilities, the consumer price index, and nominal labour productivity in prewar Japan[a]

| Dependent variable: wages | Constant | Consumer price index | | | | | Labour productivity | | | | ar(1) | Adj. R² |
		Same year	Lagged one year	Lagged two years	Lagged three years	same year	Lagged one year	Lagged two years	Lagged three years		
Local private railroads	0.01 (.62)	0.11 (1.42)	0.12 (1.79)	0.10 (1.60)	0.08 (1.50)	0.23 (1.11)	0.06 (0.44)	0.11 (.76)	−0.14 (−0.88)	0.80* (3.54)	0.92
Street private railroads	0.004 (.463)	−0.24 (−1.14)	−0.03 (−0.26)	−0.80 (−0.6)	−0.01 (−0.6)	0.54** (2.23)	0.56* (2.95)	0.29 (0.82)	0.16 (0.82)	0.44** (2.35)	0.89
Electric private railroads	−0.02 (−1.05)	−0.05 (−0.26)	−0.12** (−2.14)	0.06 (1.04)	−0.04 (−0.67)	0.06 (0.59)	0.33** (2.09)	0.13 (0.94)	0.12 (1.01)	0.81* (9.20)	0.95
Electric utilities manual	−0.23 (−0.17)	0.13*** (2.04)	0.04 (0.70)	−0.06 (−1.18)	0.12** (2.24)	−0.13 (−1.38)	−0.18*** (−1.76)	0.07 (0.75)	0.07 (0.67)	0.99 (12.75)	0.95
Electric utilities non-manual	−0.01 (−0.11)	0.16** (2.41)	0.03 (0.60)	−0.03 (−0.64)	0.11* (1.90)	−0.08 (−0.82)	0.26** (2.39)	0.13 (1.36)	−0.02 (−0.19)	0.95* (10.17)	0.89

Notes:

(a)   Regressions on the change in the logarithm of nominal daily wages as dependent variable on changes in the logarithm of nominal labour productivity and the logarithm of the consumer price index (five-year moving average for monthly wage and labour productivity) using the Cochrane–Orcutt method for first-order autoregressive correction.

*   Significant at the 1% level (two-tailed test).
**   Significant at the 5% level (two-tailed test).
***   Significant at the 10% level (two-tailed test).

Source:
See sources to Table 2.9.

The following results emerge from an examination of the four tables. First, nominal wages in the heavy industries respond to price index movements as they do for textiles, but with much smaller elasticities. Second, in the autocorrelation adjusted regressions presented in Table 2.10 there is evidence of nominal productivity increases were translated into nominal wage increases. For electric utilities the results given in Table 2.10 suggest that manual worker wages respond positively to productivity increases, but non-manual worker wages do not. In short, wages for blue-collar workers were tied to current levels of productivity, but wages for white-collar workers were not. This is what we would expect if blue-collar workers were paid on a small-commercial-firm contract basis, and white-collar workers were not. Since the effort curve shifted over the interwar period in response to the changing supply and demand for higher-education graduates there is no reason to expect a close association between firm productivity gain and the improvements in remuneration for white-collar workers.

2.9   CONCLUSIONS

Differentiation of the Japanese labour market on both the supply and demand sides into the distinct submarkets we see in the postwar period was largely achieved by the close of the interwar period. This differentiation is intimately associated with market forces – in particular the rise to prominence of heavy industry and the demise of Meiji balanced growth – and government policy. Government policies regarding the household, education, unionization, and the military all contributed. However, the differentiation in labour contracts of the 1930s is not identical to that of the 1950s and 1960s: in particular, after World War II the two-track recruitment and promotion system of large firms was replaced with a single-track system; and small, family-run firms became the beneficiaries of income redistribution policies which improved their relative per family member incomes. Social, political and economic forces set in motion during the interwar period, when differentiation in outcomes arising from market segmentation reached extreme levels, were brought to bear after the war, bringing substantial integration into postwar labour markets. How this came about in historical terms is important to our understanding of the economic logic of contracts in the various submarkets and is the subject of my next chapter.

Part II

Integrated Segmentation in the Postwar Labour Market

3 Continuity and Discontinuity

3.1 THE MEANING AND MEASUREMENT OF STRUCTURAL BREAKS

Upon Japan's unconditional surrender and acceptance of the terms of the Potsdam Declaration in August of 1945, Imperial Nationalism perished. With its demize, the linkage of expansion in the heavy industrial sector to the buildup of military hardware crumbled as well. Her capital stock decimated, her major cities mercilessly bombed into rubble, Japan's capacity for once again achieving sustained economic growth, her capacity to even struggle back to the prewar peak of per-capita income of the late 1930s, was questioned in many quarters both American and Japanese. Yet between 1952 (when the American Occupation was formally concluded and Japan's political independence and security were guaranteed under the framework of the US–Japan Security Treaty) and 1970, Japan's economy grew at hitherto unheard of rates. By 1955 she had regained her prewar peak per capita income level; and between 1955 and 1970 her income grew at annual rates which on average exceeded 10 per cent. The key to this growth was the efficient and rapid importation and adaptation of foreign, mainly American, technology. Having largely attained technological parity with the West by 1970, Japanese firms could no longer dip into a huge pool of untried foreign techniques and methods of production.[1] Growth in labour productivity and total factor productivity flagged. Hence Japanese real income growth dropped down to a new slower trend-rate-of-growth plateau: annual average growth rates tended to fall short of 5 per cent but to be substantially above the 1 to 2 per cent range characteristic of most of the rest of the highly industrial world. Within the context of this broadly painted description of postwar reconstruction (1945–55), rapid catching up with the West (1955–70), and readjustment to slower growth potential after 1970 two brief phases stand out as marking turning points, structural breaks, periods of discontinuity: the American Occupation period from August 1945 until May of 1952, particularly the initial phase from 1945 until 1950; and the period 1971–75, the era of transition to slower growth, when the capacity to draw from a vast supply of foreign techniques was exhausted, and the potential long-run stability of the economy under conditions of slower growth was called into question by the Nixon policy shock of 1971 (in particular the floating of the dollar on international money markets) and the sharp increase in costs of imported energy precipitated by the OPEC oil embargo. How was the extent of segmentation on the supply and demand sides of the labour market affected by the restructuring of social and political institutions and the remoulding of expectations about market output and labour market performance during these periods? Was there sharp discontinuity in terms of the social and institutional constraints on market outcomes for the distinct submarkets of the labour market (e.g. on the efficacy of signalling; the relative returns to effort in firms of various types) after World War II and later on in the early 1970s? In short, how continuous or discontinuous has been the evolution of the set of constraints which shape the operation and interaction of the various submarkets of the postwar Japanese labour market?

In thinking about these issues it is useful to distinguish between exogenously induced and endogenously induced changes. While easy to make in theory, the distinction is often difficult to make in practice. For instance while the impetus for the Land Reform, the remoulding of the educational system, the dissolution of the *zaibatsu*, the passage of a strong Trade Union Law, and so forth lay in the stream of directives emanating from the General Headquarters of the Supreme Commander of the Allied Powers (GH SCAP), the details of the legislation were largely worked out by the Japanese themselves. How much of the resulting legislation can be accurately described as exogenously derived? However difficult it may be to distinguish between internal and external influences in practice, the question of exogenous influence is important because it is likely that exogenously induced change is more discontinuous than endogenously induced change. Coming from outside the economic and social environment of a country, the agenda being written by foreign hands as it were, exogenously induced change is less indebted to the domestic political and social environment and hence is more likely to force legislation down untried paths. That the Americans established the general framework for Japanese legislative and policy reform during the 1945–50 era, and foreign actions induced the upward movements in the yen and oil prices, is *prima facie* evidence in support of the view that these two periods mark periods of structural break.

Now how do we measure the degree of discontinuity, how do we gauge its relative importance? Granted discontinuity exists, how telling is it? It is the burden of this chapter that the case for discontinuity is far weaker than is commonly believed. I will not marshall all my arguments in support of the continuity thesis within the confines of this chapter. But I will suggest in this chapter that (a) the capacity of the United States to remould Japan in the aftermath of the war was severely limited by political, economic and ideological constraints on both sides and (b) the most important changes in labour–management relations and labour markets commonly attributed to the Oil Crisis had either commenced before the crisis or had at least been anticipated by developments before 1970. In short, in this chapter I establish the groundwork for the view that labour market segmentation born under the political and social conditions of imperial nationalism has systematically and steadily evolved in response to secular movements in the supply and demand for labour of different types as conditioned by political and social changes following the dismantling of the Imperial Nationalist program. Discontinuities concentrated in the 1945–50 and 1971–75 periods are certainly not without significance, but that significance should not be exaggerated.

3.2   INSTITUTIONAL CHANGE IN THE AFTERMATH OF THE WAR

In moving to dismantle the program of Imperial Nationalism which the American government viewed as a threat to its own security and to its economic and political interests in the Far East, the GH SCAP attempted to rip out by the roots the social and political foundations of the emperor system, of ultra-nationalism and of militarism, and, having done so, to encourage a democratic alternative to the Imperial Nationalist regime. To this end SCAP either forced or encouraged: (a) the emperor to renounce his divinity and therefore his absolute sovereignty; (b) a purge of officials including school teachers and bureaucrats associated with promoting the ideology of Imperial Nationalism; (c) the liberalization of education and the elimination of sexual discrimination in schools at all levels; (d) dissolution of the *zaibatsu* and the other holding companies tied to the prewar military regime; (e) the formation of labour unions and collective bargaining; (f) a land reform designed to eliminate rapacious landlordism from the villages; and (g) a rewriting of the family code to eliminate the biases towards males, in particular towards the eldest son, imbedded in the inheritance rules of the Meiji code.[2] Implicit in the American program was the idea that democratically oriented American-style institutions could and should serve as useful models to the Japanese bureaucrats and politicians who were called upon to revamp the government ministries, the laws, and the administrative procedures. But no matter how sympathetic Japanese reformers were to the American program of reform, they came to their task burdened with ideological principles fostered during seven decades of Imperial Nationalism: to them democracy meant integrative egalitarianism, equality of opportunity for all members of the *Kokutai* under the aegis of the emperor; to them full legalization of trade union activity meant opening up the labour movement to a struggle between integrative, enterprize-specific unionism in which union members, government and management accepted the principles of capitalism and divisive unionism in which the union movement adopted a pro-socialist or pro-communist line and committed itself to combatting capitalism; to them a socially 'fair' (democratic, that is egalitarian) wage policy was one reflecting the economic needs of families operating under a Code which in practice, as opposed to theory, reflected Meiji concepts; to them continuity of the family line was more important than the individual welfare of particular family members; to them the scale economies fostered by *zaibatsu* type groups, and the advantages these posed for the importing and adapting of foreign technology, far outweighed the possible negative consequences to the consumer. Thus there was a large ideological gap between the American occupation administrators and reformers and their allies among the progressive wings of the bureaucracy and the politicians which served to blunt the impact of the American directives and suggestions. Moreover in the one area where there was a high degree of ideological overlap between the American officials and their Japanese colleagues, namely in their commitment to capitalism and opposition to socialism, American biases favoured the biases of those who Japanese bureaucrats who, before the War, had assiduously adopted 'candy-and-whip' (*ame* and *mushi*) policies to divide the labour movement and coopt those segments most sympathetic to a procapitalist line. Finally the resources of the United States were limited: even before the cold war buildup following the breakdown of US–Soviet diplomatic relations during 1946–7, the Americans were resigned to working through a coterie of bureaucrats who had held posts in the interwar Ministries and who, by dint of the positions they occupied, had been thoroughly indoctrinated with the Imperial Nationalist line. Let us briefly review developments during the 1945–50 period which bear on the social efficiency wage system in light of these remarks.

Of first and foremost interest to us are the three major pieces of labour legislation passed during the 1945–7 period: the Trade Union Law of December 1945; the Labour Adjustment Law of September, 1946; and the Labour Standards Law of 1947. Each of these pieces of legislation was influenced by existing American models and principles established by the International Labour Organization; but each reflected to a degree drafts of earlier legislation proposed by progressive bureaucrats in the Home

Ministry during the 1920s.[3] The Trade Union Law of 1945 was modeled on the American Wagner Act: it guaranteed the right to form unions for all workers except policemen, firemen, and employees of penal organizations; it outlawed employer discrimination against employees engaged in organizing a union; it made collective bargaining agreements binding on both labour and management; and it established a system of labour relations commissions, a central commission and regional commissions at the prefectural levels. The duties and operating procedures of the labour relations commissions were not spelled out in detail in the Trade Union Law but rather in the Labour Adjustment Law which was designed to provide a framework for conciliation, mediation, and arbitration. The second law was bitterly opposed by some segments in the labour movement, who, perhaps imagining that the new law was a resuscitated version of the interwar legislation setting up the *Kyōchōkai* (see Chapter 2), made it a political issue in 1947. Finally the Labour Standards Law built upon the Factory Law of 1911, American laws, and International Labour Organization guidelines in providing a comprehensive set of regulations governing labour contracts: forced or indentured labour contracts were prohibited; sex discrimination was ruled out; it was stated that wages were to be paid in cash and at least once a month; a paid vacation of at least six days a year was required; and restrictions were placed on female night work and on employing children below fifteen. In short, taken together the three laws provided a wholly new institutional framework for unionization, collective bargaining and the writing of labour contracts.[4]

The passage of two other laws, those reshaping the educational system, had important implications for the active labour market for new hires and labour segmentation in that market: the Fundamental Law of Education (1947) and the School Education Law (1947). The first bill struck at the hierarchical ranking, specialization, and differentiation fundamental to the prewar system by requiring nine years of coeducational public funded compulsory education open to all individuals regardless of social background. And the second established a 6–3–3–4 system (six years of elementary school; three years of middle school; three years of high school; and four years of college or university). The latter appears to have been based on the American practices prevalent at the time but, some argue that it was the Japanese reformers and not the Americans who pressed for the 6–3–3–4 format.

That the labour legislation and even the rumours of the new laws had an immediate impact on unionization and the development of collective bargaining is evident from figures on union membership: for instance in December 1945 membership stood at 381 thousand; within a year it climbed to almost 3.7 million; and by June 1949 it exceeded 6.6 million. It is almost evident from the rash of strikes and the practice of production control (*seisan kanri*).[5] Under production control, rather than strike and shut down production workers take over the plant and run it until negotiations with management are successfully achieved. The committees running the plant place any surplus of operating receipts over disbursements in bank accounts of the company itself, that is they deposit the excess revenue over operating costs to the credit of the firm. The first major production control dispute commenced at the Yomiuri newspaper company in September 1945; the next major dispute was at Keizei Electric Railway. In many ways production control can be viewed as a radical attack on the principle of private property, but it can also be viewed as an ingenious way of averting loss of company revenue and wages during a protracted labour dispute. Be this as it may, there is no doubt about the ideologically charged calls for general strikes in January of 1947 (prohibited by GH SCAP at the eleventh hour) and again in 1948. There is no doubt that during the first year and a half of the Occupation the new labour legislation opened up political divisiveness between labour and management which had been bottled up during by the integrative fascist program of the late 1930s and by the creation of Sanpo. The worst fears of the business community and the former bureaucrats of the Home Ministry had been realized: Japan's future as a capitalist economy was being called into question in the more radical wings of the labour movement, which were avowedly communist.

From the vantage point of this study, the 'reverse course' traversed by the Occupation authorities and the Japanese Diet and bureaucracy between 1947 and 1950, which began with the banning of the general strike and culminated in the Red Purge of 1950 (during which the communist newspaper *Aka Hata* was banned, communist officials were fired from public positions, and the left-leaning *Zen Rōren* labour federation was dissolved) epitomizes the constraints on American authority and the resurgence of the prewar governmental posture towards the labour movement. In order to implement the Occupation the Americans required the services of Japanese public officials at all levels. A strike threatened the supply of services. Moreover the American government was increasingly preoccupied with building up a strong capitalist bulwark to oppose communism; therefore there were many in the GH SCAP who wished on ideological grounds to move against the left wing of the labour movement. Also, within the Japanese government most of the bureaucrats had directly or indirectly been involved in the suppression of the labour movement during the 1930s and its integration into the National Front *Sanpo* organization during the war. When MacArthur proposed in a letter to the Japanese Prime Minister in July of 1948 that the public-sectors Law be amended to prohibit strikes by public officials the Diet was quick to respond. Classic divide-and-conquer tactics were employed against the labour movement: public-sector employees were segmented off into four separate categories: national-government employees; local-government employees; national-public-corporation employees; and local-public-corporation employees (see Chapter 6 for more details). For each group a separate union bill was brought in. As a result the big public-sector unions were broken up and fragmented and their members denied the right to strike. In a politically divisive situation, the government once again adopted a divide-and-conquer strategy to help tame the labour movement. During the reverse course management joined the counteroffensive against labour. The Nikkeiren, a militantly anti-union business federation, was founded in 1948, and began actively promoting enterprize unionism and opposing industrial unionism. It played an active role in breaking up strikes and opposing industrially based unions: for instance it was active in advising the Nissan Corporation during the 1953 strike against Nissan, encourageing Nissan to promote the development of a second enterprize union within the ranks of the industrial union with which it was negotiating. As a result of this action the industrial union in the automobile industry collapsed and enterprize unionism superseded it.

Hobbled by ideological and resource constraints, the United States government had no choice but to redirect the course of the Occupation away from wholesale democratization towards rebuilding Japanese capitalism under a framework which in many respects resembled that of the 1920s and early 1930s. The labour movement, ideologically divided before the War, found itself once again divided under the Occupation; and the authorities moved to further fragment the movement by breaking up the largest public-sector unions. The political integration of the labour movement achieved under fascism dissolved under the dynamics of Occupation politics, and an era of divisiveness was ushered in.

But a trend towards integration is evident in a number of the other institutions affecting differentiation on the supply and demand sides of the labour market: in the educational system which affected the degree of differentiation in terms of labour market signalling, in the tax code and in legislation guaranteeing politically acceptable levels of income support for agricultural households, and in the income tax law providing for steeply progressive taxation on personal incomes. In education the specialization and hierarchy of the prewar system gave way to a more liberal and open system: ladders leading to the highest universities were opened to all regardless of sex or social origin; the government took on the responsibility for educating the entire population of children under age 15 through the end of middle school (see Chapter 4). Moreover social integration within large enterprizes was achieved by and large because the labour movement demanded this. For instance within large enterprizes the *shain-koin* distinction was done away with: internal promotion ladders were opened up to the ranks of the shop-floor workforce (see Chapter 5). Integration undertaken to reduce income disparities between the various submarkets and/or individuals within submarkets was also a clear aim of government policy during the 1950s and 1960s. Two prominent examples are the introduction of relatively progressive personal income tax schedules and price controls for rice which would stabilize the rice market and also reduce income disparities between marginal agricultural producers and workers in manufacturing. For instance during the late 1950s and early 1960s the formula used for determining the government-controlled rice price involved '[reappraising] in terms of average wage in manufacturing industries the value of family labour of the marginal farm producers' (Ogura, 1967:208). It would be misleading to say the legislation involving rice price stabilization, or the progressiveness of income taxes, or restrictions on the floor size in department stores, was designed solely to reduce income differentiations between members of family-run small firms and workers in large firms. But it would be fair to say that a prominent political consideration of the Japanese bureaucracy and some parties or factions of parties within the Diet was reducing the maldistribution of income and income-generating opportunities which had developed in Japan during the interwar period with the end of Meiji balanced growth. The political pressure to deal with the disparities in market outcomes associated with dualism was especially severe in the years immediately following Japan's surrender because per-capita income was far lower than it was during the years of interwar dualism, and hence income redistribution was partly aimed at guaranteeing a low minimum level of subsistence income to the great mass of the Japanese people.

There is no better illustration of the integrative tendencies at work in the allocation of wages immediate aftermath of the war than the famous *Densan* wage settlement, the first settlement mediated under the new Labour Relations Adjustment Law.[6] The settlement which was based on the concept of a 'system of theoretical living costs' resulted from a strike by the electric power workers' union *(Densan)* against the group of government-owned public utility enterprizes. The union was successfully able to force the executives of the power companies to form a joint management team for the purposes of the negotiations, thus reducing the possibility of individual companies adopting divide-and-conquer tactics in their negotiations with their own enterprize unions. The union fought for the principle of payment according to family needs of workers, that is for a policy of paying workers in such a way that the consumption per consumer unit within their associated households was roughly equalized From the point of view of the model developed in Chapter 1 the *Densan* workers' demand for payment according to family responsibilities amounts to moving large-firm contracts in the direction of small-family-firm contracts. Some room but not a large amount of room was left for independent enterprize evaluation and for linkage of wages to productivity: for example under the settlement formula which was adopted 98.8 per cent of the wage took the form of the 'base' wage, and within the base wage category 63.2 per cent of the total wage was directly targeted to maintaining family livelihood (with 18.9 per cent earmarked as a direct family allowance and 44.3 per cent tied to the age of the worker). Ability pay constituted 24.4 per cent and seniority pay 4.4 per cent. Now productivity did tend to rize with age, so that in fact the *Densan* formula is not totally at odds with the large-firm-labour contract model. But the main thrust of the formula is on using concepts derivative from the economics of small, family-run firms to reduce the relative payment according to promotion and to increase the payment involving rent sharing. And this works to reduce wage disparities between highly evaluated and less highly evaluated workers. It is not surprising that enterprizes and the business federations representing companies assiduously campaigned for a system which substantially effectively eliminated constraints on firms' capacity to promote highly evaluated workers to whom premium wages would be paid. This campaign is discussed in Chapter 5. But in the years just after World War II large firms did find themselves hemmed in by integrative policies promoted by a government concerned about maintaining minimum acceptable living standards for every member of the populace.

Thus for many of the exogenous institutional constraints which helped determine the degree of segmentation and the relative labour market rewards associated with each of the differentiated submarkets, Occupation policies promoted integration and a reduction in differentiation. While the role of the United States in promoting this integration is overemphasized in some writings there is little doubt that had the Occupation not occurred Japan would not so quickly have moved towards such a state of affairs. Still it should be recalled from Chapter 2 that in many ways that the logic of Imperial Nationalism made comprehensive integration of the *kokutai* under the emperor a cherished ideal for government policy. Thus it is equally valid to view the Occupation thrust towards integration as the continuation and completion of the liberal bureaucrats' program of National Imperialism in the field of labour relations. The case for continuity rests on the idea that the most important result of the Occupation was the untying of the hands of the liberal bureaucrats: no longer facing a strident and powerful business opposition (the *zaibatsu* having been broken up), the former progressives within the Home Ministry were able to complete the program of reform which they had initiated during the interwar era.

3.3   STRUCTURAL TRANSFORMATION OF THE LABOUR MARKET, 1950–1970

The two decades of rapid growth in national output and labour productivity after the Occupation ended in 1952 encouraged the consolidation of the system of integrated segmentation forged during the Occupation. Space precludes a detailed discussion of economic growth during this period (cf. Kosai, 1986; Lincoln, 1988; Nakamura, 1981; Ohkawa and Rosovsky, 1973). Here four points culled from this literature will suffice. First productivity growth occurred both because labour was transferred from low productivity activities to higher productivity activities (structural change – cf. panel B.1 of Table 3.1), and because the technology and organization of production was rapidly reshaped, mainly through importing methods developed in the Western countries (technological progress). Second the pace of technological progress varied tremendously from sector to sector. As a result real labour productivity growth varied widely between the sectors as did the ability of enterprizes to cut their costs and (due to competition between enterprizes in the sectors) real (consumer price index adjusted) prices. Sectors enjoying the most rapid real total factor and labour productivity growth experienced the largest drops in relative price; sectors with the most sluggish productivity growth were subject to the smallest price declines. For this reason relative prices systematically changed over time. supply was instrumental in this, but demand shifts also played a role. But while wage growth for the labour force as a whole reflects the overall increase in labour productivity, at the sectoral level the connection is weaker than it is at the aggregate level. Third, because the labour force was relatively young and because the rate of output growth was high, most sectors experienced rapid increases in the number of workers hired and a large percentage of these new hires were young. As a result of rapid growth there was a continuous influx of fresh hires requiring monitoring and training. Hence promotion rates for experienced workers were high and, because there was strong demand for monitoring and training services, the marginal productivity of these promoted workers was substantial was substantial. That is, a large percentage of workers with internal firm experience were highly productive efficiency wage workers. Hence age/wage and seniority/wage profiles were steep. Fourth, because much of the technology being imported from abroad was at least partially embodied in capital equipment, investment was crucial to the rapidity of the growth process.[7]

Now the high-speed growth conditions of the decade and a half after 1955 created an environment in which there was relatively little market-driven pressure for change in the specific institutional constraints conditioning the operation of contracts in the various submarkets. Because growth was rapid, most large companies enjoyed continuous increases in their internal labour forces. Therefore the offer of employment security did not seem to be an unmanageable burden to most large enterprizes. Moreover, as noted earlier, because age/wage profiles were steep during the high-speed growth era, rapid growth in employment meant that the ratio of experienced to entrant cohorts was low and hence growth in the overall wage bill was contained. This point is discussed at some length in Chapter 5. The establishment of enterprise-based unionism and the elimination of the two-track recruitment and promotion system promoted internal, within-company-ranks, labour market integration and reduced the independent bargaining leverage which technically trained professionals in highly sought-after occupations could and did exercize. In short, integration within enterprizes made it easier for enterprizes to hold down labour costs in the face of increasing relative demand for professionals. Moreover because the postwar income elasticity of demand for higher education was large, as it had been before the war (cf. Chapters 2 and 4), that is because increases in real per-capita family income were rapidly translated into increases in per-capita demand for higher education, the expansion of demand for professionals was by and large met by the expansion of supply of new professionals on the active labour market. Finally, because the prices of goods in the sectors experiencing the most rapid real labour productivity growth tended to drop relative to those in sectors with less productivity growth, *nominal* labour productivity growth differentials were far smaller than real labour productivity differentials. For this reason less divisive pressure was imposed on collective bargaining than might have been otherwize: the sectors experiencing lacklustre productivity hikes were placed under less strain than they might have been had their relative market prices remained unchanged. Thus rapid real overall output and productivity growth promoted the diffusion and consolidation of a labour market equilibrium consistent with the institutional constraints imposed by government and by social norms.[8]

But these factors did not at first promote integration in the political dimension. Throughout the decade of the 1950s there were a series of major confrontations between labour and management: the Nissan strike in 1953, the National Railways Workers Union strike in 1957, the struggle over the teachers' efficiency rating system in 1958, and the Mitsui-Miike coal miners' strike in 1959–60. Since management tended to win these struggles, labour continually smarted under the onus of bitter defeat, and this sense of struggles won and lost at the expense of an opponent hardened the ideological lines between the left-leaning labour federations and Nikkeiren and the other business federations. This divisiveness is discussed in Chapter 6, where I will argue that it encouraged management and the government to utilize and refine divide-and-conquer tactics. Only in the later 1960s did integration in the political dimension gain serious momentum.

In short, rapid growth in output and productivity provided ideal conditions for the consolidation of the institutional constraints operating on the labour market. But once it was fully consolidated, the economy underwent a major crisis during the period 1971–5, as it adjusted to slower productivity growth potential, a fluctuating US dollar–yen exchange rate, and steep hikes in imported energy costs. How did it fare under this new environment?

3.4   STRUCTURAL BREAK AT THE TIME OF THE FIRST OIL CRISIS

By the late 1960s the engine of Japanese productivity growth was slowing its pace. Moreover as real wages climbed steadily Japan's comparative advantage in producing relatively labour-intensive manufactured goods was eroding. That these changes would eventually occur as the supply pool of untapped foreign technology dried up, and cheaper-wage countries expanded their production of labour-intensive manufactures, was appreciated and discussed in certain Japanese government and business circles even during the heady days of the early 1960s when growth rates were in excess of 10 per cent per annum. But what was not foreseen was that the slowing down of productivity growth and the upward drift in wages would occur simultaneously with a series of international events external to Japan which, in conjunction with the slowing down of productivity growth, simultaneously generated rapid inflation and recession.[9]

The first exogenous event of major importance was the decision of President Nixon in August 1971 to (a) suspend convertibility of the dollar into gold, (b) ask other industrial countries to revalue their currencies upward with respect to the dollar, (c) impose an import surcharge of 10 per cent, (d) impose a wage–price freeze in the United States. The second was the October 1973 war in the Middle East: in the middle of the month the Organization of Arab Petroleum Exporting Countries (OAPEC) announced a price increase from $3 to $5 a barrel, a cutback in shipments a total embargo on exports to the United States, and 10 per cent cut for other countries. The extent of the cutback in shipments to countries 'unfriendly' to the Arab cause in the war was further stepped up in November of 1973. The impact of these two events was striking: the yen began to appreciate against the dollar, the index of energy prices grew at a remarkably high rate, the rate of growth of industrial production markedly slowed down and the consumer price index shot up.

In understanding how and why the Japanese economy, and in particular how the large firm sector, responded to the crisis of 1971–4 it is useful to break down the responses into two main categories, market and political, and the factors triggering market and political responses into two categories, secular and short-run. First, consider the secular movements. Even before the crisis of the early 1970s it was apparent that Japanese growth eventually slow down and the economy have to be restructured, moving away from labour-intensive manufactures like textiles and shipbuilding towards knowledge- and capital-intensive industries. For instance in 1972 the Japanese politician Tanaka Kakuei (who was Prime Minister during the 1970s) published *Rebuilding the Japanese Archipelago* In this book he reflected the new set of expectations by advocating a redirecting of Japanese domestic aggregate demand towards the public-sector and housing, and away from labour-intensive industries. As for the slowing down in output growth it was understood that as expected profit growth dipped in response to lessened expectations about future productivity growth, payoffs to acquisition of new plant and equipment investment would decline and this would have a feedback effect by slowing overall demand growth even more. Hence it was recognized that if growth was to continue, a shift towards private-household capital formation and public-sector capital formation was desirable to compensate for a declining corporate-sector presence in investment markets . Again it was understood that unless industry restructured, shifting away from labour-intensive products, export potential would be sharply diminished by the secular upward drift in real wages (the price effect). Finally, because fertility and mortality rates were low after the late 1960s and the population was virtually shut off to immigration it was beginning to age. Demographic projections prepared by the Ministry of Health and Welfare clearly forecast a trend towards an older population which would pick up momentum especially after the late 1980s. And assuming age–wage profiles remained steep, the implication of ageing coupled with slow output growth was obvious: wage costs would dramatically rize. There is ample evidence that Japanese government and business leaders were aware of these secular problems and were attempting to develop policies to cope with these eventualities: the publication of Tanaka's book is a good indicator of this fact.

But this understanding and anticipation of long-run *domestic* secular movements, requiring a combination of carefully thought-out market and political responses, did not extend to the external shocks imposed by the Nixon administration's attack on US domestic inflation and an unfavourable balance of payments, and it did not extend to an anticipation of an OAPEC-engineered international hike in the price of, and shortage of, crude oil. After March 1973 and until January 1975 the growth rate of the consumer price index stayed in double digits; even before the oil shock unfolded it was growing more steeply than it had during the high-growth era; and once wholesale prices for imported oil and natural gas began soaring its growth was given even greater impetus. Both exogenous events had price and quantity implications for the Japanese economy: soaring energy prices boosted the relative cost of using capital *vis-à-vis* labour and the relative prices of energy intensive industries like aluminum production; a shortage of oil shipments meant certain enterprizes simply could not meet their energy flow requirements and had to scale down operations; the rising value of the yen meant international import prices dropped (in yen terms) but Japanese export prices tended to rize (although in so far as Japanese exports used imported raw materials the rising yen value cut both ways); and an American import surcharge meant that exporting to the United States would be more difficult. Because these unanticipated events seemed at first blush to constitute additions to the list of already anticipated secular factors expected to impede future income growth, a sense of major crisis took hold of the Japanese popular press in the early 1970s. And yet in retrospect it is clear that both the unanticipated and the anticipated factors in the crisis did not always work in the same direction, did not feed upon each other, worsening matters even more. Why?

First, consider the impact of the oil price hike. Because Japan, unlike the United States, was dependent on imported oil for all of her industrial and consumer needs, the relative price of oil had always been high in Japan, and hence the manufacturing sector and the automotive industry in particular had been biased towards energy-saving products and energy-saving production methods decades before the oil crisis. As a result when energy prices shot up on international markets Japanese products, which had been gradually developing a reputation both for high quality and for using low levels of energy input, were well positioned for export expansion even in the fact of upward yen reevaluation. Moreover the rize in energy prices raized the relative price of using capital which counteracted the rize in the relative price of labour during the high-growth era. Finally, as noted earlier, many of Japan's exports embody imported raw materials. The rize in the exchange value of the yen counteracted the rize in the yen-denominated final cost for these goods. In short the impact of the un-anticipated factors worked against the impact of the anticipated factors in some areas, making it easier, not harder, for Japan to adjust to the secular changes brought on by the closing of the high growth era. In short the Nixon shock and the oil crisis of the early 1970s helped rather than hindered Japan in coping with the secular tendencies of slower output growth, ageing, and the inexorable increase in real wages.

But at the time this was not the perception. Indeed as Lincoln (1988) points out there was a sense of panic in the popular Japanese press in the period 1973–5. Expectations for future output growth were very pessimistic. Hence enterprizes, especially larger corporations, drastically cut back on their hiring of new recruits. Those who had not already done so considered shifting away for the specific institution rules of the *nenkō* version of the large-firm labour market contract under which there was an implicit assumption that promotion rates were high (and therefore that the relative proportion of the senior labour force paid according to efficiency wage rules would be large in comparison to the proportion who would fall into the pool of rent-sharing non-promoted workers), towards the *shokunō shikaku seido* version under which it was assumed that promotion rates would be low and the relative proportion of rent-seeking senior workers would be high. Actually larger companies, anticipating a future era of slower growth and the ageing of the personnel structure, began the drive to shift the wage exchange away from market specific factors an entire decade earlier (see Chapter 5 for details). However, the frequency of switch towards the *shokunō shikaku seido* was especially high during the early and mid-1970s. Companies also began experimenting with early retirement and transfer (*shukkō*) programs whereby a firm with an excess supply of employees could 'loan' its excess workers to one or a number of other companies with excess demand for workers, thereby transferring some of its wage costs onto firms where the worker can be more productively utilized (see Chapter 5 for details). In this way large firms in the private-sector rearranged and redesigned the specific terms of the large-firm contract, redefining the meaning of employment security (to encompass *shukkō*) and reweighing the compensation formula away from market-specific wage exchange and towards firm-specific wage exchange. The government also responded: it reformed the Unemployment Insurance Law, originally passed in 1947, it provided subsidies for the retraining of workers, and it stepped up government capital formation as a mechanism for stimulating aggregate demand.

In short the period of the early 1970s witnessed an important watershed in the evolution of the system of integrated segmentation. But it would be incorrect to attribute the changes in personnel policies and government action as reactions to the Nixon shock and the oil crisis. True, these external events, by triggering a sense of panic, stimulated more rapid response than might have occurred in their absence. But if one looks at the actual changes in the institutions of integrated segmentation it is apparent that most of these, the important ones, were undertaken to cope with secular trends which were already occurring before 1970 and/or were projected to occur in the future rather than to deal with the short-run inflation and recession of the 1973–5 period. Once again the argument for continuity is strong.

3.5   STRUCTURAL CHANGE IN THE LABOR MARKET, 1975–90

The period 1975–90 witnessed the refinement of the *shokunō shikaku seido* and *shukko* responses to the challenge of ageing and slower growth in the private-sector. It also saw a rapid running up of government debt during the 1970s, followed by a strong, concerted attempt to reign in government spending and fiscal outlays after the early 1980s. The administrative reform of the period 1980–86 yielded the privatization of a number of the public corporations (the National Railways; NTT, the communications empire; the tobacco and salt corporations); and restriction of educational expenditures and other government outlays as a means of reducing the national debt. Through privatization of public corporations the private-sector of the union movement gained substantial membership at the expense of the public-sector, increasing the proportion of union membership which could legally strike under the terms of the Trade Union Law. But because ideological divisiveness between the union movement and government had been largely dissipated by the late 1970s (see Chapter 6) the political risks to the government of increasing the pool of employees legally empowered to strike were insignificant. By cutting back on its educational spending the government both reduced the quality and the quantity of its presence in the field of higher education. As a result the private-sector has substantially increased its influence over the supply of non-compulsory schooling. Thus the fifteen-year period after the oil crisis witnessed a sharp expansion followed by contraction in government outlays; and in the private-sector the period was marked by a steady trend towards a form of contract governing wages and promotion institutional-ized in the *shokunō shikaku seido* and a modified employment guarantee under which *shukkō* offers to companies burdened with an excess of workers a limited but important means of escaping the responsibility for employing its workers until they reach compulsory retirement age.

As for the growth rate of output, output growth, although far slower than it was during the high growth era of 1955–70, continued at a respectable rate usually hovering around the 4 per cent per annum mark. Partly this was due to Japan's export success after 1975, which was especially strong in the fields of automobiles, machinery and electrical machinery. I have already given reasons as to why Japanese enterprizes were unusually well positioned to deal with the oil crisis especially in comparison with enterprizes in North America which were accustomed to operating with cheap energy inputs. This was due in part to the relatively strong performance of investment demand: although private-sector investment rates fell off from the high levels of the 1960s, they remained at over 20 per cent of national income. Again this was also due to some extent to strong output growth, itself a product of earlier investment levels and the success of exports. It was due also to high domestic savings rates which helped to hold down interest rates, even in the face of a rapid increase in government spending in excess of revenues, that is in the face of a considerable increase in the accumulation of national debt.

Because income growth slowed down, so did the increase in demand for higher education. Thus the active labour market tended to stabilize after the early 1970s in terms of composition of the fresh graduate pool of job seekers according to level of school-leaving certification. As a result of the stabilization of the relative sizes of fresh graduate flows by school-leaving certification, a trend towards increases in the wage paid to entry-level junior high school leavers relative to entry-level high-school and university graduates ceased. This is documented in Chapter 4. Now since in the Japanese market for fresh graduate hires, sending a signal through the rank of the educational institution is admitted to be important during periods of high income growth when the demand for higher education has increased, so have the volumes of applicants seeking entry into the slots of the most prestigious schools. Since slot supply in the most prestigious institutions has not kept up with demand for slots, the demand for cram school services devoted to preparing students to pass entrance examinations for specific universities has increased during periods of increasing demand for higher education, this is because at this level of education, schooling is voluntary and is not substantially subsidized by public funds. Hence, increasingly over time, parental income has loomed larger and larger in determining who can successfully compete for entry into the top schools and who cannot. In short there has a been a secular drift towards divisiveness. In the aftermath of the post-World-War-II reforms, the opportunity for a child to compete in the educational hierarchy regardless of whether his or her parents were farmers, labourers, small-business owners, or white-collar employees was reasonably equal. But this equality of opportunity has tended to disappear over the course of time.

However, in the political dimension and in the collective bargaining dimension there has been a decided tendency towards integration. This is discussed in Chapter 6, and here we need only note that forces set in motion during the era of high-speed growth encouraged an reduction in the ideological divisiveness within the labour movement, between the labour movement and business, and between the labour movement and government. The slowing down of the engine of domestic growth, and the related fact that maintaining export competitiveness with fluctuating exchange rates has thereby become increasingly important for job stability, intensified the trend towards integration begun during the later years of the high-speed growth era.

In sum, the institutional constraints on the labour market have evolved in a reasonably continuous fashion over the course of the postwar period, partly in response to economic changes and partly in response to political developments and/or changes in social norms. Certainly the two periods of discontinuity, 1945–50 and 1971–5, have left their marks on the development of the institutions constraining the writing of labour market contracts and the relative net economic benefits flowing from the contracts. But it is continuous rather than discontinuous change which dominates in my account. Establishing this point is one of the key themes explored in the remainder of Part II of this volume.

4 Education and Labour Segmentation in the Active Labour Market

4.1 INTRODUCTION

By the close of the interwar period the educational system dovetailed with the dualistically segmented labour market. The school system was centralized, hierarchical, specialized and differentiated, and as a result strong signals about expected training costs, time horizons and effort capacity were effectively transmitted out of the fresh-graduate job-seeking pool to potential employers. The labour market for hired employees was also fragmented, specialized and hierarchical. Good jobs, meaning jobs paying premium wages for workers with experience and seniority, existed in the rapidly growing heavy industry sector for which implicit contracts involved long-term guarantees of employment and/or extensive training. To the extent possible, these firms drew their new hires from fresh graduates of institutions enjoying top ranking based on difficulty of admission and from the schools who trained students in the specialized areas in which particular firms had an active interest. In this way élite firms became linked to the élite schools, and particular industries became linked to particular types of schools. In the lower echelons of the labour market for fresh hires existed the plethora of light-industrial firms, small private companies in manufacturing and services, and farms. The type of contracts which these firms offered varied depending on whether the firms operated with family labour (in which case the firms 'hired' fresh entrants through marriage or incorporation of own or in-adopted children into their ranks, and most training was done in the household by the older and more seasoned family members), or with hired labour (in which case training was brief and there was no commitment to provide employment over future periods). These firms had no particular incentive to hire from top institutions, and were largely indifferent between hiring fresh graduates without previous job experience or hiring already experienced workers who commanded higher wages (depending on supply/demand conditions in the active labour markets) but who required less training and were thus likely to be more productive. Since the commercial firms in light industry and/or small-scale heavy industry who hired workers could terminate their employment of workers who were insufficiently productive with little or no cost, they were perfectly willing to hire from the lower echelons of the school system, that is they were willing to hire from a pool of fresh graduates with expected average effort capacity, expected training costs and time horizons below the means which large firms in heavy industry secured in their recruitment. Specialization in post-compulsory education was important for many of these firms but not hierarchical rank. Thus differentiation in the labour market on the supply side, and in particular the differentiation within the fresh school-graduate market, was linked to differentiation within the demand side. The two types of differentiation reinforced and strengthened one another.

Thus labour market demand was critical in shaping demand for a school system which was differentiated according to hierarchical rank and according to specialization. Moreover, because samurai values were diffused with the civil code, the income elasticity of demand for education gradually rose among all sectors of the population. Thus the demand for education increased at a brisk pace throughout the prewar period, especially so after heavy industry began to expand vigorously. But given the centralization of bureaucratic control over slots, with most of the control devolving onto the Ministry of Education in Tokyo and lesser authority onto prefectural and municipal governments, the responsiveness of supply to demand shift was far from automatic: toleration of private-sector involvement (albeit regulated) in generating slot growth, lobbying by business and direct cooperation between businesses and governmental bodies in establishing vocational and commercial schools, and political pressure applied on members of the Diet – these are examples of the mechanisms through which expansion in demand for educational slots was translated into expansion in supply of these slots. And the key to the high degree of economic efficiency in the response process was the fact that the system was specialized and differentiated, subsectors of the educational system being tailored to particular subsectors of the labour market, with the close connection between government and business mediating the two markets. For instance, as heavy industry expanded its demand for electricians, individual companies worked with the government in setting up electrically oriented vocational schools; when the silk industry shifted towards high-quality silk (owing to the introduction of rayon in the United States), vocational schools were either established within companies and were accredited by the government or were created by governments or by the private educational sector. That is, in the dynamics of change over time, the dominant factors were labour market pull and income per capita growth push, working through a combination of political pressure on public authorities and the private educational sector. But this interplay was the interplay under Imperial Nationalism. What were the dynamics under the institutional constraints of the postwar period, that is in an environment shaped by the dismantling of the Imperial Nationalist machinery by the American Occupation authorities? In short, how much continuity has there been in the interaction of educational and labour markets between the prewar and postwar periods ?

In addressing these issues I formulate a specific set of questions which are empirically tractable and which provide us with a framework for evaluating how much discontinuity occurred in the aftermath of the Second World War. (a) First, how important are labour market pull and per-capita family income growth for the shaping of demand for post-compulsory education in the period 1950–90? (b) Second, what has regulated the supply of slots and through what mechanisms have demand and supply growth been mediated? (c) Third, to what extent is the labour market pull experienced by the educational market conditioned by segmentation in the labour market, that is by a division into markets char-acterized by large- and small-commercial-firm contracts and by small, family-firm contracts and within each of these submarkets by occupational specialization? In short, how has tracking within the school system inter-acted with labour market demand segmentation and occupational specialization?

In order to set the stage for interpretation of the statistical analysis which lies at the core of my reply to these three questions, I devote the next section to a general discussion of the American-inspired reforms and their evolution after Japan had won full independence from the United States. This provides us with essential background for an understanding of how the supply of slots in the postwar educational system is regulated and what the constraints are that govern the expansion of these slots; and it gives us an overview of the content of schooling that is essential for an appreciation of what it means to be a fresh school graduate from the various levels of the educational system. Then in Section 4.3 I formulate a model of demand for post-compulsory education,which I subject to empir-ical scrutiny in the remainder of the chapter. This model puts heavy influence on labour segmentation and per-capita family income. In short, it emphasizes labour demand pull and per-capita family capacity to pay for the additional years of schooling. In Section 4.4 I consider the changing nature of the conditions governing labour demand pull over the era 1950–90 by analysing the influence of changes in the flows within the active market for fresh school-graduate hires upon the relative levels wages. Then, beginning with Section 4.5, I examine in detail the empirical character of the demand for slots in the post-compulsory education market and its interaction with slot supply: in Section 4.5 I consider high school, the choice of whether to advance from middle school to high school or to go directly into the labour market, and some of the mechanisms through which the private business sector has influenced slot supply in the public sector; in Section 4.6 I consider the parallel question for university and/or junior college education; finally in Section 4.7 I return to the three issues highlighted at the outset of the chapter and address them in the context of the results of my step by step analysis.

4.2.   POSTWAR REFORMS: CONTINUITY AND DISCONTINUITY

In dismantling the institutions of Imperial Nationalism the SCAP devoted a great deal of its energies to reform of the educational system, since it felt that the ideological roots for mass acceptance of ultranationalism and the emperor cult had been planted in the school system. For this reason the educational division of SCAP (the Civil Information and Education Section, known as CIE SCAP): ordered that teachers and officials of the educational bureaucracy guilty of documented complicity in the promotion of ultranationalism and militarism be purged; immediately set to reforming curriculum and textbooks in the hopes of eliminating the ideology of emperor worship, militarism and *kokutai no hongi*; undertook a democratization campaign designed to decentralize control over educational institutions, reducing the power of the Ministry of Education and promoting the influence of institutions independent of the Ministry such as the local School Board and the University Chartering Council; mandated that Ministry control over private schools be reduced; and ordered the Imperial University system decentralized, the distinction between the prewar imperial universities and the new national universities to be established with at least one to a prefecture muted, and the national system opened up to female applicants (cf. Pempel, 1978).[1] The key reform legislation was passed in the period 1947–9: the Fundamental Law of Education and the School Education Law in March 1947; the School Board Law in 1948; and the National School Establishment Law and the Private School Law in 1949. Taken as a body this legislation, in principle, completely restructured the educational system both in terms of the organization of schools (an American style 6–3–3–4 system open to both sexes was erected in place of the old multitrack prewar system, which was segregated by sex), in terms of the content of the curriculum (textbooks were completely rewritten), and in terms of the central control enjoyed by the Ministry of Education *vis-à-vis* teachers (who formed the Japan Teachers Union, which has been as a thorn in the side of the Ministry of Education since its inception) and educational institutions whether national, prefectural, municipal or private.

In many ways the model envisioned by the American occupation authorities and supported by those factions in the Japanese educational community enamoured by the liberal education tradition championed by many American academics was the complete opposite of the model developed by the Ministry of Education and national legislation between 1872 and 1945. The prewar system was specialized and differentiated, hierarchical, and centralized And although it gradually became egalitarian over the course of the Meiji and Taisho periods (i.e. as *minshuka* occurred, that is 'democratization' in the sense in which the Japanese use the term), with the opportunity to compete for entry into the highest echelons of the system opening up for all males, it did not become democratic in the sense in which Americans use the term; this was because ultimate control over the organizations offering education, and over the content of that education, remained in the hands of the Ministry of Education, although at the highest levels of the system this control was not exercised with the same intensity as it was at the lower and especially at the lowest, the compulsory, segment of the system. In contrast, the American model is decentralized (state governments and local communities operating at the municipal and school district level); unspecialized (the comprehensive local high school drawing on most potential students in an administratively defined catchment area and the multi-faculty four-year college are typical examples of this lack of specialization); and democratic, that is responsible to, and shaped by, local population through school boards and parent–teacher associations, and endowed with a generous supply of slots in the higher reaches of the system. Moreover, the model for the American high school and the liberal arts college in the 1940s, 1950s and 1960s was a generalist model, with choice of specialization coming relatively late in a student's career.[2] And hierarchical ranking of higher educational institutions in the United States is relatively muted: for instance, the land grant colleges in the Midwest and West have provided a education of reasonably high quality at low cost to substantial proportions of the school-aged populations in these regions. Thus even though the Americans did not unilaterally impose their organizational forms on the Japanese during the Occupation period of 1945–53, American institutions played a paramount role in directing reform legislation and administrative practice. By creating a national university in each of the fourty-six prefectures the reformers hoped to promote greater equality of opportunity and to diminish the élite status of the former imperial universities which became national universities along with the new campuses created in each prefecture (in the wake of the reform thirty-nine new national universities were established and added to a system which initially consisted of the seven former imperial universities); by passing a school board law the reformers hoped to enhance the voice of local communities in the shaping of curriculum and textbooks; by recommending a curriculum untainted by militarism and emperor worship the reformers hoped to deal a death blow to the ideology of Imperial Nationalism.

How long-lived have been these reforms? Pempel (1978: 188ff.) suggests that after the Occupation ended there has been steady drift away from many of the Occupation's reforms. The Ministry of Education's central control has been more or less reestablished And a steep hierarchy among national universities with the former imperial universities of Tokyo, Kyoto and Osaka at or near the top in almost every field reemerged quite quickly after the war (although in the last several years some private universities have begun to edge out the former imperial universities in certain fields, which would have been unheard of before the war). However, Pempel does argue that in at least one area – democracy, as understood in terms of equality of opportunity to compete for slots through the system from the bottom to the apex, as represented by entry into Tokyo University – the reforms have not been reversed. But is this surprising? For, as I have argued, because of the changes in the supply and demand for labour, the movement towards *minshuka* was gaining tremendous momentum during the interwar period. Moreover, Japanese fascism as a political movement which placed paramount value on service to the national entity, the *kokutai*, emphasized the importance of *minshuka*, understood as equality of opportunity in competing for slots in the military, the bureaucracy, the educational system and even in private firms. The trend under Imperial Nationalism was towards a diminishing of status distinctions and the lengthening of ladders of advancement to allow for the widest possible competition.

No better example of the difficulty of successfully adopting American-style educational institutions in Japan can be given than that afforded by the comprehensivisation programmes attempted by socialist governments in the late 1960s (Lynn, 1988: 33ff). The Socialist Party (and the left-leaning Nikkyoso, the Japan Teachers Union) had always been opposed the elitist orientation of the Japanese public high-school system, since (more on this below) the schools within a catchment area, which at least in the metropolitan areas tended to be extensive, had hitherto been arrayed in an elabourate pecking order according to the minimal level of performance required for a successful applicant on a weighted mixture of the average level of school grades in middle school and performance on standardized prefectural tests. As a result, in large catchment zones some schools specialized in getting students into the élite universities, some in getting students into less competitively sought-after universities and junior colleges, and some in training students for the job market or for marriage. The socialist government in Nagoya was the first to experiment with an American-style approach by so restricting the reach of the catchment areas that the ability of schools to competitively screen and select students according to demonstrated ability on standardized tests was severely curtailed The socialist government in Tokyo followed the lead of Nagoya and in 1967 initiated its own programme of limiting the size of the catchment areas. Historically, three of Tokyo's high schools – Hibiya, Nishi and Koichikawa – consistently placed in the top twenty high schools in Japan, as defined by the admission rate into the University of Tokyo achieved by their graduates. But after comprehensivisation was introduced two of these schools – Hibiya and Koishikawa – dropped out of the list of the top twenty high schools. The reason was simple: those parents enjoying incomes sufficient to exercise a private school option and having children who, if admitted to a top-ranked high school, stood a fair chance of gaining admission to a prestigious university, simply removed their charges from the public sector. As a result of having smaller catchment areas imposed on them, the average quality of the student intake in the Hibiya and Koishikawa schools fell.

The thrust of my remarks is that the hierarchical, specialized and differentiated, and centralized characteristics of the prewar system have by and large continued to thrive in the more egalitarian postwar era, and that the Ministry of education has managed to regain many of the powers seemingly stripped from it during the reform period 1947–9. Two salient characteristics of postwar schooling attest to this continuity argument. The first is the emphasis on science and arithmetic in the compulsory programme from grades 1 to 9 which, as we saw in Chapter 2, was a special feature of the Imperial Nationalist programme of importing foreign technology. There are plausible reasons for thinking that the Ministry of Education curriculum policy, which stipulates that extensive time inputs must be put into the study of mathematics and science at the elementary- and middle-school levels, accounts for the comparative and absolute advantage which they enjoy in the taking of international standardized tests in these fields. For example, compare the following means on an international mathematics examination administered to thirteen-year-olds (cf. Rohlen, 1983: 4–5, Lynn, 1988: 4ff.):

	Thirteen-year-olds	
Country	*Mean*	*Standard deviation*
England	19.3	17.0
France	18.3	12.4
Japan	31.2	16.9
Sweden	15.7	10.8
USA	16.2	13.3

Lynn (1988: 6) shows that the international test scores mean that approximately 84 per cent of Japanese children scored higher than the comparable American student. International science achievement tests administered in 1970–1 also put Japan at the top. In sum, the strong hand of the Ministry of education in formulating stringent curriculum guidelines to be followed by all schools in the country, and the stress put on developing mathematics and scientific skills within that curriculum, clearly yield a student populace with a special aptitude for science and engineering fields.

A second important legacy of the prewar period which the conservatively oriented Ministry of Education has retained in the postwar period is the use of the standardized competitive examination as a winnowing out tool for tracking students through the layers of the school system. Before the war, high schools and universities used tests requiring copious feats of memorization as a tool for deciding who would secure admission and who would not. This was one way of nullifying the influence of personal connections among social élites on the admission process; that is, it was one mechanism for stretc.hing downward the competitive admission ladder to the lowest social classes, so that only the most capable would successfully gain admission, and egalitarianism could coexist with steep hierarchy. In the postwar period the Ministry of Education has staunchly supported the continuing utilization of a standardized examination system that has now become well codified into the *hensachi* system, which is the main device for channelling middle-school graduates into the next step up the educational ladder, and the way of rationing slots at the university and junior college level. The term '*hensachi*' refers to a numerical transformation of the numbers of standard deviations above or below the median that an examinee receives on an examination. It is an indicator of relative position or rank on a test. That the Japanese student develops a strong sense of his or her academic potential early on in his or her encounter with the school system when *hensachi* rankings are handed out towards the end of elementary school is a clear indicator of the pervasiveness of the examination system in the Japanese psyche. It is interesting that a popular television programme in contemporary Japan mimics the atmosphere of a classroom taking a standardized school test by having the contestants sit in classroom chairs and compete to answer questions put to them by a programme host dressed as a teacher. Moreover, the questions he asks are based on actual school examination questions.

But while the Ministry of Education has certainly had its way in many areas it would be incorrect to conclude that it exercises the authority it did before the war. For one thing, its policies are often opposed by the Japan Teachers' Union, and if it fails to win at least grudging acquiescence in its decisions it finds it difficult indeed to implement new programmes. An example in point is the fate of the Third Educational Reform put forward by the Ministry in the mid-1970s on the basis of three reports prepared for it by a special commission of inquiry into the educational system which the Ministry had convened The Ministry argued that Japan required a third reform since the first two major reforms – that of 1872 and that of 1947 – had been carried out under foreign pressure and had ended up adopting foreign educational models (cf. Kobayashi, 1976: 151ff.). But, in attempting to formulate a new 'Japanese' vision for the educational system, the Ministry ran into the concerted opposition of the Japan Teachers' Union which felt that any new major reform would end up moving Japan even further away from the 1947–9 set of reforms which attempted to democratize and decentralize the educational system. While the outcome was not total stalemate, the Ministry was unable to carry out a comprehensive reform after all. By comparison, in the prewar period the Ministry did not have to do continual ideological battle with a determined left-leaning adversary, the postwar Nikkyoso; therefore it could get its own way with far greater frequency, as it did in 1918 when it engaged in a top-to-bottom restructuring of the educational system.

In sum, there is some continuity between the pre- and postwar periods: centralization, hierarchy, specialization and differentiation were the hallmarks of the system before the war and they are also characteristic of the postwar system. After the postwar reform the system became somewhat more democratic, but in the main this meant more egalitarian in the sense that ladders within which individuals could compete for advancement became wider and less restricted to élite socioeconomic groups, and not much more democratic in the sense of admitting the active participation of local communities in the setting of teaching standards and the content of the curriculum. And as for the trend towards egalitarianism, it is not at all evident that this was something new, brought in wholesale by the Occupation bureaucracy and those progressive Japanese parties interested in taking advantage of the Occupation to further their own programme of reform. For the fact is that there was a strong trend towards egalitarianism under prewar Imperial Nationalism, especially under the Fascist regime which emerged out of Imperial Nationalism. But the power of the Ministry of education is less than it was before the war: there are more countervailing political enemies it must contend with. In this sense the reforms of the late 1940s mark an important watershed in Japanese educational history; that is, the Occupation period was a period of true discontinuity in Japanese educational development, although the break is not nearly as sharp as it is sometimes thought.

4.3   DEMAND FOR EDUCATION AND LABOUR SEGMENTATION

That education offers a variety of rewards, some which are strictly pecuniary and some more contemplative and aesthetic in nature, is implicit in the existence of both humanistic and economic efficiency models of education. In principle, the economist's standard notion of the returns to education can accommodate both the narrow economic benefits and the more broadly conceived consumption benefits accruing to the student. To see this, consider the calculation which an individual contemplating an additional amount of non-compulsory education makes. Let us suppose it takes 1, ..., j periods to acquire the additional amount of education, and let us also assume, for simplicity, that the course of study contemplated by the individual is so daunting that part-time work/part-time study is precluded (it is easy to relax this assumption but making it facilitates the presentation of the argument). The costs of securing the education are of two types: first there are the direct costs C_t for each year t, the payment of tuition, the purchase of books and other study materials, and so forth; then there are the indirect opportunity costs, the overwhelming bulk of which are the wages w_t for each year t forgone by the individual because he or she is studying rather than working. It is reasonable to suppose that the individual possesses some notion of the expected future wages he can expect to earn throughout the remainder of his employment career with both the additional years of education and without it, and as a result forms a mental image of the expected opportunity cost wage profile he forgoes in opting for the education that, in turn, yields another wage profile lacking wage payments in the periods 1, ..., j.[3] In addition the individual electing to acquire a higher level of education may feel constrained to forgo social intercourse with relatives and former colleagues and comrades of lower educational attainment, for instance eschewing village festivals in his or her place of birth. For example, some rural communities may be less socially inhibited and freer in their mores, more fervent in their bawdy revelry at festivals, than blue-collar or white-collar workers in large metropolitan areas. This should be factored in as a forgone opportunity.

Against these expected costs are weighed the expected benefits. Let us divide these into three types: the narrow economic benefits measured in pecuniary terms; the social status benefits; and the pure consumption benefits independent of social prestige earned in workplace or the general company of one's fellows. As for social status, securing a credential from an institution of higher learning confers status, status which is greater the more competitive is entry into the organization. People lacking the drive to pursue a career – for instance the marriage-minded woman imbued with the *ryōsai kenbo* ideology who is admitted to a liberal arts faculty in a private university – may well be more interested in the status afforded to them as a result of entering an élite school where they are likely to meet high-status potential spouses than in anything they may perchance learn while they are in school.[4] Again, persons having advanced further in the educational system may be assigned less demeaning tasks in the companies they work for, thereby securing greater within-work-group status by virtue of their credentials. As for consumption benefits, there are the immediate rewards afforded to students when they are students (e.g. parties, clubs, hiking and skiing trips) as well as the opportunity after graduation of being more informed and astute consumers of the leisure activities available to them in the public and private-sectors allocate. That is, they become more efficient at consumption both in the short term and in the long-term. All of this accords with the commonly used term *gakureki shugi* (credential society), a term employed by the Japanese themselves to refer to their almost obsessive concern with formal educational attainment.

Now let us concentrate on the narrow pecuniary benefits. These are the wages w_i^q which the individual anticipates earning by dint of the incremental education planned I divide the expected benefits associated with the higher level of education into two types:

(a) *Signalling.* Gaining the certification of the higher level of education sends a signal concerning expected training costs and effort capacity since, at the minimum, it indicates that the individual was capable of securing entrance to some school at the next highest rung in the educational ladder, thereby communicating information about the graduate's time horizon. However, as far as the other features of the signal are concerned (i.e. the expected mean of effort capacity and training costs), the ranking of the schooling to which the individual secures admission is of far greater significance than the level of schooling *per se*.

(b) *Skill formation, training and occupational licensing.* In the course of study and learning, the student acquires specialized skills (e.g., the capacity to use computer software) and knowledge about how to acquire additional skills. For instance, firms in the chemicals industry have a special interest in students trained in chemical engineering and/or chemistry and/or physics; firms in the electrical machinery industry are especially interested in graduates of electrical engineering programmes; and so forth. Even though Japanese engineering graduates often change speciality within a few years of being hired by a firm, moving, say, from an electrical engineering concentration to a mechanical engineering concentration, many continue to specialize in the area within which they were originally hired, and in any case they typically continue to use their general knowledge of engineering acquired during the first few years of university study regardless of their precise job assignment. Moreover for some professions-for instance, for pharmacy, medicine, and teaching-the prospective entrant to the field must first secure a licence, and licensing standards are usually enforced through a test which is based on the curriculum taught in a specialized programme within the educational system.

Now, for many jobs with family-run enterprises or small commercial firms for which monitoring is relatively costless and specialized training requirements minimal, post-compulsory schooling is of dubious relevance. For example, those who work in the myriad of tiny family-run farms or restaurants or printing plants or manufacturing establishments producing pastries, *tatami* mats, toys and the like, or those who work as painters or unskilled construction workers, need relatively few of the skills which post-compulsory education school training provides. Now, where occupation-specific credentialism is concerned there are good reasons for believing that securing credentials through educational certification is more important for females than for males. For a Japanese woman securing professional certification sends a signal about the expected time horizon of the individual, namely that she is likely to have a low discount rate for future-versus-present earnings. After all, since many years of schooling are required in order to enter the profession a woman who is not dedicated to a long career is unlikely to persevere (nor is her family likely to persevere) in the competitive struggle for an education unless she plans on staying in the profession for a long time. Before the war women who selected teaching as a field of concentration by graduating from a normal school sent this kind of signal. After the war, with less constraints on advancement in the school system owing to the abolition of separate schooling for men and women above compulsory education, women could select from a richer array of academic fields which send the signal concerning time preference.

In any event, let us assemble the various facets of our argument concerning the rate of return to education. For simplicity of exposition, imagine we can state all costs and benefits in cardinal utility terms, evaluating the status and economic rewards and costs of the incremental schooling for the remainder of one's expected life span in the same units. Proceeding in this way, we can equate the discounted present value of the benefits B_t with the discounted present value of the costs C_t:

$$\sum_{t=1}^{N} \frac{B_t}{(1+r)^{t-1}} = \sum_{t=1}^{N} \frac{C_t}{(1+r)^{t-1}} \tag{4.1}$$

where r is the imputed rate of return to getting the additional education (r is the largest number such that the benefits exceed or are exactly equal to the costs; thus it is the 'break-even' rate of return). Note that the rate or return depends on a variety of considerations: the type of firm one expects to be hired by; the relative weight of status as opposed to financial rewards; and so forth. Also note that while, in practice, the calculation of r implied by equation (4.1) cannot be made because consumption benefits are difficult to measure in cardinal terms, the idea of including them is important. For instance, conventional measures of the rate of return for Japan (see Nakata and Mosk, 1987; and McMahon and Wagner, 1981) surely underestimate the rate of return because they fail to measure the consumption rewards from the investment. For this reason the rates of return to university education should be adjusted upward, especially for professions in which status benefits loom large relative to financial rewards.[5] Also note that at the aggregate level the rate of return is an average variable, varying substantially from individual to individual in the population. Those who are adept at schooling, or whose parents are wealthy, face lower real costs for schooling measured in terms of opportunities forgone. Thus when the rate of return r is used as an independent variable in a behavioural equation it should be understood as applying to the marginal-investor, to that person of average gifts and material endowments who just teeters on the edge, weighing the extra costs and benefits carefully before arriving at a considered decision. This point is important for the analysis which follows, because in formulating my model of demand for school advancement I assume it is the marginal investor who is making decisions each step of the way (see Freeman, 1971, for an early formulation of marginal-investor theory in the study of the economics of education). Because I am interested in analysing incremental change, and because the speed of change in school advancement is so rapid, as we shall shortly see, this assumption concerning marginal-investor behaviour is plausible.

Using the analytical framework developed earlier in this and previous chapters we can derive six useful propositions concerning the demand for incremental amounts of education:

1. *Declining rate of return.* Holding the relative demand for education of all educational groups constant, an increase in the relative supply of a higher educational group relative to a lower educational group reduces the rate of return to the extra schooling. This follows because the outward supply shift for the higher educational group, with demand unchanged, drives towards relative wages for the group.

2. *Difference between sexes.* Men are less constrained than women in the ways they can signal their effort capacity, training costs and time horizons. As a result of social norms there is an assumption that a woman's time horizon is shorter than a man's. Therefore women who wish to signal that they have long time horizons are more likely to choose careers which lead into clearly defined professions than are men with equivalent effort capacity and training costs.

3. *Firm size.* The greater is the gain in probability of securing a position in a large firm associated with getting a higher level of education, the higher is the return to education. This follows from the fact that large firm contracts offer greater opportunities for training than do those of small firms and from the possibility of promotion into efficiency wage positions which small-firm contracts do not offer.

4. *Income as a constraint on demand for education.* Because capital markets from which households might secure loans for the post-compulsory schooling of their children are imperfect, real income per household member is a factor in determining a household's demand for education for its children. The lower is the real family income per head, the lower is per-household-member demand for

advancement up the educational ladder. At low levels of average family income per capita, many capable students from lower socioeconomic strata of the population are rationed out of the market for higher education.

5. *Structural shifts in the demand for fresh graduates.* As the structure of production changes, so does the relative demand for persons with different levels of schooling. However, the greater is the willingness of firms to substitute informal on-the-job-training for formal instruction in an accredited educational institution, the more muted is the impact of demand shift in firms on the structure of demand for specialized educational services.

6. *Labour market segmentation domination of occupational special-ization.* For men, choice of field of specialization is typically of less importance than choice of terminal level of education and choice of institution from which one enters the labour market. This is due to the high priority placed on screening for effort capacity and training costs which is signalled by the ability to enter into prestigious educational institutions regardless of field.

With these propositions in mind, let us consider the decision making of a typical middle-school student who is contemplating whether or not to continue on to non-compulsory high school. Because preparing for the examinations required of applicants to high school requires a least a year of special study and effort, the student has little choice but to arrive at a decision about whether to continue on in year t one year before, that is in year $t-1$. Consider the student in the fall term of the last year before he or she is scheduled to graduate from middle school. According to my propositions, demand should increase when: (a) per-capita family income goes up; (b) the proportion of family workers in the labour force goes down; and (c) when the relative rewards of being a high-school graduate seem especially attractive relative to those obtainable as a junior high-school graduate. Now consider the students who advance on to high school. (In what follows I am implicitly assuming that there are enough slots in the high-school system as a whole to accommodate all applicants. This does not mean that there are enough slots in the most sought-after schools to accommodate applicants to that particular school; it only means there are slots sufficient to meet demand somewhere within the catchment area.) Two years after they enter the school they must decide whether they plan to continue on. For students who have entered industrial or commercially oriented programmes there is little option. Basically they have already decided to directly go into the labour market upon graduation. But for those in regular academic programmes a decision must be reached. I hypothesize that the marginal investor at this stage has his or her decision conditioned by the following variables: (a) per-capita real family income; (b) the expected probability of gaining admission to a university or college (the relative excess demand for slots observed in the current year); and (c) the total career wage payments (in discounted present value terms) currently enjoyed by high-school graduate workers relative to those enjoyed by university and college graduate workers. The actual flow of graduates out of middle schools reveals what happens to the individuals once they have actually made their choices. Some enter institutions of higher learning; some become *rōnin* and try to gain admittance in the next year; some enter the job market; and some become unemployed and/or leave both the school system and the labour market. Women marrying and not entering family work situations fall into this category.

4.4   THE CHANGING MARKET FOR FRESH GRADUATE HIRES

How important are fresh school graduates in the labour market for newly hired workers? How have supply and demand conditions for fresh graduate hires in the various educational attainment groups changed over the last four decades since the early 1950s? What has happened to relative starting earnings for fresh graduate hires over time? And regarding changes in the relative starting earnings of, and the related tightness or looseness in the separate markets for, fresh graduate hires in the three major educational groups which has been more telling: supply or demand shifts?

Consider first the figures in Table 4.1 on the distribution of the flow of new hires (family workers and the self-employed excluded) over the period 1965–84. First note that for *males* – but not for females – fresh graduate hires constitute a distinct minority of hires throughout the last two and a half decades. Those workers with previous experience have consistently been in the majority when it comes to the active labour market for males. The occupationally inexperienced, defined as fresh graduate hires plus those who have not held a job for a year before they were presently taken on, generally constitute less than 40 per cent of new hires and in the tight labour market of the 1970s approximately amounted to a mere third of hires. But for females the reverse is the case. Second, it can be seen that among fresh graduate hires there has been a secular shift away from junior high-school graduate hires towards those with higher degrees. In fact since the proportion of high-school and junior college

TABLE 4.1   Fresh hires, experienced and inexperienced, including fresh graduates by educational level completed, 1965–84.

<table>
<thead>
<tr>
<th rowspan="4">Years</th>
<th colspan="6">Percentage of new hires who are</th>
<th colspan="8">Rate of new hires per 1000 regular employees (of same sex)</th>
</tr>
<tr>
<th rowspan="3">Experienced</th>
<th colspan="5">Inexperienced</th>
<th colspan="2">Total experienced</th>
<th colspan="6">Inexperienced</th>
</tr>
<tr>
<th rowspan="2">Total</th>
<th colspan="4">Fresh graduates</th>
<th rowspan="2">Total</th>
<th rowspan="2">experienced</th>
<th rowspan="2">Total</th>
<th colspan="5">Fresh graduates</th>
</tr>
<tr>
<th>Middle school</th>
<th>High school</th>
<th>Junior college</th>
<th>College</th>
<th>Total</th>
<th>Middle school</th>
<th>High school</th>
<th>Junior college</th>
<th>College</th>
</tr>
</thead>
<tbody>
<tr><td colspan="15">(A) Males</td></tr>
<tr><td>1965–69</td><td>6.1</td><td>38.9</td><td>7.0</td><td>14.7</td><td>3.1</td><td>2.0</td><td>176.3</td><td>107.8</td><td>68.5</td><td>47.2</td><td>17.3</td><td>25.9</td><td>5.6</td><td>3.5</td></tr>
<tr><td>1970–74</td><td>69.8</td><td>30.2</td><td>3.1</td><td>10.3</td><td>0.7</td><td>6.3</td><td>156.3</td><td>109.1</td><td>47.1</td><td>31.7</td><td>4.8</td><td>16.2</td><td>1.0</td><td>9.7</td></tr>
<tr><td>1975–79</td><td>65.3</td><td>34.7</td><td>1.8</td><td>10.9</td><td>1.0</td><td>8.3</td><td>109.1</td><td>71.3</td><td>37.8</td><td>23.9</td><td>2.0</td><td>11.8</td><td>1.0</td><td>9.1</td></tr>
<tr><td>1980–84</td><td>60.7</td><td>39.3</td><td>1.9</td><td>11.9</td><td>1.4</td><td>9.2</td><td>111.8</td><td>67.9</td><td>43.9</td><td>27.4</td><td>2.1</td><td>13.3</td><td>1.6</td><td>10.3</td></tr>
<tr><td colspan="15">(B) Females</td></tr>
<tr><td>1965–69</td><td>36.0</td><td>64.0</td><td>9.6</td><td>20.7</td><td>2.0</td><td>0.2</td><td>313.0</td><td>112.7</td><td>200.2</td><td>101.7</td><td>30.2</td><td>64.8</td><td>6.2</td><td>0.5</td></tr>
<tr><td>1970–74</td><td>44.2</td><td>55.8</td><td>3.8</td><td>15.5</td><td>3.2</td><td>1.1</td><td>274.1</td><td>120.9</td><td>153.3</td><td>64.5</td><td>10.6</td><td>42.4</td><td>8.6</td><td>2.9</td></tr>
<tr><td>1975–79</td><td>39.3</td><td>60.7</td><td>2.0</td><td>16.0</td><td>5.3</td><td>1.6</td><td>207.5</td><td>81.6</td><td>125.9</td><td>51.5</td><td>4.2</td><td>33.1</td><td>10.9</td><td>3.3</td></tr>
<tr><td>1980–84</td><td>37.7</td><td>62.3</td><td>1.4</td><td>16.4</td><td>6.2</td><td>1.8</td><td>207.2</td><td>78.1</td><td>129.1</td><td>53.5</td><td>3.0</td><td>34.0</td><td>12.9</td><td>3.6</td></tr>
</tbody>
</table>

Source:
Japan Statistical Association (1987: Table 3–17, (pp. 418–23).

graduate hires has also declined in the case of males (but increased in the case of females), the net thrust of the shift has been away from the primary and secondary levels of the educational system towards the tertiary level. Third, over the period 1967–79 the flow of new hires relative to the stock of workers declined, with a slight recovery after 1980. Thus at the same time the weight of higher education graduates as a percentage of the flow of new fresh graduate hires was increasing, the relative importance of new hire flow and fresh graduate flow to the stock of workers was falling. However the shift towards higher credentials dominates over the decline in the fresh-graduate-inflow-to-worker-stock ratio, for the ratio of fresh graduate college flows to stock of workers has increased significantly over the period. As a result the proportion of employed workers possessing university or junior college degrees has significantly increased over time.

As the fresh graduate market has been transformed in terms of the distribution of credentials, so has the relative availability of new jobs for applicants, and the relative starting wages of new hires compared with workers already employed From Table 4.2 it is apparent that from the mid-1950s on, middle- and high-school graduates have enjoyed excess demand conditions. The job opening rate is the ratio of job openings posted at employment exchanges to applicants seeking jobs at these exchanges – a variable which is meaningful for general labour and fresh middle- and high-school graduates, but not for university or college graduates, who tend to spend their senior years interviewing for jobs with prospective employers and usually have a job sewn up before they graduate. It should be noted that when the job opening rate is higher then the probability of securing a job with a large or medium-sized firm in the social efficiency wage sector is greater. Now note for that non-fresh graduate hires, that is general worker (*ippan rōdōsha*) hires, in only one five-year period, i.e. the exceedingly tight labour market epoch of the early 1970's, were job openings in excess of job searchers. By contrast, for fresh middle- and high-school graduates demand has consistently outstripped supply, and during the later 1960s and 1970s the excess of demand over supply has been substantial. From 1980 to 1987 the situation has been considerably more balanced Now consider Panel B of Table 4.2, which gives the earnings of middle-school and high-school graduates relative to male higher-education graduates. Note that the relative starting earnings of middle-school and high-school graduates rose sharply through the period when the job opening rate for these groups was increasing, and that the relative levels have by and large stabilized in the post-1975 period when the job opening rates for the middle- and high-school graduates began to deteriorate. Figures from model wage tables for big firms (a thou-

Table 4.2   Job opening rates and relative starting wages for new hires, 1955–87

(A) Job opening rates

| Years | General labour | | | Fresh graduates | | | |
| | Total | Males | Females | Middle school | | High school | |
				Males	Females	Males	Females
1955–59	0.438	n.a.	n.a.	1.200	1.070	1.010	0.698
1960–64	0.908	n.a.	n.a.	2.700	2.816	3.372	1.866
1965–69	0.996	n.a.	n.a.	3.676	3.994	5.094	2.792
1970–74	1.286	1.476	1.044	6.480	5.800	5.602	3.170
1975–79	0.620	0.704	0.486	3.708	4.260	2.622	1.932
1980–84	0.654	0.766	0.466	2.080	2.776	2.172	1.480
1985–87	n.a.	n.a.	n.a.	1.660	2.000	2.150	1.470

(B) Relative starting wages (male junior college *and* college graduate wages = 100 for 1954–75; and male college graduate wages = 100 for 1976–87)

Years	Middle school		High school		Combined junior		Junior college		College	
	Male	Female	Male	Female	College males	College females	Males	Females	Males	Females
1955–59	40.7	37.2	62.3	56.4	100.0	88.5	n.a.	n.a.	n.a.	n.a.
1960–64	40.7	47.0	65.9	59.7	100.0	93.3	n.a.	n.a.	n.a.	n.a.
1965–69	60.1	59.8	74.1	69.7	100.0	91.4	n.a.	n.a.	n.a.	n.a.
1970–74	65.9	63.2	79.2	73.7	100.0	85.8	n.a.	n.a.	n.a.	n.a.
1975–79	69.1	63.9	81.8	78.0	n.a.	n.a.	87.5	85.6	100.0	94.0
1980–84	70.6	64.7	80.9	76.5	n.a.	n.a.	88.1	84.0	100.0	94.6
1985–87	69.1	65.3	79.9	75.1	n.a.	n.a.	87.5	83.3	100.0	95.7

Source:
Japan.Statistical Association (1987: various tables); and Kume (1988: various tables).

Category	1962	1972
Male college graduate		
(*shokuin* – staff member)		
age 25	119.4	112.3
age 30	127.8	122.8
age 55	206.9	178.3
Male high-school graduate		
age 25	106.9	102.9
age 30	108.4	104.8
age 55	141.7	111.9
Female high-school graduate		
age 25	86.8	86.1
age 30	81.5	82.4
Female middle-school graduate		
age 25	81.2	84.4
age 30	74.9	80.0

sand employees or over) in 1962 and 1972 reveal that the gap in wages shrank not only for starting earnings, but also for workers who were older and had experience. Consider the following figures on the relative wages of males and females compared with the wages of male middle-school graduates (set at 100) at various ages in 1962 and 1972 (figures from Kume, 1988: 280–1):

Among the various educational grades of male workers there has been considerable convergence in wages, mirroring the changing market supply/demand balance conditions for fresh graduate hires.

But even as relative earnings for junior-high-school and high-school graduates have improved, their relative occupational status has declined For instance, middle-school graduates have increasingly taken jobs as assembly workers and machine operators, while high-school graduates have also been assigned work which in the 1950's would have been considered beneath them. And the proportion of high-school graduates placing into professional/technical and office jobs has steadily declined, while the proportion of university and junior-college graduates doing this work has risen. Among higher-education graduates the shift towards technical and office worker has partly occurred because of a proportionate shift out of the field of education. One can put this one of two different ways, either saying that there has been a substantial educational upgrading for the technical and office worker occupations (associated, perhaps, with increasing sophistication in the content of the work assigned to workers in this category), or alternatively saying (in line with the arguments by Ichikawa, 1977, for Japan, and by Rumberger, 1981, for the United States) that occupational downgrading for has been occurring throughout the ranks stratified by education. As far as college and university graduates are concerned, the upshot of these findings is that the rate of return to a college degree has declined in both financial terms. Long-term estimates of the rate of return for Japan given in Nakata and Mosk (1987) bear this point out. At one time, holding a university degree made one a member of an exclusive and privileged club, but by the late 1960s this was no longer the case. However, it is not clear that the relative status of college and university graduates has fallen or at least has declined as fast as their relative wages. For in the case of status the matter is more complex: it is true that with the recent 'grey-collarization' of the labour force brought on by a relative shortage of middle- and high-school graduates, some university graduates now find themselves assigned to blue-collar tasks which two decades earlier would have been considered fantastic, but at the same time the occupational status of both middle-school and high-school graduates has slipped in comparison with the duties and responsibilities to which they might have been assigned three to four decades ago. The relative increase in the higher educational groups has caused the lower educational groups to be 'bumped down' in terms of the occupational categories into which the workers are pigeon-holed In understanding the *supply* side causes for these deterioration in the job assignments given to university and college graduates we must consider two separate interpretations: one is based on the idea that the pressure put on the educational system by the rapid expansion of university enrolments has caused a deterioration in the quality of universities and hence of the graduates produced by these organizations; the other more plausible interpretation is that change in the relative supply of university graduates compared with junior and high-school graduates, that is the sheer force of the change in the ratios of numbers of people in the educational classes, has reshaped the levels of remuneration despite little if any quality slippage. And, of course, it is quite possible that a weighted combination of changes in relative numbers of workers, and of the relative quality of those workers, within the various educational grades constitutes the supply side input into the reshaping of relative wages.

But shifts in the supply of graduates by type of terminal certification are, in principle, only part of the story. Demand matters as well. With Table 4.3 I attempt to assess the importance of demand. Basically the

TABLE 4.3   Growth in demand for, and supply of, fresh graduate hires, 1956–1985[a]

| | Males | | | | Females | | | |
| | Demand (D) | | Difference (D–S) | | Demand (D) | | Difference (D–S) | |
Years	Supply[a]	Industrial weights[b]	Occupational weights[c]	Industrial weights	Occupational weights	Supply(s)	Industrial weights[b]	Occupational weights[c]	Industrial weights	Occupational weights
					(A) Lowest educational level[d]					
1956–60	n.e.	0.96	1.53	n.e.	n.e.	n.e.	0.40	0.72	n.e.	n.e.
1961–65	n.e.	0.83	−0.04	n.e.	n.e.	n.e.	−0.10	−0.88	n.e.	n.e.
1966–70	0.39	0.80	1.42	0.41	1.03	0.78	0.10	0.44	−0.68	−0.34
1971–75	0.18	0.44	0.70	0.26	0.52	0.33	−0.28	−1.28	−0.61	−1.61
1976–80	0.10	0.54	0.41	0.44	0.31	0.16	0.80	0.93	0.64	0.77
1981–85	0.10	0.02	0.06	−0.08	−0.04	0.12	0.70	0.59	0.58	0.47

TABLE 4.3   (continued)

| | Males | | | | | Females | | | |
| | Demand (D) | | Difference (D–S) | | | Demand (D) | | Difference (D–S) | |
Years	Supply[a] Industrial weights[b]	Occupational weights[c]	Industrial weights	Occupational weights	Supply(s)	Industrial weights(b)	Occupational weights(c)	Industrial weights	Occupational weights
			(B) Middle educational level[e]						
1956–60	n.e.	2.13	2.86	n.e.	n.e.	n.e.	1.70	2.42	n.e.	n.e
1961–65	n.e.	1.72	1.82	n.e.	n.e.	n.e.	1.20	2.19	n.e.	n.e.
1966–70	1.01	1.54	2.12	0.53	1.11	1.99	1.50	3.04	–0.49	1.05
1971–75	0.66	0.87	1.76	0.21	1.10	1.58	–0.70	1.01	–2.28	–0.57
1976–80	0.56	0.58	1.06	0.02	0.50	1.37	1.70	3.06	0.33	1.69
1981–85	0.64	0.51	0.98	–0.13	0.34	1.44	1.20	2.63	–0.24	1.19

TABLE 4.3   (continued)

| | | Males | | | | | Females | | |
| | | Demand (D) | | Difference (D–S) | | | Demand (D) | | Difference (D–S) | |
Years	Supply[a]	Industrial weights[b]	Occupational weights[c]	Industrial weights	Occupational weights	Supply(s)	Industrial weights[b]	Occupational weights[c]	Industrial weights	Occupational weights
				(c) Highest educational level[f]						
1956–60	n.e.	3.22	2.65	n.e.	n.e.	n.e.	2.80	2.86	n.e.	n.e.
1961–65	n.e.	2.53	2.34	n.e.	n.e.	n.e.	1.70	2.98	n.e.	n.e.
1966–70	0.38	2.22	2.29	1.84	1.91	0.26	2.00	3.87	1.74	3.61
1971–75	0.48	1.87	3.03	1.39	2.55	0.48	0.80	4.22	0.32	3.74
1976–80	0.49	1.16	1.68	0.67	1.19	0.62	2.30	6.07	1.68	5.45
1981–85	0.57	1.08	2.31	0.51	2.24	0.70	1.80	5.09	1.10	4.39

Notes:
(a) Flows per 100 persons employed (including family workers and the selfemployed) of the same sex. Supply figures for 1981–5 are actually for 1981–4.
(b) Estimated from age specific figures on the concentration ratio, for males and females separately, in the three educational classes for agriculture and forestry; fishing; mining; construction; manufacturing; communication, transportation, electricity, gas, heat supply and water; wholesale, retail, eating and drinking trades; services; and government and other. Demand estimated for each sector and then, weighting by the percentage of the mployed (for each sector separately), overall demand secured by summing the sectoral demands.
(c) Estimated from the overall concentration ratio, for males and females separately, in the three educational classes for professional and technical workers; managers and office workers; clerical and related; sales; farmers, lumber workers and fishing workers; miners; transportation and communication workers; craft workers; labourers; and service sector workers.
(d) Lowest level = elementary school plus middle school plus prewar higher elementary school plus (old) prewar youth schools.
(e) Middle level = high school plus (old) prewar middle school.
(f) Highest level = junior College plus *kōsen* plus university graduates (4-year college and graduate school).

Sources:
Nihon. Sōmuchō Tōkeikyōku (1984: various tables); and Japan Statistical Association (1987: various tables).

demand growth figures in a given year, which are measured here as the flow of new hires per hundred employees presently working whether as paid employees or family workers, reflect the industrial and/or occupational structure of the labour force in terms of the relative concentration of the three educational classes in each sector or occupational group. Thus, for example, consider the impact of the decline in agriculture on the demand for labour in the various educational groups. Agriculture intensively uses family workers, many of whom complete their formal schooling at the end of middle-school. Thus as the labour force shifts away from agriculture and primary industrial pursuits, the demand for middle-school graduates drops. And for the labour market as a whole the impact of this decline in demand depends upon the weight which agriculture occupies in the overall demand for middle-school graduate labour input. Using separate industrial and occupational weights, I derive two separate sex-specific sets of demand growth estimates for the three educational groups (all flows are relative to the stock of male and female workers taken separately). It is reassuring that the estimates based on sectoral weights are close to the estimates based on occupational weights. What story do these estimates tell us? They show that demand has most increased for higher educational graduates and least for junior-high-school graduates. Given the sectoral shifts away from primary industry and family worker production towards manufacturing, and in particular after 1975, towards technologically sophisticated service sector activity, these demand estimates are plausible. But are supply and demand completely independent of each other? As educational upgrading occurs demand for persons with advanced credentials increases at least on paper, even if there is little or no change in the nature of job content. For example, owing to a shortage of junior- and high-school graduates on the market of fresh graduate hires in contemporary Japan, some college graduates are being assigned to positions on the assembly line. Thus the estimates in Table 4.3 overstate the expansion of demand for college graduates. Still, the shift in economic activity has definitely promoted an expansion of demand for college graduates.

In quantitative terms, how important have been shifts in demand for, and supply of, graduates by level of schooling for the reshaping of job opportunities? For middle-school and high-school graduates we can address this question since we have figures on job opening rates. In Table 4.4 I report on regressions with the (sex-specific) job opening rate as dependent variable and the proxies for growth in demand and supply as the independent variables. It is apparent from the estimates that supply shifts are important, and demand shifts are not, in the shaping of job

TABLE 4.4   The job opening rate and the growth rate of supply and demand for middle and high school graduates, 1965–84[a]

Dependent variable	Growth rate of demand for group				Growth rate of supply of group				
	Constant	Year	Same year	Previous year	Same year	Previous year	ar(1)	Adjusted R^2	Durbin–Watson statistic
log of job opening rate, male middle-school graduates	246.73* (6.19)	–0.12* (–6.17)	0.10 (0.99)	n.e.	–3.36* (–4.78)	n.e.	n.e.	0.68	1.32
log of job opening rate, female middle-school graduates	221.53* (8.61)	–0.11* (–8.56)	-0.02 (-1.16)	n.e.	–1.58* (–6.72)	n.e.	n.e.	0.83	1.71
log of job opening rate, male high-school students	96.24* (2.73)	–0.05* (–2.74)	–0.01 (–0.11)	0.05 (0.51)	-2.10* (-2.76)	2.84* (3.76)	–0.17 (–1.13)	0.69	1.77
log of job opening rate female high-school students	79.09* (3.04)	0 .04 (-3.08)	–0.02 (–1.00)	0 .03 (–1.57)	–0.83*** (–1.90)	1.31* (3.44)	–0.10 (–0.91)	0.81	2.43

Notes:

(a) Regressions use demand flow estimates based on industrial composition rather than occupational demand variables; ar(1) adjusted regressions are for 1966 to 1984.

opening rates for middle- and high-school graduates. Moreover, as Table 4.5 shows, the job opening rate is an important determinant of the relative starting wages of middle- and high-school graduates. Thus it is evident that as the demand for higher educational attainment has expanded, partly responding to improvements in per-capita income (which I have documented for the prewar period in Chapter 2 and which I document for the postwar period later on in this chapter), the relative levels of wages *between* the three main educational classes have been reshaped

4.5   FROM COMPULSORY MIDDLE SCHOOL TO HIGH SCHOOL: THE CHANGING ADVANCEMENT RATE

Upon completing middle school, the student enters the world of voluntary schooling as a full-time student, enters the job market as a full-time worker, enters both markets as a part-time student/part-time worker, leaves both the educational and the labour markets. Within their catchment districts, which in the case of major cities like Tokyo and Osaka is a subdistrict of the city, public high schools can fill their available slots in a competitive manner (that is by selecting students according to a mix of course work achievement and *hensachi* ranking, taking the best first and cutting off admissions when slots are filled), and private high schools are free to admit whomever they wish subject to some general guidelines. Thus once middle schooling is complete, the Japanese school system becomes quite specialized, schools differentiated themselves from one another according to the types of programmes they offer, and according to their reputed 'quality' based on the success of their graduates in either advancing on to prestigious universities or locating positions for their graduates in large prosperous companies.

Now as we saw in Chapter 2, a salient characteristic of the prewar education was differentiation and specialization, with a strong orientation towards channelling students advancing past compulsory schooling into public sector positions (e.g. subsidized normal and military schools training future teachers or soldiers), or into private business sector positions (e.g. the *jitsugyō gakkō* which trained blue-collar workers and lower-level managerial employees, and the *senmongakkō*, which trained technical personnel and white-collar employees). An important element in the development of the *jitsugyō gakkō* system was the active cooperation of businesses with municipal and prefectural authorities in the setting up of schools which trained workers in specific skills useful to the company or

TABLE 4.5   Relative starting wages and the job opening rate for middle and high school graduates, 1966–84[a].

(A) Based on logarithms of levels in variables

Dependent variable	Constant	Log of job opening rate for the group	Log of the percentage of new male hires who are either junior college or college graduates	Adjusted R^2	Durbin–Watson statistic
Middle-school male graduate, relative wage (log)	3.49* (34.50)	0.05* (3.92)	0.26* (11.95)	0.89	1.63
Middle-school female graduate relative wage (log)	3.62*	0.05* (2.69)	13* (6.03)	0.64	1.15
High-school male graduate, (log) relative wage	3.72*	06* (3.57)	20* (7.22)	0.76	0.93
High-school female graduate, relative wage (log)	3.66*	0.06* (3.14)	0.20* (7.99)	0.81	1.34

(B) Based on first differences in logarithms of dependent and independent variable (A)

Dependent variable	Constant	First different in log of job opening rate for the group	First different in log of percentage of new males hires who are either junior college or college graduates	Adjusted R^2	Durbin–Watson statistic
Middle-school male graduate, relative wage (difference in logs)	0.011** (2.12)	0.065** (2.675)	0. 038 (0.759)	0.29	2.62
Middle-school female graduate, relative wage (difference in logs)	0.006 (0.901)	0.058 (1.428)	0.740 (1.224)	0.11	2.66
High-school male graduate, relative wage (different in logs)	0.004 (0.864)	0.035** (2.156)	0.09** (2.140)	0.29	2.74
High-school female graduate, relative wage different in logs)	0.003 (0.526)	0.023 (0.891)	0.092*** (1.852)	0.10	2.88

Notes:
Wages relative to either male junior college and college graduates combined (for 1966–1975) or male college graduates.

companies and at the same time provided the worker/students with credentials: witness, for instance the establishment of silk-production-oriented *jitsugyō gakkō* which trained the kyofu actively sought after by the silk industry during the 1930s. Since the Occupation, Japanese education has drifted back to a system and practice of linking up with private commercial enterprises reminiscent of that in the prewar era. A good example of this is the so called '*renkei hō*' of 1961, the Cooperation Law, an amendment to the School Education Law, which permitted companies, labour unions and school officials to jointly fashion programme and curriculum for *teijisei* (evening) high schools tailored to the specific needs of particular industries or even particular firms (cf. Uchibara, 1968: 202 ff. for a concrete example giving details of a curriculum worked out in 1962 between a Kansai area firm and a Kobe city commercial high school. Also see Dore and Sako (1989) for more contemporary examples of similar phenomena.) It is interesting that the Ministry of Education (in consultation with the Ministry of Labour) agreed to the legislative reform, promoted it and administered it, because the Japanese business associations, in particular *Nikkeiren* published pamphlets calling for the plan and actively lobbied for it with the bureaucracy. This is similar to the business–government cooperation in education characteristic of the prewar era. There is one important area of difference however: organized labour, voicing its demands through unions and union federations, played an important role in the development of the *renkei hō* and continue to be consulted today. But since the late 1940s the party in power has invariably been pro-business, and since the Liberal Democratic Party (*Jimintō*) was founded in 1954, out of a coalition of conservative pro-business/pro-agriculture parties, it has been the sole majority party in the national diet. Therefore it is hardly surprising that the voice of the two major business associations, the *Nikkeiren* and the *Keidanren*, has been actively listened to by the Ministry of education and that business demands have been important in the specialization of the postwar higher educational system. This is an important aspect of continuity between pre- and post-war post-compulsory education.

Another feature of the postwar system which strongly smacks of continuity in the area of specialization and differentiation is the *hensachi* score system, discussed earlier in this chapter. Given the prewar pattern of excess demand for post-compulsory education, and given the use of competitive examinations as a mechanism for winnowing out successful applicants from a large pool of potential admits during the era 1870–1940, it is not surprising that Japanese high schools have made extensive use of standardized test results as a method of being 'fair' by not strictly relying on pre-high-school grade performance which may reflect the competitiveness of individual elementary and middle schools rather than the actual ability of the individual student.[6] Recall in this context that the Japanese notion of democracy in education means, more than anything else, egalitarianism, i.e. the broadest and widest possible competition for a narrow set of élite slots. This is one reason centralization in the setting of examination content is widely tolerated in Japan. And it also gives us an important clue as to why the average Japanese youth develops a 'realistic' set of expectations about his or her capacity to advance through the higher reaches of the school system and subsequently through career tracks within the labour market. For from a very early age on students are given a rough sense of how they are faring on standardized tests, and therefore their *hensachi* scores usually come as no surprise to them. Parents and school counsellors use the scores as goals and as indicators of ability, and children learn to be realistic about what they can be expected to accomplish given their native talents and the amount of effort they feel comfortable putting forth. In this manner slots are allocated so that students of high 'quality' and academic promise are matched with institutions of high 'quality', and students who have given up on their chances for admission to universities or junior colleges are channelled either directly into the labour market, into a high-school programme with an industrial or commercial orientation, or into a less competitive regular academic programme leading to the labour market or marriage (or both) upon graduation.

To see how realistic expectations are consider the following figures (for 1968) on the average accumulated grade (scale of 1 to 5) of applicants to the various types of high schools and the average of those who actually secure entry (data from Nihon Monbushō Daijinkanbō Tōkeika, 1970a and 1970b). 'Regular' refers to academically oriented programmes designed for college and university aspirants; and 'industrial', 'commercial' and 'occupational' designate programmes and/or educational institutions training students for direct entry into the labour market. *Kosen* are five-year technical schools which a student enters after completing middle school, and which owe their origin to the push for an expansion in the number of engineers and technicians during the Income Doubling Plan era of the 1960s.

Because national and public (prefectural or city) high schools charge far lower tuition than do private schools, other things equal they are preferred to private schools. As can be seen from the data immediately listed above, the prestigious national high schools maintain the highest admission standards and the private high-school sector on average maintain the lowest. But this statement refers to types of schools as a whole and to a situation which obtained in the two decades after 1950; for individual schools within each of the school types, and even for the average school types themselves, the rankings do change, albeit gradually. The alert reader may recall the experience of Hibiya and Koishikawa high schools in Tokyo regarding the potential for a precipitous drop in ranking.

School	Type	Applicants	Accepted	Difference
National	Regular	4.4	4.7	+0.3
National	Occupational	3.6	4.1	+0.5
Public	Regular	3.8	3.9	+0.1
Public	Industrial	3.3	3.4	+0.1
Public	Commercial	3.2	3.4	+0.2
Private	Regular	2.7	2.7	0
Private	Industrial	2.4	2.4	0
Kosen	National industrial	4.4	4.5	+0.1
Teijisei	Public	2.7	2.7	0
Teijisei	Private	2.8	2.8	0

Now consider the marginal student, who is not outstanding but performs adequately and who is considering, or more accurately is considering in consultation with his/her parents and school counsellors, whether to continue on in school after middle school. What considerations dominate in the decision making process? Household income is one important variable as attested to by countless official surveys. Consider the following figures for 1968 (from *Nihon Monbushō Daijinkanbō Tōkeika*, 1970a) on the distribution of students continuing on to high school, and those going directly into the job market. The six income classes (I, …, VI; I is the lowest and VI the highest) are used to classify the families of the students and the numbers given here are the percentages of all youths either continuing on or taking a job falling into the various parental income classes:

Type	I	II	III	IV	V	VI	Total
Continuing	13.2	44.9	25.8	9.0	4.8	2.4	100
Taking job	47.1	42.5	7.5	1.7	0.7	0.4	100

Note that the overwhelming proportion (over 89.6 per cent) of students taking jobs have their origins in the lowest family income stratum. To go beyond this descriptive statement it is useful to statistically explore time-series and cross-sectional data with an eye to formulating a demand function for advancement which takes into account the family income supply constraint as well as labour market demand variables. Because change in the advancement rate over the 1950–80 period has been extremely rapid, analysis of the marginal investor is eminently possible.

Over the period 1948–80 both the advancement rate to, and the composition of, high schools underwent dramatic reshaping. For instance the advancement rate to high school, which in the later 1950s was around 55 per cent had risen to over 90 per cent by the 1970s. Moreover, the composition of schools by *type* which students were entering changed as well: there has been a sharp increase in the proportion of middle-school graduates going into full-time (non-*teijisei*) schools and into private high schools; the proportion electing agriculture as a speciality programme has fallen off; and there has been some increase in the proportion going into engineering courses and other programmes with a manufacturing orientation.[7] In modelling the advancement rate for time-series analysis I include in the list of independent variables household income per household member (assumed to have a positive impact), the job opening rate for middle-school students (assumed to have a negative impact), the job opening rate for high-school students (assumed to have a positive impact), and the percentage of workers who are family workers (assumed to have a negative impact). All of these independent variables are lagged one year in accordance with my earlier discussion. I present my results twice: once using the job opening rates for the nation as a whole, and once using the average job opening rates for Tokyo, Osaka and Aichi prefectures. In adopting the latter specification I follow Kato (1984) who points out that a great many of the junior-high-school, and some of the high-school students from rural prefectures were recruited into the Tokyo, Osaka and Nagoya (Aichi prefecture) job markets by company recruiters who established solid connections with school counsellors in rural middles and high schools (connections similar in many ways to the long-term ones established by textile recruiters with the village heads during the interwar period). My analytical results appear in Table 4.6. As can seen, the specification employing the average of the job opening rates for Tokyo, Osaka and Aichi prefecture yields a very good statistical fit. This suggests that the network of connections between labour recruiters and school counsellors was efficient in directing students towards rational calculating decisions, however irrational certain individual members of the student population may have been.

TABLE 4.6   Determinants of the advancement rate from middle school to high school, 1959–75

[A] With job opening rates for the whole country, 1959–85

Dependent variable	Constant	Year	Log of real household income per capita, previous year	Job opening rate for middle school graduate, previous year (same sex)	Job opening rate for highs school students, previous year (same sex)	Percentage of workers who are family workers, previous year (same sex)	ar(1)	Adjusted R^2	Durbin–Watson statistic
Advancement rate from middle school to high school, males	680.2 (1.3)	−0.39 (−1.33)	15.83** (2.31)	0.04 (0.13)	0.09 (0.52)	−2.93 (−4.42)	0.41***	0.99	2.04
Advancement rate from middle school to high school, females	1150.1 (1.4)	−0.67 (−1.50)	24.42* (2.86)	0.04 (0.13)	0.49 (1.04)	−1.16* (−2.76)	0.40 (1.61)	0.99	1.84

[B] With average of job opening rates for Tokyo, Aichi and Osaka Prefectures, 1968–1985

Dependent variable	Constant	Year	Log of real household income per capita previous year	Job opening rate for all middle-school students, graduated, previous year	Job opening rate for all high-school students, previous year	Percentage of workers who are family workers previous year (same sex)	Adjusted R^2	Durbin–Watson statistic
Advancement rate from middle school to high school, males	1930.44** (5.46)	–1.12 (–5.11)	32.60* (3.36)	–0.39* (–2.90)	0.60*** (2.14)	–2.15* (–2.08)	0.98	2.30
Advancement rate from middle school to high school, females	2165.06* (3.65)	–1.36* (–4.54)	52.40* (5.19)	0.46* (–3.09)	0.85** (2.69)	–0.16 (–0.33)	0.97	2.09

*   Significant at the 1% level (two-tailed test).
** Significant at the 5% level (two-tailed test).
*** Significant at the 10% level (two-tailed test).

4.6 FROM HIGH SCHOOL TO UNIVERSITY OR JUNIOR COLLEGE: THE ADVANCEMENT RATE

The trends in postwar high school education parallel those for prewar higher education: growing participation of the private-sector in a system heavily regulated by the central authority of the Ministry of Education. But, in the case of the high-school system in which by the 1980s almost all persons in the age group 15 to 18 are enrolled, the give and take between demand growth and the supply of bureaucratically determined slots is naturally mediated by local community politics. The school districts are local administrative units and their administrators who answer to elected politicians must take into account parental demands (politicians who ignore an essential facet of economic and social life like education risk being quickly turned out of office). For this reason I have treated high-school slots as demand-driven, although in the short-run there have been occasions when supply and demand are out of balance. On the other hand, the curriculum taught in high schools both public and private is heavily determined by Ministry of Education (for instance Ministry of Education influence over entrance examinations for the national universities exercises is a powerful force shaping what students want to study and what teachers feel they must teach). Thus we can view the interaction of supply and demand for slots at the high-school level as the outcome of market driven demand influenced heavily by family income and supply/demand conditions for middle- and high-school graduates with a relatively pliant supply constraint, in which political factors play a crucial role in determining the response of supply to demand expansion, and the private-sector response is relatively muted

But at the level of the university and the junior college the interaction is considerably different: each school determines its own curriculum (although the Ministry of education has the power to review curricula, and will not grant accreditation to schools or approve proposals for new programmes in accredited institutions if it disapproves of the course offerings; on the operation of the postwar accreditation system see Kitamura, 1977) and professors select their own texts, but the Ministry of Education must approve changes in the number of slots allocated to individual departments within individual universities and colleges. In principle, curriculum control is relatively weak but slot control is relatively tight. Moreover, as can be seen from the following figures on number of four-year-degree-granting institutions (from Nakata and Mosk, 1987: 386), the private-sector looms far larger in university and college education than in does in high-school education:

Year	National	Public	Private	Total
1950	70	25	104	199
1960	72	33	140	245
1970	75	33	274	382
1980	93	34	319	446

Note that of the 247 universities added between 1950 and 1980, 215 (87 per cent) are in the private-sector. Not only has private university education been important from the very beginning of the postwar period; it has become increasingly important over the course of the last four decades. How have supply of slots and demand growth accommodated each other?

To begin with it is clear supply of slots has tremendously expanded This follows from the fact that the number of high-school students has increased rapidly *at the same time* as the advancement rate of high-school students into university and college has increased In fact the dramatic increase in the advancement rate from junior high school to high school is matched by an equally impressive increase in the advancement rate from high school to universities. Table 4.7 shows just how rapid the expansion was. In light of the figures in the table four conclusions seem warranted First, the application rate of graduating high-school students to combined university and junior college has increased from slightly under 30 per cent in the early 1960s to nearly 50 per cent in the late 1980s. Second, the total advancement rate has increased from around 20 per cent to slightly more than 30 per cent, which means that the gap between graduating high school applicants and those directly admitted upon graduation to departments in universities or junior colleges has increased (reflecting the specialization characteristic of post compulsory schooling through Japan, individual university departments admit students on the basis of examinations which faculty members at the university write). Thus total applicants consisting of graduating high-school senior applicants plus *rōnin* have increased more rapidly than graduating high-school senior applicants. Third, junior-college applications and admissions have grown faster than university applications and admissions, a trend which in part reflects the growing proportion of women in the pool of high school seniors attempting to secure a higher degree (for instance in 1990, 94.4 per cent of junior-college students were female). And finally the number of applications to departments (*gakubu*) per applicant has significantly increased, reflecting a shift away form the public and national universities towards private

TABLE 4.7   Fresh graduating high school seniors – applications, applicants and those advancing on to college and junior college, Japan: 1961–90

Years	[A] Application rates			[B] Advancement rates			[C] Advancement/applicant ratios		
	College	Junior college	College and Junior college	College	Junior college	College and Junior college	College	Junior college	College and Junior college
1961–65	23.5	6.3	29.8	14.89	5.3	20.0	62.7	84.3	67.2
1966–70	25.6	8.5	34.0	13.8	7.0	20.8	53.9	83.0	61.2
1971–75	30.8	11.8	41.8	19.2	10.2	29.4	62.4	91.8	70.2
1976–80	33.3	13.1	46.4	20.1	11.9	32.0	60.4	91.0	69.0
1981–85	31.7	13.0	44.7	18.7	11.5	30.2	59.0	88.9	67.6
1986–90	33.5	14.2	47.7	18.2	12.3	30.5	54.2	86.8	63.9

| Years | [D] Growth rates | | | | | [E] Percentage of college and junior college who are college bound (fresh graduates only) | | [F] Applications to university departments per university bound applicant[b] |
| | Total estimated | | Applicants (fresh graduates only) | | | | | |
	College applicants[a]	Graduating high school student	College	Junior college	College and junior college	Applicants	Admitted	
1961–65	6.8	5.4	9.7	15.4	10.8	79.1	73.8	3.2
1966–70	9.0	4.9	4.8	9.3	5.8	75.1	66.3	3.2
1971–75	3.1	−1.1	4.9	6.3	5.3	73.5	65.4	3.9
1976–80	0.6	1.1	−0.2	1.6	0.3	71.7	62.8	4.5
1981–85	0.3	−0.3	−0.5	−0.6	−0.5	71.0	61.9	4.2
1986–90	6.6	5.4	7.0	8.1	7.3	70.3	59.7	4.7

Notes:

(a)   Total applicants in year t, app_t estimated as follows:

$\text{app}_t = \text{fgapp}_t + (\text{fgapp}_{t-1} - \text{fgacc}_{t-1})$ where

fgapp_t = graduating high school seniors applying to college in year t,

fgacc_t = accepted (and actually entering a *gakubu*) graduating high school seniors in year t.

(b)   Applications per total number applicants, including *rōnin*

Sources:

Nihon. Monbushō. Daijin Kanbō Chōsa Tōkeika (various years: various tables); and Japan. Prime Minister's office (various years: various tables).

universities. Under the examination system used throughout most of the postwar period (it has been reformed several times), students can at most take two examinations for the national and public system because the tests are conducted on only two days, but they can take a considerable number of private university examinations, since the private universities can and do give their tests on a variety of days and locales, usually in the period January to March.

The hierarchical dualism characteristic of the prewar educational system, a financially favoured national system coexisting with a less-well-off (on average) private system, has continued in the postwar era. James and Benjamin (1988) and Fujino (1986) provide ample evidence that: (a) tuition is far higher in private than in the public schools (the ratio was 7.4 to 1 in 1965, but had fallen to 2.5 to 1 in 1982); (b) the ratio of students to resources is far less in the national and public system than it is in the private system (for instance private university floor space per student was only 25.8 per cent of that in the public-national universities in 1965, and only 38.2 per cent in 1981); (c) as a result the private rate of return for the student is far higher for the national system than it is in the private system but the social rate of return is far higher in the private system than it is in the public because the public system is far more lavish than the private in expenditures per student. Nakata and Mosk (1987: 398) show that the crowding ratio for the private-sector (total enrolment of new college students divided by slots allocated by the Ministry) considerably deteriorated during the era of rapid enrolment growth (1961–75). However, after 1975, matters have improved to a degree:

Years	Crowding ratio	Years	Crowding ratio
1960–64	135.5	1970–74	152.2
1965–69	147.4	1975–79	140.6

That the Ministry allows crowding to take place in order to accommodate surges in demand suggests that demand may take precedence over the bureaucratic supply of slots. Pempel (1978: 142–5) indicates that the Ministry has allowed deterioration to occur in a variety of ways. First, minimum standards for accreditation are based on a student quota which is supposed to ensure that there are a minimum number of library books, library seats and faculty per student. But in fact a survey of 69 major institutions revealed that all but one exceeded their quota, and 47 were in excess of their quota by over 50 per cent. This phenomenon is known as *mizumashi* and is knowingly condoned by the Ministry. But dilution of standards does not stop there. By regulation, half the faculty members of a university faculty must be full-time. However, a survey of 34 universities revealed that 16 had more part-time than full-time faculty. Violations in the number of library seats per student also abound. In short, the Ministry of Education allowed slot supply to expand in response to demand growth by accrediting many marginal institutions, by condoning *mizumashi*, and by non-enforcement of its own regulations.

Given the highly variable quality of the different systems and institutions within each of the systems, it is natural that there is a sharp hierarchical ranking of schools with the former imperial national universities at the head of the legion of national/public schools, and the old, well-established former prewar *senmongakkō* like Keio, Waseda and Doshisha universities at the head of the ranks of private schools. For example, in 1968 the average high-school grades of graduating students in five main subjects were compared for entrants into the various types of universities (Nihon Monbushō Daijin Kanbō Tōkeika, 1970b):

These differences in selectiveness among the institutions have important implications for the distribution of excess demand which exists for higher education as a whole. For some individual organizations continually enjoy excess demand and can pick and choose from a large pool of potential applicants, while other schools find it difficult, perhaps impossible, to fill their allocated slots. This explains why there are so many *rōnin* (note from Table 4.7 that the growth rate of total applicants consisting of graduating high school seniors plus *rōnin* generally exceeds the growth rate of graduating high senior applicants by a considerable margin). Thus for the former imperial universities there are large *rōnin* pools, but for more newly established private universities there are none. This 1968 study cited immediately above has data on distribution of high-school students (in regular academic programmes) applying to universities by type of school they wish to enter:

Institutional type	Grade	Institutional type	Grade
National university	4.0	Public university	3.8
Private university	3.3	Public junior college	3.6
Private junior college	3.3		

Desire to enter	Get in	Become *rōnin*	Work
National university	27.7	47.6	5.2
Public university	13.0	51.3	4.3
Private university	61.6	25.4	3.3
National junior college	24.1	10.3	14.4
Private junior college	84.7	2.0	3.0

Most *rōnin* could have gained admission to some institution of higher learning in the year they graduated from high school. They become *rōnin* because they expect a greater return on their investment in a higher education (even taking into account their fees at cram *yobiko* schools, and the forgone earnings which they sacrifice in order to carry out an additional year of preparatory schooling) if they can manage to secure entry into a prestigious university. From Figure 4.1 it is evident that the national system pays off with a higher rate of return than the private system; but these figures apply to national and private systems as a whole. However a word of caution is in order: these estimates do not take into account the costs of pre-entry *rōnin* schooling: if included the differences between estimated rates of return would probably be considerably reduced. On the other hand, the figures do not take into account social status benefits; including these would increase the advantages accruing to acceptance in the most élite schools.

Because the universities operate with a *hensachi* system similar to that for the high schools, students can easily secure a relatively reliable indicator of the minimum hensachi level required for entrance into any *gakubu* department in any given university or college (in fact the *hensachi* scores needed in order to have an 80 per cent chance of entering a specific university *gakubu* are widely published in magazines and books released by yobiko examination preparatory schools). Thus a student who has failed to gain entry into a particular department in a particular school can make a fairly careful calculation of the chances of getting in a year later and weigh this against the option of attending a less-desired university or college in the current year: if he/she attends a *yobiko* with an *x* per cent success rate (given the 'quality' of students measured by the *hensachi* scores on the tests required for entrance into the *yobiko* and/or other information on the student intake into the *yobiko*) then he or she knows with a high degree of certitude what is the probability of getting into his or her first-choice institution a year later. More generally, students learn how they are likely to fare on standardized tests throughout their careers in the compulsory educational sector; moreover, they take mock examinations for universities in high schools. Thus information necessary for informed decision making is available to the students, their school counsellors, and their parents. One consequence of this predictability is that applications to the more competitive schools have a tendency to adjust to the number of admissions. In regard to this point, consider Table 4.8. It is evident that a very small minority of students attempt to get into the national system (in 1986–90 applications to the national system were only 12 per cent of all applications, but in 1956–60 they were almost 36 per cent of all applications), reflecting the fact that the growth rate of admissions to the national and public sector fell far short of the growth rate of the private. In sum the composition of demand for slots adjusts to the composition of the supply of slots: as the 'cost' of securing entry into a particular school rises (in terms of expected number of *rōnin* years needed to secure entry into it) applications for the school naturally fall off.

But demand is driven by far more than slot availability. Nakata and Mosk (1987) show that changes in demand for higher education in Japan are strongly driven by: (a) increases in real disposable household income (positive factor); (b) the expected rate of return on the investment (positive factor); (c) the percentage of new college graduates who secure employment in large firms (positive factor); (d) direct college costs (negative factor); (e) the crowding ratio (negative factor); and (f) the acceptance rate, the ratio of acceptances to applicants (negative factor). All of these decision-making variables are lagged one year, reflecting information available to potential applicants when they arrive at their decisions. (Also see Organisation of Economic Cooperation and Development, 1973; Japan. Ministry of Education, 1963, for slightly less analytical approaches which nevertheless point towards similar determining variables.) Note that only the last variable cited, the acceptance rate, reflects the bureaucratic supply of slots. In turn this suggests that demand for slots is important in shaping the number of slots available in the system as a whole.

4.7   CONCLUSIONS

In the prewar period the Japanese educational system was built around the needs of Imperial Nationalism. Though its goals were not monolithic, it had a strong bias towards a definite programme: to instill discipline and loyalty to the national entity as represented in the personage of the emperor and the trappings of imperial power in the compulsory com-

TABLE 4.8   Applications and admissions–national, public and private universities: 1956–90

| | [A] Admission rates (%) | | | | | | [B] Percentage of applications and admissions (%) | | | | | |
| | National | | Public | | Private | | of applications (total) | | | of admissions (total) | | |
Year	Total	Same-year graduates	Total	Same-year graduates	Total	Same-year graduates	National	Public	Private	National	Public	Private
1956–60	19.0		12.6		25.4		35.6	8.0	56.4	30.5	4.6	64.9
1961–65	18.6		12.0		22.6		26.9	7.1	65.9	24.1	4.6	64.9
1966–70	16.1		10.0		18.9		21.9	6.1	72.0	19.9	3.4	76.7
1971–75	17.9	18.6	12.0	12.0	18.3	20.8	18.1	4.1	77.8	18.1	2.7	79.2
1976–80	22.2	22.8	13.0	13.2	13.8	16.3	14.0	3.0	83.1	19.2	2.6	78.2
1981–85	35.2	35.0	17.1	17.7	13.4	16.0	9.2	2.4	88.4	21.0	2.7	76.4
1986–90	22.7	22.6	11.4	11.6	11.3	13.7	12.2	3.1	84.8	21.0	2.7	76.3

TABLE 4.8   *(continued)*

[C] Growth rates (%)

Year	Applications			Admissions		
	National	*Public*	*Private*	*National*	*Public*	*Private*
1956–60	−1.3	+2.1	+8.6	−0.5	+4.2	+6.5
1961–65	+4.3	+8.6	+10.9	+3.3	+3.9	+10.7
1966–70	+4.5	+4.2	+13.2	+4.3	+3.9	+7.2
1971–75	+3.9	+0.6	+8.7	+2.4	−0.5	+5.3
1978–80	−8.1	−7.9	+1.3	+2.3	+0.3	−1.2
1981–85	0.5	−0.3	+0.6	+0.8	+1.0	−0.3
1986–90	+21.7	+20.8	+10.7	+2.8	+4.6	+3.9

Sources:
Nihon. Monbushō. Daijin Karbō Chōsa Tōkeika (various years: various tables); and Japan. Prime Minister's Office (various years: various tables).

ponent of the system, and to train an élite corps of technically competent experts who would staff positions in large firms and government. Thus the system which developed was centralized at the national level, hierarchical, and specialized and differentiated With the rapid expansion of heavy industry in the interwar period the demand for an expansion of specialized higher education and middle-level vocational and commercial education intensified and was transmitted to the educational bureaucracy both through the market (in the forms of applications and expanding *rōnin* pools) and through business lobbying; and with the increase in family incomes the per-capita demand for education as a vehicle for economic advancement and as a basis and for the pure consumption benefits flowing directly and indirectly from it expanded, especially for females. Despite centralized bureaucratic control over slots the system proved remarkably responsive to demand shifts.

That the educational establishment was responsive to market conditions and to the goals of Imperial Nationalism was crucial to the linking of labour market segmentation on the supply side with labour market segmentation on the demand side. The close coordination of supply and demand was achieved through the creation of an educational system which was centralized, hierarchical, specialized and differentiated Despite the active efforts of American reformers and their allies among the reform-minded academic community in Japan, the postwar educational system is in many respects virtually identical to its prewar forerunner. It is centralized, hierarchical, specialized and differentiated, and coordination between labour market demand segmentation and fresh graduate supply segmentation remains high. But there were changes brought on by the occupation, for instance democratization. But democratization mainly served the interests of egalitarianism: it helped guarantee that all sectors of the population would have access to the ladders through which competition for advancement in the educational system and later on in the labour market. In so far as this democratization worked to equalize opportunities for advancement to the very highest rungs of the corporate and political communities to all citizens, it helped to promote the notion that the resulting state of affairs was fair. Thus change was important but should not be exaggerated. Most of my results in this chapter point towards continuity rather than discontinuity. Imperial Nationalism as a system may be virtually dead, its ideology lingering on only among small communities of right-wing fanatics, but in the educational system and its linkage with the labour market we see many vestiges of the system put in place by the Meiji oligarchies during the first seven decades of Japanese industrialization.

5 Competition and Cooperation: Wage Profiles, Job Retention, and Dualism

5.1 INTRODUCTION[1]

Building upon the two-track contracting of the prewar period, the institutional framework for a decidedly more egalitarian contract was established in large firms through the protracted negotiations between unions, management and government in the wake of Japan's defeat in the Second World War. Guarantees of employment stability, extensive training and the potential for rising into the ranks of management were extended down to the shop floor. As a result, internal dissension stemming from blue-collar resentment over being excluded from the ranks of 'company membership' was mitigated. This increased the viability of the large-firm contract from the viewpoint of internal firm morale and training. But were the resulting labour contracts viable in terms of the performance of the aggregate economy? The combination of high rates of economic growth and a youthful age structure ensured that viability over the period 1952–70. Facing an active supply pool teeming with young fresh graduates and family firm workers looking for more attractive employment opportunities, and enjoying rapid output and hence employment growth, most large firms during the high-speed-growth era had, year after year, labour forces heavily weighted towards entrants. As a result, promotion rates were high. And the marginal productivity of both promoted and non-promoted trained workers tended to be high, resulting in steep age-wage and seniority-wage profiles. However, the force of rapid technological progress stemming from the import and adaptation of Western technology did erode the skills of veteran workers in some sectors of heavy industry. For instance, in iron and steel and shipbuilding during the 1950s and 1960s, a common complaint was that the skills of veteran and new recruits were often equalized when new machinery and production methods were introduced. Still, in most industries veteran workers were more productive than entrants, part of the productivity stemming from their capacity to teach younger workers how to function effectively with the machinery and within the organization of the shop floor. But in the early 1970s the engine of rapid growth faltered. Could the institutional rules embodied in large firm contracts weather this structural break? How could firms handle the potential adverse consequences to employee morale of promotion denied? How could they keep rent seeking, sabotage and shirking in check? What modifications had to be made in the precise institutional rules governing labour contracts? These are the issues of concern to us in this chapter.

Fundamental to the argument I develop here is that from their very inception, Japanese contracts between workers and companies and between companies and companies have forged a tight connection between cooperative (in Japanese *kyōchōteki*) and competitive (in Japanese *kyōsōteki*) behaviour. To be competitive one must be cooperative. In this respect, within-ladder competition for promotion resembles team bicycle racing: a rider races within a team and, in one's role as team member, one's marginal revenue contribution lies in the support one gives to other team members because overall team performance is important in determining which teams receive generous sponsorship in the future and which do not; but at the same time the rider competes against other members of his or her own team for the lead spot in the individual ranking. By making cooperation crucial to competition the Japanese large-firm contract creates a set of incentives for workers which render the system highly flexible. In our opinion this is one of the most important sources of viability for the system under conditions of ageing and slow economic growth.

To better understand how and why the terms of labour contracts adjusted as they did – in particular to understand how and why they changed during the transition from an environment with a young labour force and rapidly growing employment, to one characterized by slow-growing employment and a rapidly ageing labour force – it is essential that we sketch out a theory about how competition and cooperation operate within and between separate enterprise-specific labour markets. In the next section the argument is laid out. On the basis of the reasoning in this section I derive implications for job stability and turnover and for age-wage profiles which we test, mainly on data for the subsectors of manufacturing over the period 1961–80. To properly appreciate the analysis of retention, however, it is helpful to put Japanese retention patterns in comparative perspective at the outset. To this end, in Section 5.3 I compare postwar US and Japanese job stability patterns, focusing especially on the relationship between age and job retention. Then in Section 5.4 I turn to a statistical analysis (at the level of the twenty subsectors of manufacturing in 1961, 1970, and 1980) of the ratio of senior to junior worker and wage ratios. Although I limit my analysis to three cross-sections I advance an thesis which explains how and why the two sets of ratios have changed over time. But our goal in this section is not restricted to statistical estimation. I link up the analysis of senior/junior worker and wage ratios to the emergence, refinement and diffusion of the *shokunō shikaku seido* (the functional status system) which, steadily but surely, has replaced *nenkō* as the particular institutional embodiment of the large firm labour contract. Finally, in Section 5.5 I turn to retention and the wage profile in the labour market populated by workers employed in small firms.

5.2   COMPETITION AND COOPERATION

In understanding how competitive and cooperative behaviour are integrated in the modern Japanese labour market it is useful to consider how labour-related competition and cooperation operate both *between* firms as well as *within* them. Let us first consider between-firm behaviour, and then within-firm behaviour.

Most Japanese subsectors within the private-sector (e.g. iron and steel and automobiles in manufacturing; hotels in the service sector) are formally or informally organized along territorial lines. By 'territorialily' I mean that a subsector is dominated by one or several large enterprises who are connected through labour exchange and/or subcontracting contracts with subordinate producers. Often the overall national market is segmented into regional markets dominated by one or two major firms and their subordinates (e.g. Toyota City with Toyota Motors and its many parts suppliers in Aichi Prefecture). That Japanese industrial structure developed along territorial lines is partially a carryover from the feudal period when fiefs exercised regional control, taxing and taking responsibility for only those villages and towns lying within their boundaries. And it is partially a result of demand and supply conditions in labour and capital markets during the interwar and postwar high-growth periods. As for the legacy of the Tokugawa period, it must be kept in mind that during the first half-century of Japanese industrialization former samurai and their descendants played a major role in creating, financing, directing and manageing corporations. The model of political and economic organization which they best understood was one based on the divide-and-conquer feudalism of the Tokugawa period. Hence it was natural for entrepreneurs who were former samurai to attempt to build up hierarchically organized industrial networks. Second, as we saw in Chapter 2 the supply pool of effort-giving workers was small during the first four decades of industrial development. Therefore large firms were reluctant to expand their labour forces too rapidly; reluctant because they were guaranteeing employment over long periods; reluctant because they wished to restrict their intake to workers recruited out of institutions with which they had built up long-established ties of mutual trust; reluctant because by securing components from smaller firms – subcontractors – which enjoyed lower monitoring costs and hence wages (the scale of small firms making direct supervision by the owner possible) they could secure certain types of inputs at lower costs than they could themselves produce the components at. Third, capital was scarce during the pre-1970 period. Possessing collateral, large firms could negotiate better interest rates with banks, and acquire capital at lower costs and more quickly than smaller firms. Now technological advance is either embodied in capital to some degree, or at least is complementary to capital formation. Therefore large firms tend to be in the avant garde in terms of new techniques, especially techniques imported from abroad. For this reason large companies encouraged the development of close connections with subordinate suppliers to whom it, the large firm could sell off their technologically depreciated capital, and with whom could share the fruits of technological progress which, by reducing supplier production costs, reduced its (the large firm's) expenses for purchases of inputs from subcontractors. For these reasons (and undoubtedly for others as well) Japanese industries tend to be organized along territorial lines.

Because of territoriality in product and labour markets there is a natural tendency, stemming from lower job search costs within a territorial sub-sector, for labour either to stay within a firm or to move between firms in the same territorial group. Large firms must respect territorial limits because if they invade an rival's labour market territory they risk retaliation: retaliation in product markets, retaliation in labour markets, retaliation in the halls of the government agencies with administrative control over licensing and distribution regulations in the industry. For this reason employers offering large-firm labour contracts have been reluctant to bid away employees from each other. Of course, the development of skills specific to a particular firm also acts as a barrier to between firm mobility. For instance, the lack of firm specific skills and the relative shortness of training probably helps to explain why in the prewar textile industry firms attempted to aggressively recruit employees from their rivals. (Cf. Kidd, undated: 14–15). But these firms did not offer large-firm labour contracts except to a favored few: they provided no incentives which locked workers in and kept them from going elsewhere with whatever skills they had managed to acquire in the previous employment. And even in this industry manufacturers did on occasion attempt to form industrial associations at which representatives of individual enterprises pledged to not hire away workers from competitors. Thus in the context of large-firm labour contracts, recruiters have attempted to hold down their screening costs by limiting their hiring to fresh school graduates from schools with which they have established long-term relations. Or, failing this, they have concentrated on recruiting experienced workers who are employed with their territory. Regarding the occasional hiring of experienced workers, by restricting the compass of their recruiting, large firms minimize the risk of setting off boundary disputes with potential large-scale rivals.

In short, within a territorial group cooperation is extensive and interfirm labour mobility occurs. And there is relatively little tension between one and the other because the principal locus where cooperation (in capital and/or technology transfers) and competition for labour rub up against each other is the interaction of large firms with small firms. When an exchange of labour occurs between a large firm and a small firm (e.g.an upward transfer from a subcontractor to the parent company to stave off a shortage of workers in the parent company; or a downward move, involving reassignment of a regular worker in a large firm to a subcontractor due to the redundancy of workers in parent companies), the moves are usually negotiated by the enterprises rather than by workers with enterprises. For this reason the potential for friction between cooperation and competition is held in check. By operating within territorial groups large firms reduce their firing costs.

Now let us consider competition and cooperation within enterprises. By promoting some workers and not promoting others, the large firm effectively operates a two-track system in terms of actual outcomes as opposed to opportunities, which differs from its prewar predecessor which worked along two-track lines in terms of both outcomes and opportunities. Firms are well aware of the risks associated with such a bifurcation: for instance, the resulting potential for deterioration in morale among, and for sabotage or harassment of new entrants by, non-promoted senior workers. This is certainly a major impetus for managerial evaluation of workers according to a broad rather than a narrow range of criteria. In particular the use of a diffuse set of criteria for evaluating workers permits managers to partially grade workers on the degree of cooperativeness evidenced in their behaviour. In so far as enterprises have (limited) leverage to adjust the rents accruing to individual senior workers through evaluation (known as *satei* in Japanese), they can penalize workers for sabotage or harassment. But given expensive and hence imperfect monitoring, management's ability to proceed in such a manner is circumscribed. However, its leverage over the evaluation of entrants is considerable. By making displays of cooperation a criterion for favorable promotion recommendation, the firm attempts to inculcate cooperative norms into its entry cohort on the hope that in the future even non-promoted workers will not backslide against internalized behavioural rules promoting cooperation. One important consequence of the priority placed on cooperation is that the non-promoted employee incurs high costs if she or he actively resists a forced out-transfer to another company. To resist vociferously is to be uncooperative. A worker might be able to get management to relent and cancel the transfer at the cost of being branded uncooperative and suffering the associated economic loss in subsequent evaluations.

The argument linking cooperation to competition explains why the costs associated with a poisoning of morale due to a rationing of higher-level posts are usually kept in check by enterprises operating with large firm contracts. For this reason, I assume that a firm can adjust downward its promotion rate, thereby flattening its age–wage profile, at relatively little cost (there are costs attributable to voluntary quits of able but unsuccessful workers and to a requisite increase in monitoring intensity to counteract morale loss). By the term 'relatively low cost' I mean at a cost which is low compared with the efficiency loss associated with promoting too many individuals given the state of demand for managers. This being the case, it can be seen that there are mechanisms operating for both large and small firms within any given industry whereby age–wage and seniority–wage profiles are flattened as the relative number of experienced workers within the industry increases relative to the number of inexperienced workers. For small firms who hire and fire experienced and inexperienced workers, the relative supply and demand for workers in each grade who are on the active labour market or who are potential hires determines relative wages. Thus, because of the on-going turnover of workers in the world of small commercial firms an increase in the relative supply of experienced workers tends to drive down their wages relative to inexperienced workers. And in large firms which are partially insulated from the active labour market by dint of their contracts, an increase in the relative supply of senior workers depresses promotion rates and therefore flattens internal firm age-wage profiles. As a result at the industry level, ageing of the labour force *ceteris paribis* flattens age–wage profiles; and the more rapid is employment growth *ceteris paribis* the steeper are the industry wide age–wage profiles.

Thus in the large firm the age–wage and seniority–wage profiles are negative functions of the ratio of senior to junior employees within its ranks. But the profiles depend on more than promotional probabilities.

They also depend upon the per-worker rents which the firm shares with its non-promoted senior staff, and these rents can be most easily approximated by value added per worker. In industries where value added per worker is comparatively high, training of new entrants is extensive, leading to considerable skill acquisition; and/or the capital labour/ratio is unusually high; and/or the firm earns monopoly or oligopoly rents. In any of these three cases the non-promoted worker, either through individual or collective action, is able to secure some incremental rent from the firm which workers in low-productivity firms cannot. For in capital-intensive firms the threat to sabotage capital gives the workers leverage; and in firms with high levels of skill acquisition the threat to quit (and/or strike) gives the worker leverage; and in firms enjoying monopoly or oligopoly rents the worker's threat to quit or harass entrant workers enhances the bargaining position of seniors.

Drawing from these arguments, we can specify two functions governing the ratio of senior to junior workers (E_S/E_J) and senior to junior wages (w_S/w_J) in year t:

$$(E_S/E_J)_t = f([w_S/w_J]_{t-1}, \text{empg}_t) \tag{5.1}$$

for the ratio of senior to junior employees; and for the ratio of senior to junior wages:

$$(w_S/w_J)_t = g(\text{empg}_t, q_t) \tag{5.2}$$

where $t-1$ refers to the period before t when current senior workers were junior and faced lower costs to moving than they do in period t; q is labour productivity; and empg_t is the growth of employment between period $t-1$ and period t. We expect that $f()$ is a positive function of the previous period's senior/junior wage ratio and a negative function of the employment growth rate (rapid recruitment of new hires driving down the ratio of the senior ranks to junior ranks) and $g()$ is a positive function of the employment growth rate and a positive function of q, labour productivity. The functions are designed to explain behaviour at the territorial level; in practical terms this means at the level of subsectors of manufacturing for the analysis we carry out below.[2]

It is important to emphasize that the model laid out in equations (5.1) and (5.2) captures behaviour at the subsector level and it is specifically designed to deal with job retention and the ratio of workers and wages with seniority to those for workers who are their juniors. At the aggregate level of the entire labour market, or at least at the level of the wage-earning employee labour market, the situation is more complicated, since ageing does not automatically imply an increase in the mean age of seniority. Whether it does or not depends on the rate of employment retention for the labour force (or the employee labour market) as a whole. Mosk and Nakata (1985) explore the relationship between age–wage and older to younger workers in the Japanese labour market as a whole, and find that the growth in demand and the ratio of older to younger workers is instrumental in determining the aggregate level ratio of older to younger worker wages.[3] They also find that 1975 marks a structural break in the response of age–wage profiles to ageing because of the sharp dropoff in demand growth after the early 1970s. But this overall aggregate relationship is not central to our analysis in this chapter. Rather we are most interested in the age–wage profiles in terms of seniority patterns within territorial subsectors of the labour market, specifically within subsectors of manufacturing.

5.3   SENIORITY AND EMPLOYMENT RETENTION OVER THE POSTWAR PERIOD

Because the large-firm contract involves extensive training and the possibility of promotion into the ranks of an efficiency wage élite the large firm attempts to hire only workers with a long time horizon. But regardless of what the rate-of-time preference held by a worker is, the steeper is the age–wage profile the less likely is an entrant to quit at the end of the entry period. For the steeper is the profile then the greater is the probability of promotion and/or rents to be shared with the firm as the worker becomes a senior employee. By the same token the flatter is the age–wage profile then the more likely is the worker to quit (both of these statements are meant to refer to the case where the two firms face identical external labour market demand conditions). My analysis also, suggests that at the level of industries or subsectors of manufacturing the steeper is the age–wage profile the greater is the retention capacity of the firm and therefore the greater will be its future senior/junior worker ratio, other things equal. But as we know from the analysis in Chapters 2 to 4, many workers in the Japanese labour market are employed as family workers in family-run enterprises or as self-employed members of the labour force, both in and outside agriculture. What do we expect to be true for the employment stability of the labour force as a whole, inclusive of family workers? And how much does the retention pattern for the entire labour market deviate from that characteristic of the non-family-worker labour market?

We address this issue with Table 5.1, which compares retention rates for the entire (civilian) labour forces of the United States and Japan over the period since the late 1960s (panel A), and these rates with those for the

TABLE 5.1   Mean length of uninterrupted employment tenure (seniority) and retention rates, postwar Japan and the United States

[A] Estimates based on entire job holding population[a]
[A1] Mean seniority lengths

Country, sex, year	By age					
	under 25	25–34	35–44	45–54	55–64	65 and over
Japan, male, 1987	2.7	7.8	15.3	21.7	21.5	24.2
Japan, female, 1987	2.6	5.8	8.9	14.2	20.8	25.0
United States, male, 1987	1.5	4.2	8.0	12.5	16.1	18.7
United States, female, 1987	1.4	3.6	5.9	8.4	11.2	13.2

Overall (total job holding population)

Year	Males			Females		
	U.S.	Japan	U.S./Japan	U.S.	Japan	U.S./Japan
(1) Unstandardized						
1973 (Japan), 1974 (U.S.)	8.40	13.39	0.63	6.15	10.92	0.56
1987	7.70	15.14	0.51	5.40	11.08	0.49
(2) Standardized on 1983 U.S. employment structure						
1973 (Japan), 1974 (U.S.)	7.93	12.75	0.62	5.25	10.13	0.52
1987	7.87	13.01	0.60	5.52	9.22	0.60
(3) Standardized on 1982 Japanese employment structure						
1973 (Japan), 1974 (U.S.)	8.95	14.24	0.63	6.31	11.84	0.53
1987	9.05	14.64	0.62	6.29	10.76	0.58

wage earning (wage census) population of Japan only after 1970.[4] First consider the figures in panel A which include self-employed and unpaid family workers. As can be seen, employment stability is considerably higher in the postwar Japanese labour market than it is in the American market, especially in the younger age groups. This statement holds for both males and females; it holds for retention rates and it holds for mean

TABLE 5.1 Mean length of uninterrupted employment tenure (seniority) and retention rates, postwar Japan and the United States (continued)

[A2] Male retention rates (10-year)

[1] Japan, 1977–87

1977 seniority/1977 age	*25–34*	*35–44*	*45–54*	*55 and Over*
0–9 years	0.704	0.645	0.482	0.225
10–19 years	0.813	0.845	0.563	0.239
20 years and over	—	0.824	0.550	0.369

[2] United States, 1968–78

1968 seniority/1968 age	*25–34*	*35–44*	*45–54*	*55 and over*
0–19 years	0.342	0.381	0.297	0.082
10–19 years	0.639	0.688	0.521	0.125
20 years and over	—	0.653	0.483	0.153

[B] Estimates based on wage census sample (Japan Only)[b]
[B1] Retention rates (10 Year): all males in samples (1975–85)

Seniority in 1975/age in 1975	*25–34*	*35–44*	*45–49*	*50–54*
0–4 years	53.3	53.0	38.8	19.1
5–9 years	67.4	64.5	43.9	19.4
10 years or over	70.0	64.4	34.7	9.5

lengths of job tenure, age-standardized and non-age-standardized. It confirms the commonly held view that in general Japanese retention rates exceed those in the United States: because Americans engage in more voluntary job switching; or because they are involuntarily let go (through firing or layoff) at higher rates; or because the self-employed experience higher rates of business failure in the United States. Since most American firms tend to fire according to the seniority rule, letting their employees go in inverse order of seniority, the last hired being the first fired and so forth,

TABLE 5.1   (*continued*)
[B2] Retention rates (10 year): by education, males (1970–80)

Seniority in 1970/ age in 1980	Old middle-New high school graduates		College graduates	
	25–34	*35–44*	*25–34*	*35–44*
0–4 years	51.2	54.9	63.4	58.5
5–9 years	62.0	65.6	74.0	73.8
10 years or over	69.9	68.2	79.3	85.4

[B3] Retention rates (5-year): by education, males, manufacturing only (1975–80)

Seniority in 1975/ age in 1975	New middle-school graduates		New high school graduates	
	20–24	*25–29*	*20–24*	*25–29*
0–4 years	57.1	62.5	66.7	78.4
5–9 years	69.7	71.8	81.6	77.1

Notes:
(a)   For the United States the entire civilian working population, including self-employed workers and farmers. For Japan the entire working population (*yugyōsha*) including the self-employed and unpaid family workers.
(b)   Based on estimates of employees in firms of 10 workers or over in the sectors, and subsectors of manufacturing, covered in the *Chingin Sensasu* (Wage Census).

Sources:
For the estimates in panel A, Nakata (1990: various tables) for panel B, the wage censuses (*Chingin kōzō kihon chōsa*) of the Ministry of Labour.

and because large Japanese firms eschew this practice, some of the difference in retention between the two labour markets, especially at the young ages, stems from this difference in labour–management institutional rules. In any event, it is evident that the high rate of self-employment and family work in the Japanese labour market does not significantly erode job stability in the Japanese labour market. If anything it enhances it.

What about retention in the male wage earning segment of the Japanese labour force, that segment in which the social efficiency wage sector resides? As can be seen from panel B of Table 5.1, retention rates are high for this population before age 55, especially for those workers who have achieved high seniority by age 25–34 (mostly but not exclusively standard workers). Regarding retention in this population, however, it is interesting to compare college graduates with high-school graduates (panel B2), and highschool graduates with middle-school graduates (panel B3). As can be seen, the higher the level of education the greater the level of retention. This suggests that either because of the way the postwar labour market contracts promote and reward the different educational groups, or because of the inherent attitudes of school leavers at the various levels, college graduates are most closely linked to the standard worker model central to the system. During the prewar period the formal 'permanent employment' guarantee only applied to white-collar workers, mainly to college and/or technical-school graduates; after the war the differential in retention between blue- and white-collar workers stems not from formal rules but rather from the nature of promotional opportunities. While job ladders are far more open to all inductees after the war than before the war, it is still difficult for the blue-collar worker to advance up into the ranks of management, especially with the rapid expansion in the proportion of college graduates in the labour force. The socially divisive nature of the prewar large-firm labour contract has not completely vanished in the postwar period. The other point I would like to stress is that retention rates are only high up to age 55. Until recently this was the standard compulsory retirement age. (Since the early 1970s firms have heavily pressured by both their unions and the government to raise the age of compulsory retirement. As a result today, the mean retirement age is a bit over age 60.) The so-called 'lifetime employment' guarantee is only a guarantee of job stability over a moderate length of time, namely over that portion of the life cycle when family responsibilities are the most pressing for the household head.

However, while behavioural differences between Japan and the United States can account for the differences in retention patterns between the two labour markets, one reason why Japanese retention rates are higher than the corresponding rates for the United States is semantical. That is, it is a function of the way Japanese personnel departments keep their books for, and the way they respond to, government surveys such as the wage census regarding, their employees. Especially after the mid-1970s Japanese firms building up excess supplies of workers, especially older workers, began to engage in *shukkō*, forced transfer to another company usually but not always in the same territorial group (cf. Watanabe, 1988; Larger firms are more likely to engage in the practice than smaller firms; it is usually associated with downward mobility within a territorial entity from parent firm to subcontractor; in most but not all cases the balance between the wages which would ordinarily be paid to the employee if he or she was not transferred and the wages which the receiving company actually pays and would ordinarily expect to pay are paid by the sending company (cf. Sugeno (1989). In some cases the transfer is temporary; in some cases permanent. But in most cases the transferred employee is treated as if he or she remained in the employ of his or her original employer. Thus from the point of view of retention rates the employee is treated as a retained and not separated worker. To some extent this is perfectly reasonable, especially because wage subsidies are paid to the firm taking in the transferred worker and the worker's potential return to the parent company is possible. But it is a bit of a fiction: a fiction which allows for efficient reallocation of labour in response to changing excess demand and supply conditions in particular firms without undermining the principle of guaranteed employment over the period of greatest family obligations central to the social efficiency wage system. And of course the threat of *shukkō* is one of the sticks which management wields in countering discontent and morale loss under conditions of ageing and a shortage of higher level posts. In effect under *shukkō* rules, the concept of employment security has been fundamentally redefined. In any case, from a data point of view the impact of *shukkō* is to bolster the length of retention rates measured for the Japanese labour market.

5.4   THE CHANGING AGE-WAGE PROFILE AND THE EMERGENCE AND DIFFUSION OF THE *SHOKUNŌ SHIKAKU SEIDO*

My purpose in this section is threefold: to demonstrate that age–wage profiles for males have considerably flattened over the course of the postwar period as the labour force has aged and the mean length of seniority with the wage-earning sector of the labour force has increased; to present empirical estimates consistent with our formal model which explains how seniority, employment growth, labour productivity and age–wage profiles interact; and to provide a brief account of the institutional changes in evaluation and promotional components of the social efficiency wage system which accompanied, and to an extent shaped, the changes in the age-wage profile. In reference to the last point, the process may be succinctly described by the transition from the age driven *nenkō* system of the late 1940s and 1950s (conceptually captured in the classic *Densan* formula) and the *shokunō shikaku seido* system of the late 1960s, 1970s and 1980s in which a worker's functional status within a company (his or her *shokunō shikaku*) overshadows age in determining the overall wage paid. Because the shift from one system is a subtle one, and in the case of many firms involves very little actual change in evaluation and/or payment, we do not want to overemphasize the contrast between *nenkō* and *shokunō shikaku*. But there is a very clear change in the practices governing wage compensation in the sense that age-wage profiles have dramatically flattened and the possibility of promotion has been sharply curtailed. In order to ensure workers that the changes made do accord with the basic principles of the large-firm labour contract lest morale and effort supply be undermined, firms felt compelled to recast the rules governing their personnel procedures. This is the most useful way of looking at the shift from *nenkō* to *shokunō shikaku*.

Let me begin my investigation with the age-wage profile. In Table 5.2 I present some summary figures on the ratio of wages for persons in their fifties relative to those in their early twenties covering the period between the mid-1950s and 1985.[5] The figures in panel A refer to all workers; those in panels B and C to standard workers who are inducted into a firm upon graduation from school and remain with that firm until compulsory retirement (the ideal worker type under the large firm labour contract); finally, those in panel D refer to model wage tables, tables created by companies for the guidance of their personnel sections (in Japanese *jinjibu*) in assigning wages to their standard workers. The terms 'standard worker' (in Japanese *hyōjun rōdōsha*) and 'model wage table' are intriguing and go to the heart of large-firm labour contracting in the private-sector. The standard worker is the ideal type under the terms of the contract, each year adding on a year of seniority as he or she ages; because the standard worker is so common in the large firm sector there is a demand for model wage schedules in firm personnel departments and publishers of the tables find a ready market for their wares. It is interesting that up through the 1980s the published model schedules for women stop at age thirty, reflecting the assumption that a woman leaves work upon marriage which is built into the assumptions about the rate-of-time preference for females. Social norms dictate that the typical woman either completely withdraws from the labour market upon marriage or pursues a broken career: working, then marrying and bearing children, and only later on returning to the market when the children have entered the school system. Upon re-entry the female worker must start her career anew. Thus the re-entering

TABLE 5.2   Age-wage profiles: overall; for standard workers; and model

[A] Relative wages (monthly contracted including overtime) of workers aged 55–59 to those aged 20–24 (=100): 1954, 1965, 1985[a]

Year	Males			Females	
	Total	Old middle school/ new high school	College	Total	Old middle school/ new high school
1954	190.8	242.3	315.0	96.7	140.3
1965	185.0	223.6	318.9	111.6	158.6
1985	178.7	182.2	268.7	120.0	141.7

Table 5.2   (*continued*)

[B] Male standard worker (*Hyojun rodosha*) relative wages (scheduled hours only excluding overtime) of workers aged 50–54 to those aged 20–24 (=100): 1970, 1975, and 1985[b]

Year	All firm sizes			Firms of 1000 workers and over			Firms of 10–99 workers		
	Total	Old middle/ new high school	College	Total	Old middle/ new high school	College	Total	Old middle/ new high school	College
1970	225.3	329.7	476.7	n.e.	n.e.	n.e.	n.e	n.e.	n.e
1975	n.e.	n.e.	n.e.	n.e.	295.2	346.8	n.e.	295.2	346.8
1985	n.e.	287.5	351.2	n.e.	290.1	365.9	n.e.	236.5	296.2

[C] Female standard worker relative wages as in panel B: old middle/new high school graduates

Year	All firm sizes	Firms of 1,000 workers or over	Firms of 10–99 workers
1970	230.3	n.e.	n.e.
1975	n.e.	194.9	182.8
1985	217.9	217.3	202.9

TABLE 5.2   (*continued*)

[D] Model wage table relative wages of male workers aged 55 to those aged 22: 1965, 1982 and 1985[c]

	Large firms			Medium-small firms		
Year	Middle-school graduate (production) workers)	High-school graduates (production) workers)	College graduate (white collar)	Middle-school graduates (production) workers)	High-school graduate (production) uction workers)	College graduates (white collar)
1965	300.4	374.8	508.6	261.7	300.4	350.5
1982	n.e.	n.e.	n.e.	156.8	260.0	295.6
1985	252.7	268.0	396.6	n.e.	n.e.	n.e.

Notes:
(a) For all workers covered in the wage survey (*Chingin kōzō kihon chōsa*). Monthly contracted earnings (*kimatte skikyūsuru genkin kyūyo*) include overtime payments but not bonuses.
(b) For all workers covered in the wage survey (*Chingin kōzō kihon chōsa*). A 'standard worker' is one who enters a firm at the time of his graduation from the school system and continues with that firm until compulsory retirement age is reached.
(c) For all sectors, not just manufacturing. Data for older female workers is unavailable in the model tables.

Sources:
Kume (1988: various tables).

female competes in the active market with fresh graduates. This is the reason I emphasize the social norms of the *ie* system in explaining why time horizons for women differ from those for men. Hence we do not expect the age-wage patterns for females to mimic those for males who dominate in the large-firm sector. In fact, the patterns for the two sexes are different, as can be seen from the table. Note the strong trend towards a convergence in wages between younger and older male workers over the three decades after 1954, a trend which is absent in the case of females. A similar convergence is evident for standard male workers (cf. panel B) and can also be seen in the model wage table data for males (panel D). In fact there is a close correspondence between the figures for male standard workers which is drawn from the company personnel information sampled by the wage census and worked up into the wage census averages, and the model wage table figures. Also note, again for males, that the convergence in wages for standard workers and in the model tables, is greater for college graduates than for high-school graduates. As we saw in Chapter 4 male college graduates rapidly increased as a share of the labour market during the high growth era, and, therefore, the senior-to-junior worker ratio increased more rapidly for college graduates than for high-school graduates (also recall that retention rates for male college graduates exceed those for high-school graduates). In short, overall male and standard male worker age-wage profiles have flattened over the period 1954–85, especially for college graduates. But for females who are by and large excluded from large firm labour contracts (even if they work for large firms) and whose age-specific employment pattern differs markedly from the standard male pattern there is no evidence of age-wage profile flattening. Because I am primarily interested in the operation of the large firm labour contract in this chapter I restrict my subsequent analysis to age-wage profiles to males.

I concentrate on the subsectors of manufacturing over the period 1961–80 , working from three cross-sections: those for 1961; those for 1970; and those for 1980.[6] Consider the data in Table 5.3. In this table I cross-classify the 20 subsectors of manufacturing by an index of sectoral employment based in 1951 (1951 = 100) and by net value per worker. For four categories of subsectors I calculate averages for various measures of seniority, ageing, wages and senior–junior worker and wage ratios (males only throughout): rapid employment growth and high labour productivity subsectors ($eei \geq 280$ and $nvaw \geq 200$); rapid employment growth and low labour productivity subsectors ($eei \geq 280$ and $nvaw < 200$); slow employment growth and high labour productivity subsectors ($eei < 280$ and $nvaw > 270$); and slow employment growth and low labour productivity sub-

TABLE 5.3 Seniority, ageing, worker and wage profiles in the subsectors of manufacturing classified by the Index of Employment Expansion (eei) for 1980 (with 1951=100) and net value per worker (nvaw) in 1970: 1961, 1970, 1980 (males only)

[A] Composition of employment, average age and average seniority

Group[a]							Average seniority					
	Percentage college graduates in employment			Average age			High school graduates			College graduates		
	1961	1970	1980	1961	1970	1980	1961	1970	1980	1961	1970	1980
eei ≥ 280												
nvaw ≥ 200	6.1	12.9	25.4	30.2	33.0	36.9	5.7	7.7	11.7	5.5	6.8	9.6
nvaw ≥ 200	4.9	12.2	26.7	29.9	33.0	37.0	5.1	6.9	10.1	4.6	5.9	7.5
eei < 280												
nvaw < 270	9.8	17.5	24.6	32.5	34.7	37.7	7.6	10.3	14.2	6.6	8.4	11.5
nvaw < 270	5.2	10.7	18.2	32.2	35.7	39.6	6.2	8.5	12.1	5.7	7.5	10.2
maximum	15.6	22.6	42.3	34.9	39.1	42.6	9.1	11.6	15.6	7.5	9.0	12.9
minimum	2.1	6.8	14.5	27.9	30.3	34.8	4.1	6.3	8.4	3.7	4.7	5.7
mean	6.5	13.3	23.8	31.2	34.1	37.8	6.1	8.4	12.0	5.6	7.2	9.7

TABLE 5.3   (*continued*)
[B] Relative subsectoral wage level and standard worker wage profiles[b]

Group[a]	Relative wages (all of manufacturing = 100)						Standard worker peak to starting wage (=1.0) profile					
	High-school graduates			College graduates			High-school graduates			College graduates		
	1961	1970	1980	1961	1970	1980	1961	1970	1980	1961	1970	1980
eei ≥ 280												
nvaw ≥ 200	98.7	100.3	101.1	100.6	100.6	99.8	7.5	4.2	3.9	7.1	4.5	3.5
nvaw < 200	88.3	90.3	92.1	88.4	91.0	91.0	6.9	4.2	4.4	4.5	3.9	3.2
eei < 280												
nvaw ≥ 270	120.5	113.2	112.0	115.4	111.6	114.3	6.7	3.8	3.8	7.8	4.5	3.8
nvaw < 270	92.6	96.3	94.8	5.5	96.9	95.0	5.7	3.3	3.1	6.6	3.7	3.2
maximum	139.2	129.7	118.5	122.5	127.3	126.5	10.7	3.3	4.8	10.0	5.1	4.2
minimum	74.4	82.7	82.6	76.0	79.3	82.0	2.8	5.1	2.6	3.1	2.8	2.7
mean	100.0	100.0	100.0	100.0	100.0	100.0	6.7	2.1	3.8	6.5	2.8	2.7

TABLE 5.3   (continued)
[C] Senior–junior worker and wage ratios[c]

| | Senior–junior worker ratios (%) | | | | | | Senior–junior wage ratios | | | | | |
| | High-school graduates | | | College graduates | | | High-school graduates | | | College graduates | | |
	1961	1970	1980	1961	1970	1980	1961	1970	1980	1961	1970	1980
eei ≥ 280												
nvaw ≥ 200	8.7	15.5	53.9	7.0	12.6	35.7	2.1	1.7	1.7	2.4	2.0	1.8
nvaw < 200	4.1	11.4	41.0	3.0	8.9	20.0	2.0	1.7	1.7	2.0	1.9	1.7
eei < 280												
nvaw ≥ 270	15.2	33.3	83.2	11.0	21.7	57.0	2.1	1.7	1.7	2.5	2.0	1.8
nvaw < 270	7.1	26.4	68.2	5.9	19.6	43.7	2.0	1.5	1.6	2.3	1.8	1.7
maximum	20.7	41.8	118.5	17.7	35.2	69.7	2.3	1.8	1.8	2.7	2.1	1.9
minimum	2.4	8.3	25.1	1.2	5.7	6.7	1.5	1.2	1.4	1.6	1.7	1.6
mean	8.8	21.7	61.6	6.8	15.7	39.1	2.0	1.7	1.7	2.3	1.9	1.8

Notes:
(a)   Each group has 5 subsections in it. Averages for the groups are unweighted.
(b)   Standard worker wage profiles are the ratios of peak monthly earnings (contracted including overtime but not bonus payments) to starting earnings for standard workers (hyōjun rōdōsha).
(c)   Senior workers are defined as those workers who are aged 35 to 49 years having at least 15 but less than 30 years' seniority; junior workers are defined as those workers who are aged 15 to 34 years with less than 15 years' seniority. Worker ratios have a base of 100, so the ratio is the relative number of senior workers as a percentage of junior workers.
Source:
Nakata (1987: various tables).

sectors (*eei* < 280 and *nvaw* ≤ 270). I also provide the mean, and the maximum and minimum for the twenty subsectors in the table.

Several points concerning the 1961–80 trends can be gleaned readily from the figures. First, college graduates have rapidly increased their shares of employment in all subsectors regardless of productivity level. In and of itself this trend works to reduce average seniority for workers as a whole, since college graduates enter firms later than middle-school and high-school graduates. Second, the average age of employees has increased by about seven years in all groups. Third, mean seniority has increased for both male high-school and college graduates about six years in all groups. Fourth, the relative wages (of the subsectors relative to all of manufacturing) have converged towards a common level over the period. Fifth, the peak-earnings-to-starting-wage ratio for standard workers has sharply dropped for both high school and college graduates in all subsectors, as has the ratio of earnings of senior to junior employees. In this context it should be noted that in tabulations not reported here it has also been found that intersectoral variation in the wage profile is far greater than the variation in starting earnings for fresh hires (cf. Nakata, 1987). Therefore variation in wages for senior workers is mainly due to variation in the wage profile, and not due to variation in starting wages.

Sixth, senior-to-junior worker ratios have increased in all sectors. Seventh, senior-to-junior worker ratios are higher in the slower growing subsectors; and, other things equal, in the higher labour productivity subsectors. Wage profiles are steeper in the faster growing subsectors and, other things equal, in the higher productivity subsectors. These latter relationships are what we would expect given our hypotheses advanced in equations (5.1) and (5.2). They suggest that the labour market has become increasingly integrated over the course of the 1960s and 1970s; bothin the sense that within subsectoral wage profiles have flattened and in the sense the intersectoral wage variation has diminished. Earnings of junior and senior workers have converged, as have wages in the various subsectors.

It is possible to use the data underlying Table 5.3 in regressions with which we can explore the validity of the relationships postulated in equations (5.1) and (5.2). To statistically test for the relationship indicated by equation (5.1) we use two specifications: one with logarithms and the other without. The two variants are:

$$(E_S/E_J)_t = a_0 + a_1(empg_t) + a_2(w_S/w_J)_{t-1} + \epsilon \tag{5.3a}$$

and

$$\ln(E_S/E_J)_t = b_0 + b_1(empg_t) + b_2[\ln(w_S/w_J)_{t-1}] + \epsilon \tag{5.3b}$$

where $t-1$ is 1961 when t is 1970, and $t-1$ is 1970 when t is 1980, and employment growth for year t is between 1961 and 1970 when t is 1970 and between 1970 and 1980 when t is 1980. According to my model we expect $a_2 > 0$, $b_2 > 0$, $a_1 < 0$, and $b_1 < 0$. For analogues to equation (5.2) I use either a linear equation without logarithms, (5.4a), or with logarithms, (5.4b):

$$(w_S/w_J)_t = c_0 + c_1(empg_t) + c_2 q_t + \epsilon \tag{5.4a}$$

$$\ln(w_S/w_J)_t = d_0 + d_1(empg_t) + d_2[\ln(q_t)] + \epsilon \tag{5.4b}$$

where, again, I fit the regressions for both $t = 1970$ and $t = 1980$; and, in conformity with my model, I expect $c_1 > 0$, $d_1 > 0$, $c_2 > 0$, and $d_2 > 0$. My results appear in Table 5.4. As can be seen, the findings are fully consistent with my expectations.

In light of these findings it is interesting to ask whether employment growth depresses the overall wage bill per worker or not. We can pose this question in two different ways: does it depress the average wage bill because employment growth promotes a younger age structure? Does it raise the age standardized wage bill by promoting a steeper age-wage profile? An answer to these queries appears in Table 5.5 in which I present estimates for equations (5.5a) and (5.5b) and (5.6a) and (5.6b)

$$aw_t = e_0 + e_1(empg_t) + e_2(q_t) + \epsilon \tag{5.5a}$$

$$\ln(aw_t) = f_0 + f_1(empg_t) + f_2(q_t) + \epsilon \tag{5.5b}$$

where aw_t is the average wage in year t, either unstandardized (see panel A) or standardized to a fixed age structure (see panel B). I also report on regressions with the starting wage sw_t as dependent variable, namely:

$$\ln(sw)_t = g_0 + g_1(empg_t) + g_2[\ln(q_t)] + \epsilon \tag{5.6a}$$

$$\ln(sw_t) = h_0 + h_1(empg_t) + h_2[\ln(q_t)] + \epsilon \tag{5.6b}$$

These results appear in panel C of the table. As can be seen, because retention rates have generally been high (due to previous period's age-wage profiles) and because the employment growth rate has tapered off rapidly, especially after the early 1970s, the ratio of senior to junior workers has rapidly increased, depressing senior–junior wage profiles in the next period. It is also apparent that while there is a tendency for wages to be slightly depressed by overall employment growth the effect is not very great. However, it is notable that the sign for the estimated coefficient on the employment growth variable is either consistently negative (in the case of the non age-standardized wage regressions) or positive (in the case on the age-standardized wage regressions) as was anticipated.

TABLE 5.4 Senior–junior worker and wage profiles, employment growth and labour productivity in the subsectors of manufacturing: 1970 and 1980

[A] With the senior–junior wage ratio as dependent variable

Group, year	Without logs[a]				With logs[a]			
	Constant	Employment growth, previous decade[b]	Net value added per worker	Adjusted R2	Constant	Employment, growth previous decade[b]	Net value added per worker	Adjusted R2
High-school graduates, 1970	1.48* 20.67	0.03** (2.54)	0.003 (1.64)	0.21	0.004 (0.02)	0.02* (2.79)	0.08* (2.13)	0.27
High-school graduates, 1980	1.69* (60.80)	0.03* (3.84)	−0.00001 (−0.37)	0.40	0.55* (4.66)	0.02* (3.81)	0.01 (−0.31)	0.40
College graduates, 1970	1.69* (25.07)	0.04* (3.02)	0.001* 2.85	0.37	0.05 (0.34)	0.02* (3.75)	0.10* (3.82)	0.50
College graduates, 1980	1.71* (59.56)	0.02* (1.84)	0.00007** (2.41)	0.31	0.24* (2.20)	0.01** (2.27)	0.05* (3.08)	0.40

TABLE 5.4   (continued)

[B] With the senior–junior worker ratio as dependent variable

Group, year	Without logs[a]				With logs[a]			
	Constant	Employment growth, previous decade[b]	Senior-junior wage ratio ten years earliar[c]	Adjusted R2	Constant	Employment growth, previous decade[b]	Senior-junior wage ratio ten years earlier[c]	Adjusted R2
High-school graduates, 1970	18.57 (1.27)	−4.30* (−5.88)	7.82 (1.08)	0.63	2.88* (6.88)	−0.22 (−0.70)	1.04*** (1.75)	0.71
High-school graduates, 1980	−56.45 (−0.91)	−9.78* (−3.92)	66.08*** (1.81)	0.42	3.04* (6.75)	−0.17* (−4.45)	1.75** (2.05)	0.49
College graduates, 1970	−2.41 (−0.26)	−2.24* (−4.05)	10.77* (2.88)	0.62	1.54* (2.87)	−0.13* (−3.25)	1.80* (3.06)	0.57
College graduates, 1980	−84.46 (−1.54)	−5.57* (−2.76)	61.59** (2.19)	0.27	0.85 (0.73)	−0.21* (−3.17)	3.84* (2.21)	0.32

Notes:
(a) In the regressions with logarithms, the employment growth variable is not entered in logarithmic form but the dependent and other independent variable(s) are.
(b) For 1970 the growth rate is for the 1961–70 period.
(c) For 1970 the wage ratio is for 1961, not 1960.
*   Significant at the 1% level (two-tailed test)
**   Significant at the 5% level (two-tailed test)
*** Significant at the 10% level (two-tailed test)

TABLE 5.5 Subsectoral wage levels (weighted and unweighted), employment growth and labour productivity in the subsectors of manufacturing: 1970 and 1980[a]

[A] With the average wage level as dependent variable

Group, year	Without logs[a]				With logs[a]			
	Constant	Employment growth, previous decade[b]	Net value added per worker	Adjusted R2	Constant	Employment, growth previous decade[b]	Net value added per worker	Adjusted R2
High-school graduates, 1970	140.90* (15.20)	−0.86 (−0.52)	0.07* (3.08)	0.35	4.05* (18.31)	0.001 (−0.08)	0.19* (4.74)	0.56
High-school graduates, 1980	189.06* (27.70)	−0.15 (−0.08)	0.03* (4.49)	0.49	4.25* (22.68)	0.004 (0.55)	0.17* (5.97)	0.64
College graduates, 1970	183.64* (15.09)	−1.19 (−0.54)	0.08** (2.42)	0.24	4.40* (18.42)	−0.002 (−0.160)	0.17* (3.93)	0.47
College graduates, 1980	212.20* (28.37)	−0.21 (−0.10)	0.05* (5.90)	0.64	4.24* (22.43)	0.005 (0.59)	0.20* (6.75)	0.70

TABLE 5.5   (*continued*)
[B] With wages weighted by fixed labour forces as dependent variable

Group, year	Without logs[a]				With logs[a]			
	Constant	Employment growth, previous decade[b]	Net value added per worker	Adjusted R2	Constant	Employment growth, previous decade[b]	Net value added per worker	Adjusted R2
High-school graduates, 1970	140.86* (17.84)	1.35 (0.95)	0.05 (2.28)	0.15	4.32* (21.20)	0.01 (1.62)	0.13* (3.59)	0.37
High-school graduates, 1980	175.46* (40.49)	1.39 (1.13)	0.02* (4.29)	0.50	4.49* (33.25)	0.01*** (1.98)	0.12* (5.69)	0.64
College graduates, 1970	183.60* (22.71)	1.91 (1.31)	0.04** (2.02)	0.12	4.73* (29.46)	0.01** (2.08)	0.10* (3.45)	0.61
College graduates, 1980	214.86* (51.45)	3.13** (2.64)	0.02* (3.66)	0.53	4.91* (41.59)	0.02* (3.45)	0.08* (4.37)	0.61

TABLE 5.5   (*Continued*)
[C] With starting wages as dependent variable

Group, year	Without logs[a]				With logs[a]			
	Constant	Employment growth, previous decade[a]	Net value added per worker	Adjusted R2	Constant	Employment growth, previous decade[a]	Net value added per worker	Adjusted R2
High-school graduates, 1970	61.00* (31.54)	0.03 (0.08)	0.02* (3.58)	0.39	3.75* (26.10)	0.001 (0.15)	0.08* (3.12)	0.32
High-school graduates, 1980	78.75 (40.79)	−0.26 (−0.70)	0.02* (5.17)	0.61	3.76* (30.23)	−0.003 (−0.62)	0.11* (5.75)	0.66
College graduates, 1970	100.98* (33.77)	−0.03 (−0.06)	0.03* (4.07)	0.47	4.10* (39.90)	0.002 (0.55)	0.11* (5.91)	0.66
College graduates, 1980	135.46* (35.74)	1.22 (1.13)	0.01 (1.21)	0.06	4.60* (26.36)	0.01 (1.44)	0.05 (1.90)	0.16

Notes:
(a) In the regressions with logarithms, the employment growth variable is not entered in logarithmic, form but the dependent and other independent variable(s) are.
b) For 1970 the growth rate is for the 1961–70 period.
(c) For 1970 the wage ratio is for 1961, not 1960.
*   Significant at the 1% level (two-tailed test).
**   Significant at the 5% level (two-tailed test).
*** Significant at the 10% level (two-tailed test.)

The twist in the age-wage profile occurring between the mid-1950s and the mid-1980s is strong and the model does a reasonable job of explaining it in statistical terms. But the statistical changes are only part of the story. Equally important are institutional changes in the nature of large-firm labour contracts which accompanied the twist. Basically these changes involved the development and diffusion of the *shokunō shikaku seido*, the functional status system which has come to supplant the *nenkō* system. To understand the significance of the shift it is useful to begin with the words themselves. The word '*nenkō*' is a two-character combination, '*nen*' signifying age and '*kō*' merit or meritorious achievement. Thus *nenkō* as a term describing a system of evaluation puts weight on both age and performance, age coming first. In contrast the term *shokunō shikaku* combines two words, each combining two characters, none of which signify age *per se*. '*Shoku*' designates occupation and '*nō*' ability or capacity; the word '*shikaku*' means functional status (as opposed to *chii*, which designates social status). Thus there is an important difference in the words used to describe the two systems. The *shokunō shikaku* system seems to put less weight on age (although as we shall see age and status are typically correlated) and more on occupation specific work ability or capacity. How does the system work in practice? And how and why did it come to supplant a system explicitly based on age and performance rating?

As typically implemented, the *shokunō shikaku seido* bases wage payments on five main criteria: (a) family and individual needs; (b) age, education and perhaps seniority; (c) performance rating by supervisors and the personnel department; (d) shikaku, status ranking in occupationally defined job ladders; and (e) occupation (for a myriad of case studies of actual *shokunō shikaku seido* see Sangyō Rōdō Chōsabu, various years, and Takisawa, 1981). Items 1 to 3 are also found in the classic *nenkō* system, even in the egalitarian *Densan* formula; but items 4 and 5 are new. Moreover,the *weights* placed on the components are different. Under *nenkō* the weight placed on items 1 and 2 is very large; recall the Densan formula discussed in Chapter 3. Under the *shokunō shikaku seido* the weight placed on 1 and 2 is comparatively small, and the weight placed on performance, on occupation, and on functional status (grade, rank, in the hierarchy) is large (see Inagami, 1983, 1988, for survey evidence which bears on the issue of the shifting weights). During the era of high-speed growth, promotion was common and hence the correlation between age, seniority and position held in the company was high; with the slowing down in growth, age and position increasingly came to diverge and the change in the weights reflects this.

The important point to keep in mind is that *shikaku* and occupation (*shokugyō*) are different: *shikaku* is a indicator of grade, similar to the corporal or general designations in a military organization. Regardless of one's speciality – technician, programmemer, superintendent for the mess hall – a soldier is placed into a definite rank category which describes his status level in the pecking order. So it is under the shikaku system. Employees doing completely different jobs have the same status ranking. How is status determined? In the early years of a person's career within a company most companies make promotion up the status labour automatic. As one takes on an additional year of seniority one gets an automatic hike in status. But then at a certain point the candidate reaches a 'break point'. To move up to the next main class one must survive a competition among potential applicants. This competition is typically based on a combination of factors: personnel evaluations from previous years (including evaluation of the degree of cooperation exhibited by the candidate); interviews; and, most important, stellar performance on detailed examinations. Drawing a leaf from the system used to grade samurai in the fiefs, the managers write (or purchase from independent suppliers) test questions and administer these examinations to the applicants. These tests are detailed: they test for technical knowledge of the production process and the organization of the shop floor; they test for knowledge of government regulations in labour and product markets; and they solicit the worker's opinion about what he or she thinks the future direction (*hōshin*) of the enterprise should be. Using these wide-ranging criteria,the managers select the candidates to be advanced and those to be held back: in this way the company slows down the promotion process; it also imbues the selection process with an aura of fairness since the process is based on competitive examination (just as is *hensachi* style promotion within the school system which for most workers was the first place where they encountered a brutal weeding out process); and effort and skill is enhanced at the workers' expense since they usually cannot use company time for examination preparation. In short, the system serves to ration higher-level slots, but does so in a way which to some degree takes into account age and seniority.

The shift from *nenkō* to *shokunō shikaku* began in the 1960s. Ishida (1985, 1990) describes in detail the ideological battle between Nikkeiren and the national union federation centres, especially Sōhyō, over the introduction of an occupation- and performance-oriented system in place of the more purely age-oriented system of the 1950s (see Chapter 6 for a discussion of Sōhyō and the national centres). The impetus to move in this direction came from larger companies many of whom, even during the high-growth era, found themselves saddled with a rapidly ageing stock of employees and, because of high retention rates, a rising senior-to-junior worker ratio. But the period of most rapid adoption of the new system was in the 1970s, after the era of slow growth was ushered in. For instance Matsuda (1985: 43) shows that of companies with 30 workers or more introducing a *shokunō shikaku seido* on or before 1980, over 63 per cent embraced the system between 1970 and 1979, and 34 per cent between 1975 and 1979. However, among larger enterprises (with 1,000 workers or over) around 27 per cent had already introduced the new system by 1969, whereas among all companies with 30 workers or over only 21 per cent had introduced the system by 1969. In short the initial impetus for introducing the new institutional rules governing labour contracts was concentrated in the world of the largest firms – that is among firms which committed to strategies which generated high firing costs, which most relied on the possibility of promotion as a motivating device for securing effort from entrants, and which had the highest retention rates and therefore the most rapidly increasing senior-to-junior worker ratios. These companies pioneered the shift towards a new set of institutional rules guiding the actual realization of the large-firm contract: towards a set of rules which assumed fairly low rates of promotion (*shokunō shikaku seido*) rather than high rates of promotion (*nenkō joretsu seido*).

Why did the national union federation centres go along with the shift? Ishida (1985, 1990) argues that the unions acquiesced because the shift accorded with a sense among the rank and file that the new system was 'fair', i.e. that it met their critera for fairness. True, socialization in the school system did make this type of system seem 'fair' to many workers. But there are two other factors which need to be stressed: the rising level of income which reduced the marginal value of market specific efficiency wage exchange; and the fact that during the high-growth era young workers constituted a large share of the unionized labour force in the private-sector. It was in the immediate short-run interests of junior workers to reduce the steepness of the firm-specific wage exchange profile, and embracing the *shokunō shikaku seido* helped to achieve this outcome. That is, demographically based divisiveness between older and younger workers was helpful to the cause of management in its programme of sweeping aside *nenkō*.

5.5 DUALISM

One salient feature of efficiency wage models developed by American economists is their focus on explaining the existence of involuntary unemployment as the outcome of a situation where some firms pay premium above-market clearing wages in order to secure effort, these jobs being rationed out to the fortunate. Indeed in some models of efficiency wage behaviour the efficiency wage firm pays a premium wage in order to raise the cost of 'shirking' to the worker: were this premium not to be paid then a worker, fired for shirking, would simply secure alternative employment at similar wages, and shirking would in fact be widely observed in the economy. This type of reasoning links up unemployment and/or underemployment to being outside the part of the economy governed by efficiency wage contracts. In my model the closest analogue to unemployment and underemployment is the sum of unemployment, employment in small family-run firms, and employment in small commercial firms (which in the Japanese reality includes some medium-sized firms).

While this may or may not be a valid characterization of the way the American labour market operates, it is not a valid characterization of the way the Japanese labour market operates. Many reasons for this assertion can be given but the first and most obvious point one can make is that unemployment in Japan has been very low throughout the postwar period. For instance, compare the following estimates of unemployment rates (those declared as unemployed relative to the labour force) for the United States and Japan over the 1950s and 1960s:[7]

Years	*United States*	*Japan*
1956–60	5.2	2.2
1961–65	5.5	1.4
1966–70	3.9	1.2

Since the oil crisis rates have climbed a bit in both countries, but the point remains true throughout the postwar period: measured unemployment is far lower in Japan than in North America. Some of this stems from the definitions of unemployment in the two countries: Taira (1983) provides convincing arguments that the way unemployment is measured in the two countries reflects different conceptual frameworks about, and attitudes towards, being unemployed. Japanese are far more likely to withdraw from the labour force when the economy falters than are North Americans; because some factory jobs are second jobs held down by part-time farmers and part-time factory workers, during a downturn the laid-off worker can return to full-time agriculture; and so forth. Thus it is probably true that if unemployment in Japan were measured according to American concepts the rate would be higher, perhaps even double what is measured using Japanese concepts. But even so, it is true that Japan has a considerably lower rate of unemployment than the United States.

To understand how the aggregated Japanese labour market, consisting of three distinct submarkets which interact with each by transferring labour to a degree, creates an 'underclass' of economically less advantaged individuals similar to the unemployed in the United States, it is useful to talk about underemployment in Japan rather than unemployment. By underemployment I mean a concept encompassing unpaid family work, (most) self-employment, employment in small commercial firms and pure unemployment. Now a significant share of underemployment defined in this way arises from transfers out of the sector of the economy governed by large-firm labour contracts, through retirement at the mandatory retirement age, forced transfers to subcontracting companies and the like.

Recall the notion of territoriality in the Japanese labour market. According to this concept labour can and does move back and forth with a fair degree of fluidity between large enterprises and small enterprises within the territorial industrial group without significantly disturbing the cooperation linking enterprises within the group. This is because most territorial groups are vertically integrated through subcontracting relationships. Large firms can dispose of their less-hard-working employees and their depreciated capital among their smaller subordinate subcontractors. Older workers and those forcefully retired from the main firm in the group typically end up taking up employment in the smaller firms within the same territory, or they start up their own small firms, sometimes with the assistance of their former employer. In this way a network of former employees of the parent firm is created within the smaller firms of the territorial group, a network which binds together all of the firms in a cohesive manner (cf. Brunello, 1988). And by playing off the subcontractors against one another through classic divide-and-conquer tactics the parent firm can assure itself that smaller enterprises within this territorial unit remain competitive.

This reasoning suggests that a key strength of the way segmented labour markets interact in Japan, an important rationale for the high levels of effort and productivity it elicits, lies in the fact that small firms with minimal monitoring costs hire and fire workers at reservation wages, and large firms take advantage of this by integrating their production operations and labour force adjustments with small firms within their territories. Under large-firm labour contracts, large firms face a high cost of firing workers. Therefore they are reluctant to aggressively expand their own internal labour forces during periods of rapid expansion, preferring to pursue a balanced programme of own-firm expansion and the encouragement of expansion of smaller subcontractors within their territorial group.

At one time it was widely believed by Japanese economists that Japanese dualism would disappear as the Japanese economy matured, that it was a transitory phenomenon attributable to a shortage of capital during the era of catching up, and one that would eventually wither away as the hectic pace of technological advance slowed after the late 1960s. But this has not proven true, and indeed in light of the arguments advanced in this chapter the fact that this is not true is not surprising. Regarding this point, consider Table 5.6. As can be seen, dualism was very much a product of the rise of heavy industry (it was largely non-existent around 1909), but since it emerged in the period after 1910 it has persisted. Moreover, the

TABLE 5.6 Dualism in Japanese manufacturing: 1909–85

[A] Percentage of employees in firms size group – both sexes

Year	1–49	50–99	100–499	500–999	1000+
1964	41.5	11.3	22.0	8.2	17.0
1982	46.2	9.1	17.0	5.5	22.2

[B] Percentage of male employees in firm size groups

Year	1–29	30–99	100–999	1000+
1965	23.5	17.1	26.4	32.7
1985	16.9	16.9	27.0	32.5

[C] Wage differentials by firm size (average wages for firms of 1000+ = 100)

Year	1–9	10–19	20–29	30–49	50–99	100–199
1909[a]	80.7		85.9	90.8	94.5	96.8
1914[a]	71.3		75.4	79.4	83.4	84.4
1951[b]	41.7	46.0	50.0	54.4	60.3	68.5
1967[c]	33.2	56.6	63.3	64.2	65.9	69.6
1985[c]	n.a.	n.a.	57.2	59.8	60.2	63.7

TABLE 5.6 (*continued*)
[D] Value added per worker and capital per worker by firms size (firms of 1000+ = 100)

Year	1–9	10–19	20–29	30–49	50–99	100–199	200–299	300–499	500–999
				[D1] Value added per worker					
1955	24.9	33.0	37.2	42.4	51.0	63.0	74.6	83.2	95.7
1967	27.3	39.5	44.1	46.0	48.7	58.0	67.9	71.9	84.1
1985	n.a.	n.a.	36.9	38.6	40.5	45.3	67.2	75.2	80.2
				[D2] Capital per worker					
1985	n.a.	n.a.	30.1	33.4	34.6	38.1	43.7	56.6	65.1

Notes:
n.a.: not available
(a) Smallest firm size group is 5–9 employees and the values for 100–199 are actually for 100–499. These figures are standardized for age structure and sexual composition and are based on daily wages.
(b) Smallest firm size group is 4–9 employees. These figures have been adjusted for sexual composition and are based on monthly wages.
(c) Based on unstandardized average annual wages.

Sources:
Japan. Prime Minister's Office. Bureau of Statistict (various years: various tables); Japan. Ministry of Labour. Minister's Secretariat (1986: various tables); Japan. Ministry of International Trade and Industry (various years: various tables); Yasuba (1976: p. 258); and Napier (1972: various tables).

proportion of workers working in the world of small firms remains large, especially in the case of females but even in the case of males (compare panels A and B in Table 5.6). In short, dualism emerged in tandem with the large-firm labour contract and both have persisted, despite institutional changes which effect the precise way they operate, ever since.

With this in mind consider wage dualism for experienced male workers (aged 35 to 39) in 1967 and 1985. Figures appear in Table 5.7. As can be gleaned from the table, in those subsectors in which large firms make comparatively generous wage payments, the magnitude of the wage differential between large and small is substantial; and in subsectors in which

TABLE 5.7 Dualism and subsectoral hourly wage levels: 1967 and 1985[a]

Quarterlies	Large-firm hourly wage levels			Differentials[b]		
	Total	Production	Non-production	Total	Production	Non-production
[A] 1967						
Highest wage quartile	0.43	0.38	0.47	172.5	170.7	153.4
Next highest wage quartile	0.37	0.33	0.41	145.2	152.0	133.4
Third wage quartile	0.34	0.31	0.40	141.5	141.5	126.6
Lowest wage quartile	0.31	0.28	0.36	136.4	136.0	123.1
[B] 1985[c]						
Highest wage quartile	2.57	2.40	2.86	159.5	162.0	154.8
Next highest wage quartile	2.32	2.01	2.48	157.2	150.4	144.3
Third wage quartile	2.18	2.01	2.37	149.6	146.6	144.3
Lowest wage quartile	1.97	1.80	2.14	146.2	143.0	135.9

TABLE 5.7   (continued)

Quarterlies	Small firm hourly wage levels for males 35–39			Differentials (large firm/small firm = 100), males 20–24		
	Total	Production	Non-production	Total	Production	Non-production
[A] 1967						
Highest wage quartile	0.25	0.23	0.31	126.4	127.5	123.8
Next highest wage quartile	0.25	0.22	0.31	117.1	115.6	115.1
Third wage quartile	0.24	0.22	0.32	111.0	109.7	109.2
Lowest wage quartile	0.23	0.21	0.29	105.0	104.2	106.9
[B] 1985[c]						
Highest wagequartile	1.62	1.49	1.84	141.6	148.7	129.7
Next highestwage quartile	1.48	1.34	1.72	139.4	144.7	126.3
Third wagequartile	1.46	1.38	1.65	125.7	130.7	119.5
Lowest wagequartile	1.35	1.26	1.58	127.2	131.2	116.0

Notes:
(a) Subsectors ranked into four quartiles according to hourly wages (in 000 *yen* for males aged 35–39 in large firms (including over-time and bonus payments). The figures in the table are unweighted averages for the quartiles. Large firms have 1000 employees or more, and small firms have 10 to 99 employees.
'production' stands for production workers; 'non–production' for white collar or professional workers.
(b) Small-firm levels = 100. Large firms relative to that.
(c) Only 19 subsectors in manufacturing in the 1985 are used for 1985 because of reclassification and recombination of two of the subsectors.

large firms pay relatively low wages the wage differential is slight. In short, most of the variation in wages between subsectors is in the large-enterprise component of the subsector, not the small-firm component. Despite differences in the skills required by small firms in the various sub-sectors, there is sufficient mobility between subsectors to virtually equalize wages at the small-firm level everywhere. Training costs in these firms are generally sufficiently low, so that the skill-related barriers to intersectoral movement, and within sectors to interfirm movement, do not deter a significant tendency towards wage equalization. As for large firms, differences in scale economies and/or oligopoly power, in capital intensity, and the pace of technological advance in so far as it affects the productivity of skills acquired by workers, and in senior/junior worker ratio, are the primary determinants of variation of age-wage profiles and hence of the wages paid senior workers.

This analysis implies that mobility is considerably higher in the world of small firms than among large ones. The literature on Japanese dualism frequently mentions comments on the fact that while most employees in small firms have changed jobs at least once before entering the firm, the proportion of older workers who have never held another job is the highest in the small-enterprise category. Certainly this is because the owner usually does not fire himself or herself and/or his or her family workers and because small firms have no mandatory retirement age.

According to the perspective advanced here there is a continuum running from the large firm in high-productivity sectors down through smaller enterprises down to self-employment and unpaid family work and finally to unemployment at the bottom of the Japanese labour market. In characterizing self-employment in this manner I am implicitly excluding self-employment among professionals like doctors, lawyers, architects, writers and musicians. This is not an unreasonable characterization, since a large number of the self-employed are older workers who have had to retire from large firms or are former workers of smaller firms who learned how to run a small enterprise by observing the practices of their former employes (on entrepreneurship among former employees of small firms cf. Koike, 1983). That is, I assume self-employment for the non-professional represents a calculated gamble for individuals who by dint of experience in the educational system or personality or age are not able to secure or retain employment in the world of large firms. Most are forced down into this kind of employment because of the limited capacity/unwillingness of large firms to absorb labour under the contract terms they offer. Job availability in the large-firm sector is a key factor conditioning the degree to which dualism prevails in the Japanese labour market.[8]

That a significant share of the labour force is concentrated in the family-run business sector, and that workers move in and out of that sector, is one reason measured unemployment is low in Japan. It is also part of the explanation for the fact that in Japan hours worked adjust with a high elasticity to fluctuations in aggregate demand, but the number of workers in the labour force does not adjust with nearly the same responsiveness. For during downturns the marginal benefits of additional hours worked decline for family workers, who accordingly cut back on hours worked. This is only a partial explanation, however. Equally important in accounting for the flexibility in aggregate hourly input is the existence of job guarantees and variable intensity of effort in large firms. This is an issue I return to in the next chapter.

5.6   CONCLUSIONS

That Japan's postwar labour market is simultaneously strongly segmented and tightly integrated is one of the most remarkable characteristics of her postwar economic performance. Part of the explanation for the persistent coexistence of integration and segmentation lies in the linking of cooperative to competitive behaviour. Because cooperation is an integral component of competition both within large firms and between firms within a territorial group, the basic segmentation of the private labour market into three interacting submarkets, each of which functions with a distinctive type of labour contract, has weathered the strains imposed by a slowing down in economic growth and population ageing. For instance, the fact that the specific institutional rules governing the large-firm labour contract have flexibly adjusted to the growth slow down and ageing – as the rules shifted from the *nenkō/shūshin koyō seido* rules consistent with high promotion rates and extremely high firing costs towards the *shokukō shikaku seido/shukkō* rules consistent with low promotion rates and reduced firing costs – is testimony to the strength of the welding of co operation to competition within large firms as well as between firms within territorial groups. As a result the basic principles governing the large-firm contract have not changed, but the specific parameters characterizing promotional probabilities and firing costs implicit in the contract have changed as the aggregate economy has evolved. Flexibility is a definite hallmark of the integrated segmentation of the postwar Japanese labour market and this flexibility is closely related to the linking of competition with cooperation.

6 Collective Bargaining and Capital Accumulation

6.1 INTRODUCTION

Why are Japanese unions cooperative in their wage demands? Why has there been so little disruption of work through strikes over the last quarter of a century? Why have rates of capital accumulation been so high over the last four decades? In this chapter I address these disparate questions using my theory of integrated segmentation and my model of large-firm labour contracts, drawing from these theoretical concepts implications about the divisiveness of union bargaining strategy as constrained by the contracts governing employment in firms. Because the securing of costly on-going collective bargaining rights is of little interest to workers who work for their own families or work in small firms where the probability of job separation is high, most private-sector unions tend to be in companies operating with large-firm labour contracts and tend to be enterprise-specific (since extensive within-company training and the overriding importance of within company seniority make both unions and management ambivalent about interference from non-company outsiders), fissures have opened up not only within the membership of individual unions;but also between unions attempting to operate in consolidated federations, and between one federation and another. These fissures weaken the ability of unions to carry on protracted strikes, that is they dilute the capacity of labour to extract rents from the owners of capital. By dint of the large-firm labour contract, workers within the typical private-sector union are divided by the degree of stake they have in their firm's performance, senior workers (and junior workers who expect to be promoted) enjoying greater vested interests than rank-and-file entrants. Thus senior workers and highly rated entrants within a typical unionized firm have a strong self-interest in the competitiveness of their firm. And for this reason unions attempting to maintain a common front against a group or groups of employers tend to distrust one another. For if one of the unions within a union federation launches a protracted strike against its employer, it incurs a risk of undermining the position of its firm within the sector (or in the worst case bankrupting the firm). And if the present or future profitability of the firm is imperileed the union, by putting at risk the interests of those employees tightly bound to it because of their seniority and/or their status as efficiency-wage employees, faces the attendant possibility of an internal split into two rival unions, and a consequent loss of membership and influence within the union movement. But large-firm labour contracts and supply-side segmentation are not the only source of debilitating divisiveness within the ranks of organized labour. Ideological competition within the ranks of the union movement has also weakened the influence and integrative capacity of labour. Moreover, unionized public-sector workers are divided by legislation and by government policy: they are divided from their colleagues in the private-sector and within the public-sector by the agency which employs them. In short divisions in the ranks of organized labour are an essential feature of the ritualized annual spring offensive (*Shuntō*) through which collective bargaining in postwar Japan occurs. Management and a succession of business-oriented Liberal Democratic cabinets have seized on the divisions offered by the large-firm labour contract and by ideological divisions in the labour movement to develop and hone divide-and-conquer tactics as a response to labour demands.

But integrative forces are at work as well. A key to the history of the emergence and evolution of the *Shuntō* system over the 1950–90 period is the movement towards integration, albeit incomplete and unsteady (rapid in some periods and painfully slow, perhaps even retrograde in others). In the first period, 1950–60, the era of the radical *Shuntō*, division – within the ranks of the labour movement; between government (and public-sector corporations) and government workers; and between private-sector management and workers – was at its height. Not surprisingly as the union movement groped towards a strategy which would serve both to unify it and to bring unorganized workers into its camp, thereby increasing its leverage in bargaining with private firms and local and national governments and public corporations, it seized on the concept of a radical, confrontational *Shuntō* organized around the threat of a protracted across-the-board strike. The outcome was unanticipated by the architects of the system: true, participation in the *Shuntō* rapidly increased, and the expansion partially fuelled by wage increases won under the early *Shuntō* were substantial. But the confrontational theory behind the radical *Shuntō* was shaken: management and government beat back major strike attempts; and the actual impact of the *Shuntō* bargaining process on wage hikes, that is the degree to which the *Shuntō* exercised any influence independent of the forces of supply and demand in the active market for new hires and productivity gain, became an open question. In so far as unorganized workers answered this question in the negative, the organizing impact of the *Shuntō* was blunted.

The high-growth era *Shuntō* ensued. In the second period, 1961–74, with rapid gains in industrial employment and labour productivity guaranteeing a hefty expansion in the capacity of companies and governments to pay wage hikes, and with the confrontational strategy of the strike confounded by events in the formative decade of the 1950s, integrative forces gained momentum within the *Shuntō* system. This is apparent in three areas: in the outcomes of *Shuntō* wage bargaining; in the process of *Shuntō* wage bargaining; and in the content of *Shuntō* wage bargaining. First, the variance in wage increases both between sectors, and between firms within the same sector, narrowed despite substantial variation in the productivity growth of these sectors. This occurred despite the fact that most of the *Shunto* wage bargaining occurred within the private confines of enterprises and their enterprise unions. Second, the *Shuntō*, along with the *Chintō* (wage struggle) waged almost simultaneously by federations reluctant to nominally submit themselves to the discipline of a common struggle committee joint leadership, became *the* recognized mechanism for publicly arguing over the theory and practical realities of annual wage increases. Each year the federations and the Nikkeiren (the business federation specifically devoted to collective-bargaining issues) published their views on wages and related issues including the operation of social efficiency wage promotion and individual worker evaluation practices (e.g. on the shift from a 'pure' *nenkō/shūshin koyō seido* towards a *shukkō/shikaku seido* system). Thus *Shuntō* bargaining took on a wider public meaning, serving as a vehicle for *public* debate over the socially acceptable norms of fairness in the distributional and effort related rules of the efficiency wage system, as well as a vehicle of debate over the average socially acceptable wage hike for the employed labour force as a whole. Third, within the ranks of the unions in the key private heavy-industrial sectors there developed a coalition (the IMF-JC) committed to expanding the role enjoyed by unions in the decision making of their associated enterprises through joint consultation committees and the like. This signalled a decisive movement towards integration: first by steering a course around the ideologically divided federations and second by proposing greater accommodation with management in exchange for influence.

The third period treated here, that stretching from 1975 to 1990, witnessed the emergence and refinement of the consensus *Shuntō*. The period is characterized by unification of most of the organized union movement under the umbrella of the *Rengō* federation; the inclusion of the unified labour movement in national and regional government–business–labour policy-making committees; and a decline in strike activity as enterprise unions increasingly work through firm information sharing channels like the joint consultation committee to influence company decision making, especially in areas crucial the to the current interests of workers. These issues include transfer (*shukkō*) and forced-retirement practices, the closing and/or relocation of plants, structural changes in the composition of the firm's output, the retooling of workers and their reassignment within divisions of the company (*haichi tenkan*). The movement towards a consensus *Shuntō* has its roots in two conditions: the changing labour market environment (in particular on the demand side the slowdown in per-worker labour productivity and income per-head growth rates, the fluctuation in the US dollar–yen exchange rate, and the rapid rise in energy prices which imperilled energy-intensive heavy industries; and on the supply side the ageing of the labour force); and the historical movement towards integration in the high-growth era *Shuntō*. In short, the functions and meaning of the *Shuntō* have radically changed over the course of the four decades since it was originally conceived at a time of great division and disintegration; changes in the economic environment have fostered a new, much more integrative system, far less confrontational and more comprehensive in terms of the issues covered in the bargaining which occurs.

The material in this chapter weaves together the two main topics touched on above, the one concerned with developing out of the Japanese integrated segmentation model implications for the behaviour of Japanese unions and *Shuntō* collective bargaining and the testing of these implications, and the other concerned with the historical development of the *Shuntō* system, in the following way. In the next section I develop the theoretical argument; then in the third section I discuss in greater institutional detail the evolution of the *Shuntō* as it moved from its formative radical phase through the high-growth era phase to the integrative, consensus form it exemplifies today; finally in the remainder of the chapter I present statistical findings in support of my model of Japanese collective bargaining behaviour and of the historical periodization and, in Section 6.8, findings concerning the impact of *Shuntō* wage increases on new union organizing. Other than historical description, the evidence I offer in support of my model falls into four main categories: time series results concerning the response of nominal wages (and the bonus taken separately) to increases in nominal labour productivity and the consumer price in the subsectors of manufacturing cross-classified by labour productivity growth; cross-sectional regressions on wage levels and wage increase rates and volumes for medium-sized firms in the subsectors of manufacturing in selected years; time-series regressions on new union organizing rates in the subsectors of manufacturing; and, finally, analysis of the *Shuntō* wage increase in 1985 for individual enterprise unions attached to firms for which I have profitability measures.

6.2　DIVIDED LABOUR

Recall from the discussion in Chapter 2 that the large-firm labour market contract was initially, during the interwar period, limited to a relatively small subgroup of the labour market, that is mainly to white-collar workers in large firms in heavy industry. After the war, in part owing to the demands of the labour movement this contract type became widely diffused among most large and many medium-sized companies in both the heavy and light industries, and the coverage of the contract was extended to all 'regular' company workers. Unionization and the demand for a large-firm contract were linked historically. And this is hardly surprising: for in the private-sector, in few companies other than those operating with a large-firm contract does there exist a substantial body of employees who can expect to extract rents from management through collective bargaining. For instance, in firms operating with small-firm contracts of either the commercial or the family sort there is no obvious advantage to workers in unionization. In reality, of course, small firms operate with implicit contracts which differ somewhat from the theoretical model of the small firm contract. However as long as the rents which can be secured from management are sufficiently low then the benefits from unionizing fall short of the costs, and this is likely to be the case in almost all real-world small companies in Japan. With this in mind note that the overlap of large-firm employment with unionization with private-sector union membership during the postwar period offers a decided contrast to the situation regarding union membership before World War II. Also characteristic of the postwar period but not of the prewar period is the fact that the government has very high (and increasing) rates of unionization. Unionization rates are relatively high in mining, which since the 1950s has been a declining sector, and in manufacturing, which expanded in terms of total employment up until the early 1970s and has been on the wane ever since. Analysis of data on unionization by firm size reveals that union density is very high in the large firms within the manufacturing sector, that is in enterprises operating with large-firm labour contracts.[1] In short, excluding government, the overlap between the unionization and employment under large-firm labour contract terms is substantial. For this reason I develop my analysis of union behaviour and collective bargaining in terms of the private-sector operating under large-firm labour contracts, and in terms of the public-sector.

First, consider the implications of large-firm labour contracts for the organization forms unionism takes. The firm naturally is opposed to industry-wide and craft-based unions which organize workers across a broad range of enterprises because negotiation over wages, effort levels and amenities with union officials who lack company experience severely constrains the capacity of the firm and develop and shape separate packages of wages and amenities for efficiency wage and for non-efficiency wage workers. If the firm is to set wages and amenities in order to minimize the cost of output per efficiency wage worker in a fashion separate from its rent-sharing agreements with non-promoted senior workers then it must have a relatively free hand in determining the internal distribution of wages and its promotion rates. For this reason, management fought hard to break the back of industrial unionism in the late 1940s and early 1950s, and encouraged the spread of enterprise-specific unionism. Two institutional rules concerning labour union formation facilitated management's push for enterprise-specific unionism. First, according to the postwar Constitution private-sector, and most public-sector, employees have a legal right to establish unions. Thus multiple unionism within an enterprise is possible. On the tendency of unfair labour practice complaints to emerge from situations where there are two rival unions within an enterprise, see Hanami, 1988, and Sugeno, 1988). Hence if management finds itself bitterly opposed to a union, for example because it is an industrial union or because it advocates policies subversive of the firm's plans, it can legally encourage the development of a second union which, typically, is enterprise-specific and more accommodating to the employer in its negotiating stances. Second, ideological factionalism within the labour movement, which as we saw in Chapter 2 divided the prewar unions into right, left and centrist factions with the left and centrist factions, emerging out of groups of unions expelled from the Sōdōmei, which was intent on pursuing an integrative programme, cooperating to a degree with the Home Ministry and enterprise owners, has plagued the postwar movement, especially in the period prior to the formation of *Rengō* in the late 1980s.[2] Until recently most unions have belonged to industrial federations which in turn belong to one of the national centres allied either with the Communist Party or one of the socialist parties. This can be seen from panel A of Chart 6.1. Because of the ideological divisions many union organizing campaigns have made it a goal to secure enterprise-wide union shop agreements since this precluded the possibility of rival national centres attempting to organize the same company.[3] As a result of these developments, private-sector collective bargaining is enterprise-specific bargaining with the terms of the firm's wage system at stake. The union becomes the collective voice for almost all of the firm's employees, except those in the higher ranks of management.[4] This voice expresses employee demands filtered through a political process of voting about the size or

Chart 6.1   Evolution of the postwar Japanese national centres and the laws under which they organize and bargain

Panel A   Approximate membership of the national centres in (000s);
percentage of all union members in ( )

Before Rengō formation

	Left Leaning			*Centrist Right Leaning*			*Independent*	
Year	Sanbetsu[a]	Shinsanbetsu[b]	Sōhyō[c]	Sōdōmei	Dōmei[d]	Zenrō[e]	Chūritsurōren	*Others*
1946	1,600	–	–	850	–	–	–	n.e.
1950	290	55	2,765	835	–	–	–	4,714
1957	n.e.	41 (0.6)	3,549 (50.8)	n.e.	–	797 (11.4)	–	2,680 (38.4)
1964	–	58 (0.6)	4,207 (42.9)	–	1,466 (15.0)	n.e.	949 (9.5)	n.e.
1968	–	71 (0.7)	4,214 (38.8)	–	1,848 (17.0)	n.e.	1,270 (11.7)	n.e.
1975	–	n.e.	4,573 (35.2)	–	2,266 (17.5)	n.e.	1,369 (10.6)	n.e.

After Rengō formed

	Rengō	Sōhyō	*Others*
1987	5,500	n.e.	n.e.
1990	5,445 (40.4)	3,907 (29.0)	4,138 (30.7)
1991	7,610 (merged)		n.e

CHART 6.1   (*continued*)

Panel B   Number of union members and/or the percentage of union members governed by various laws; when absolute figures are given the percentage distribution is in ( )

| Laws | All union members percentages of total | | | Membership by national centres (000s) 1975 | | | | 1990 | | |
	1965	1975	1990	Sōhyō	Dōmei	Chūritsurōren	Other	Rengō	Sōhyō	Other
T.U.C.[f]	71.0	72.9	78.1	1,635 (35.8)	2,106 (92.9)	1,368 (99.9)	4,265 (89.3)	5,443 (99.96)	1,568 (40.1)	3,804 (91.9)
Public corporations and enterprises	11.6	9.9	4.0	1,037 (22.7)	140(6.2)	1(01)	73(1.5)	2(0.04)	382(9.8)	100(2.5)
PCNELR[g]	9.9	8.1	2.3	n.e.	n.e.	n.e.	n.e.		199(5.1)	77(1.9)
LPELR[h] [Local]	1.7	1.8	1.7	n.e.	n.e.	n.e.	n.e.	2(0.04)	183(4.7)	23(0.6)
Civil Service	17.3	17.2	17.0	1,901 (41.6)	21(0.9)	–	237(5.0)	–	1,957 (50.1)	234(5.7)
N.P.S.[i]	2.5	2.3	2.3	n.e.	n.e.	–	n.e.	–	218(5.6)	59(1.4)
L.P.S.[j]	14.8	14.9	15.7	n.e.	n.e.	–	n.e.	–	1,739 (44.5)	175(4.2)
Total	100.00	100.00	100.00	4,573 (100.0)	2,266 (100.0)	1,369 (100.0)	4,775 (95.8)	5,445 (100.0)	3,907 (100.0)	4,138 (100.0)

Notes:

n.e. = not estimated and/or not available

(a) Disbanded in 1958.

(b) Created in 1949 out of some of the Sanbetsu unions.

(c) Created in 1950 out of some of the Sanbetsu, some of Sōdomei, and some of the unaffilated unions.

(d) Created out of some of the Sōdomei unions, some of the Zenrō unions, and other unions.

(e) Created out of some of the Sōdomei unions and some of the Zenrō unions.

(f) Trade Union Law (enacted in 1945).

(g) Public Corporations and National Enterprise Law, enacted in 1952. National railways and the tobacco monoply were governed by this law.

(h) Local Public Enterprise Labour Relations Law.

(i) National Public Service Law.

(j) Local Public Service Law, enacted in 1950. All of the laws governing public corporations and enterprises were amended in 1965 to comply with Japan's ratification of the International Labour Organization Convention #87 (Freedom of Association and Protection of the Right to Organize Convention).

Sources:

Kawada and Komatsu (1973), Koshiro (1983a, 1983b, 1983c, 1983d, 1983e), Mitsufuji (1971), Nitta (1988), Okochi (1958), Nihon Rōdō Daijin Kanbō Seisaku Chōsabu (1986), and Sumiya (1974a, 1974b).

rate of increase in the wage bill and, depending on the period and union involved, over the weights which workers wish to see management place on the various components of the wage settlement: how much importance should be attached to age and/or worker-specific family requirements; how much weight should be given to firm-related performance in the summer bonus; how much overtime work is to be assigned, the premium attached to it, and the distribution of the overtime assignments by age and type of worker; and so forth. In short, private-sector collective bargaining in the spring and the continuing dialogue concerning the implementation of the agreements during the remainder of the year institutionalize the large firm in terms of specific rules and weights on various criteria, helping to insure that both the wage system and the wage level are viewed as fair by rank-and-file workers and hence deserving of the effort supply levels implicit or explicit in the agreement.[5]

But because the wage agreement negotiated in the *Shuntō* tends to be an enterprise-specific agreement giving management a relatively free hand in internal wage distribution, the labour movement tends to be divided when collective bargaining occurs. Fissures are opened up not only *between unions* within industry-wide federations, which are expressively set up in order to strengthen the hand of enterprise unions in their bargaining with management, but also *within* the memberships of the unions themselves. For fresh entrants, promoted and non-promoted senior workers have different vested interests in the financial health of their enterprises upon which their present and expected future wages and amenities rest.[6] For instance, promoted workers earning premium efficiency wages (or white-collar entrants graduating from prestigious schools with high probabilities of being promoted) have the strongest vested interest in company perform-ance because in the event of bankruptcy the probability of their reaching similar status in another large company is low. In contrast is the position of a young blue-collar worker in the company who quite possibly anticipates not being promoted and is therefore considering alternative employment in another firm. Thus in its negotiations with management the union is best equipped in terms of its internal politics to press for an overall percentage and/or absolute wage bill increase with an guaranteed minimum wage increase for all grades of workers and for an overall, across-the-board bonus rate settlement, and least well equipped to press for wage increases which involve designation of particular rates for partic-ular occupations.[7] Management's goals centre around retaining maximum flexibility in the internal distribution of wages and in determining who gets promoted and who does not.[8] In principle, a wage bill settlement with a minimum increase for all workers eliminates much of the tension between union and management because management retains a relatively free hand in setting wages for promoted workers with due regard for the interests of non-promoted and entrant employees.

Now consider the problem of striking under conditions of enterprise-specific collective bargaining. Enterprise unionism and firm-specific efficiency wage payments for promoted workers and rent sharing for senior non-promoted workers implicitly divide the unionized workers within the industry into competing groups, squaring off against each others' vested interests in own firm performance (and hence potential future union membership size). Trust between unions is limited: hence the potential for wageing a joint strike is blunted. For if the workers in one union engage in a bitter strike against their own company, they may end up simply hurting their own enterprise, thereby endangering the discounted present value of the future rents which they expect to share with management, and/or their efficiency wage payments. Unions in competing enterprises which either manage to reach settlement on the terms of a new contract without a strike, or with only a brief disruption in normal business due to work stoppage or slowdown, may end up gaining at the expense of the union which wages a protracted struggle. The likely outcome of this is the splitting of the union which held out into two smaller unions: one populated by militant workers, especially younger workers who can move more easily if the company's fortunes are endangered; and the other by company employees who, by virtue of promotion, seniority and/or a long history of favourable performance ratings, presently enjoy substantial wage benefits which would be endangered should the company's fortunes decline and which cannot be transferred should they be forced to take up employment in another enterprise. Ohta Kaoru, the original architect of the Shuntō during the early 1950s when he headed Gokaroren, one of the chemical industry federations, pinpointed this problem in his book *Shuntō no shūen: Teiseichōka no rōdō undō* (1975; 'The Demise of the *Shuntō*: The Labour Movement Under Slow Economic Growth')[9]: '*Kigyōbetsu kumiai shoshiki de aru koto kara, shihongawa to taiketsu suru tsuyoi sutoraiki o dekinai jakuten o motte iru*' (page 61). ('Because union organization is enterprise-specific, it has the defect of being unable to confront capitalists with a strong strike.')

In Ohta's original radical conception of the *Shuntō*, coordinated strike activity of the unions in an industry or several industries or sectors, with the general strike as the ultimate weapon, is designed to overcome this defect.[10] By simultaneously striking, each union can carry on its own struggle with management and wield the strike 'blackjack' with which it secures rents from its firm (cf. Reder, 1984 for the blackjack theory of

American strike activity). But in the case of most union industry-wide federations, the firms with which they deal enjoy varying levels of labour productivity and economic success. In this case the willingness of the unions to carry out a unified strike of unlimited duration varies from firm to firm. Workers in firms with relatively poor business prospects, especially those workers enjoying efficiency wage status within these troubled firms, have a strong incentive to settle early on so that they can avoid a bruising confrontation which may ultimately do harm to the survival prospects of their company. Since ultimate power over bargaining and the strike resides in the hands of the enterprise union (regardless of what prior agreement is reached among the unions in the federation), the union in a weak firm can withdraw from an industry-wide federation strike agreement earlier than its affiliated unions if it strenuously insists.[11] Management knows this; the federation of businesses facing the federation of unions share information and can and do use divide-and-conquer tactics to secure wage settlements which do not imperil the weakest firms in the federation. Thus the incentive for a union in a weak firm is to settle as quickly as possible. Once a settlement is joined which permits the least productive enterprise in the industry to stay afloat, the better-off firms can settle at levels close to those reached in the less well-off firms. The management of the more favourably situated firms know that their own union members can be divided if their opposing unions attempt to wage a protracted strike. Thus they have little incentive to settle for a regular wage which greatly exceeds that arrived at between weak firms and their unions. In this way wages are settled at levels more in line with that which the least-productive unionized firms can afford. Bonuses are settled in separate negotiations. In principle the bonus, which represents one of the most important components of the firm-specific wage payment, could fully compensate the workers in the more productive firms for settling for a regular wage below that which their firms can potentially 'afford' to pay.[12] And more successful firms *do* reward their workers at a *slightly* higher level than do weak firms. By giving their workers this incremental reward firms above and beyond that offered by their less favourably situated competitors, they shore up worker effort levels in the present and in future periods, since union officials and some rank-and-file union members have at least a general awareness of recent company performance and would view a failure of the company to pay an above-average bonus as a rejection of the firm's implicit obligation under the principles of rent sharing and efficiency wage payment. But the incentive of the company to fully compensate their workers is small, for its officers know that the potential strike weapon which the union possesses cannot easily be wielded by the union. Moreover, the union officials have a direct incentive to bolster the profits and growth potential of the companies with which their unions are affiliated. To see why we need to systematically the costs and benefits of unionism, and the objective function of the union as a collective body represented by its officers.

Japanese unions are both political and economic entities and a proper assessment of their costs and benefits must take into account both factors.[13] During the course of the evolution of the *Shuntō* from its radical origins to the high-growth era phase to its consensus form, the political implications of union membership have changed, but in all periods politics have mattered to a degree, although it is fair to say that bread-and-butter economic issues are probably always of greater concern to the average rank-and-file union member than the less tangible rewards offered through political voice and potential influence on the policy, making process. Still, some union officials move up into political positions in the national Diet after their active union careers are finished (often to the relief of their former union members) and, if nothing else, they do propose legislation beneficial to union organizers and attempt to block legislation injurious to the labour movement or at least some factions of it. On the political aspects on unions see *inter alia* Cook, 1966; Koshiro, 1983d; Nitta, 1988). I take account of this in Chart 6.2, which considers the costs and benefits of unions to workers and management in terms of both economic considerations (wages, effort, amenities and employment stability) and the political calculus. Note that employment security, employment growth, and political power of the union are linked, in the sense that unions with greater member retention rates (which are basically identical to firm retention rates in the case of enterprise unions) and greater membership growth rates can, over time, exercise increasingly potent political muscle in their national centres and federations than can slow-growing and/or unstable unions.

But how do Japanese unions grow? In general growth has two sources: new union organizing and automatic additions to membership stemming from employment growth in the enterprises with which the union is affiliated. Because Japanese unions are mainly organized along enterprise lines, their principal source of growth is growth in enterprise employment.[14] Of course, industrial federations or national centres may and do hire organizers to organize hitherto unorganized workplaces, usually but not always in the sector where the union federation has its base. But for most unions and certainly for the enterprise union which, in terms of share of union movement resources, is the backbone of the union movement, the main source of growth is expansion of company labour force. We can

CHART 6.2 Potential costs and benefits of union to union members and to management in Japan

	To employees		To management	
Item	Costs	Benefits	Costs	Benefits
		[A] Economic		
Wage (W) Average wage per worker (W_a)	(1) Depending on relative labour productivity level and/or productivity growth of the firm, the ranking principle implicit in unionized collective bargaining may depress average wage level and/or the gain in wages. (2) Union dues (expensive in enterprise unions, especially in smaller and/or smaller unions companies).	(1) Depending on relative labour productivity level and/ or productivity growth of the firm, the ranking principle implicit in unionized collective bargaining may enhance average wage level and/or the gain in wages.	(1) In firms with relatively low labour productivity and/or low productivity growth of the firm, unionized collective bargaining may depress profits. In the case of government, unionized collective bargaining may put pressure on parliament and/or Ministries to recommend tax increases, endangering re-election chances of some politicians.	(1) In firms with relatively high labour productivity and/or high productivity growth unionized collective bargaining may enhance profitability. In the case of government, it may yield the possibility of cuts in taxes.

| | To employees | | To management | |
Item	Costs	Benefits	Costs	Benefits
Wage (W) Distribution [by occupation and age]	(1) For those in occupations with excess demand, the egalitarianism of enterprise unionism may reduce potential wages. (2) The above remark applies to cohorts in relative excess demand.	(1) For those in occupations with excess supply, the egalitarianism of enterprise unions may enhance wages. (2) The above remark applies to cohorts in relative excess supply.	(1) Reduces managerial discretion over relative wage payments for individuals in certain posts and/or occupations. (2) Enhances wage costs for some employees in potential excess supply.	(1) Reduces potential wage costs for some cohort and/or occupational groups.
Effort (e)	(1) For some individuals with a high opportunity cost for leisure time, a collective bargaining agreement stipulating long hours of mandatory overtime may beonerous. (2) For salaried white collar workers who are not paid for overtime work, the use of overtime may increase their work time but not their remuneration.	(1) For most individuals, socialization in the school system and in the household keeps the opportunity cost of leisure low. Hence the fact that most unionized enterprises can negotiate a higher overtime premium in comparison to non-unionized enterprises is a plus.	(1) Impairs managerial discretion over the use of overtime work, and/or the introduction of new methods for speeding up production.	(1) The fact that labour is represented by a collective union voice reduces the transactions costs of negotiating increments in overtime work and/ or the speeding up of the production line.

CHART 6.2   (continued)

Item	To employees		To management	
	Costs	Benefits	Costs	Benefits
Amenities (a) Working conditions and non-work related amenities	(1) For some occupational groups (e.g. white collar workers in a mining corporation) most direct work related company amenities are irrelevant and come at the expense of amenities for themselves. The same holds for persons in a geographical region where housing is relatively cheap.	(1) Enhances the "voicing" of workers' demands regarding the amenities provided to them. (2) Puts pressure on the enterprise to adhere to legislatively mandated standards governing the work place (e.g.: the articles on the Labour Standards Law).	(1) Constrains the company to more scrupulously adhere to governmental regulations governing welfare standards. (2) May limit the company's ability to offer its own individualized package of welfare benefits.	(1) Reduces transactions costs of finding out what welfare enhancing programs workers desire. (2) Useful in determining the efficient allocation of non-mandated amenities in large and medium sized companies having high transactions costs for gathering information.

CHART 6.2   (continued)

Item	To employees		To management	
	Costs	Benefits	Costs	Benefits
Employment (*L*) Employment security for the individual employee, and overall union membership	(1) In the case of enterprise unions, concern over the company's competitive position which is linked to the company's ability to compete against rivals in the industry and hence to offer future employment, reduces the union's ability to carry out protracted strikes. (2) In the case of the public sector where strikes are illegal, those promoting illegal activities may lose their jobs.	(1) Employees can collectively exercise voice concerning managerial decisions involving labour force rationalization like automation, redeployment of workers from one work group or plant to another work group or plant (*hachi tenkan*), transfers to other firms (*shukko*), firings and 'requests' for early retirement.	(1) Impairs managerial discretion over rationalization. Raises costs to firm of firing workers, or of passing over incumbent employees in favour of an outsider when the firm is filling higher level posts.	(1) Because management must consult the union before taking major action regarding retrenchment and rationalization measures, unionization reduces the morale loss experienced when transfers, redeployment of forces, or firings occur.

CHART 6.2   (continued)
[B] Non-economic

| | To employees | | To management | |
Item	Costs	Benefits	Costs	Benefits
Political Voicing of political positions and ideology	(1) For some employees affiliation with an ideologically national centre may be distasteful. Thus union ideology works to split employees within a firm into separate unions or into factions which impairs decision making. (2) Since union political prowess is tied to the size of the union membership, the union's giving voice to ideology raises the value of union size in the eyes of union officials at the possible expense of larger wage gains.	(1) Gives union members political voice, and possible influence in the determination of outcomes of mediation or arbitration for public sector employees, and may influence the fashioning of legislation which governs mandated amenities. (2) Over the postwar period, the value of political voice seems to have diminished, partly because of new legislation governing mandated welfare amenities, and partly because of the monopoly of political power enjoyed by the pro business Liberal Democratic Party at the national level from 1955 until 1993.	(1) Increases the potential for politically and ideologically motivated friction in the work place. (2) Increases the pressure for legislation mandating compulsory amenities. (3) For the government as employer, the ideology harboured by the unions to which employees belong, may affect the way they carry out their duties (e.g. the way school teachers teach their subjects as opposed to the way the Ministry of Education wants them to teach their subjects).	(1) Increases the probability of a split within the union, weakening the bargaining power of workers. In particular the political nature of unionization makes it easier for a management finding its enterprise union difficult to deal with, to encourage a subgroup of its. employees to create a second union.

see this in two ways. First consider Table 6.1, which gives figures on union density for subsectors of manufacturing cross-classified by employment growth and union density. Note first that sectors with high levels of union density in the early 1950s have persisted in having high union density throughout the postwar period. (These density rates are calculated by computing the ratio of union membership with headquarters in the subsector relative to subsectoral employment; thus workers employed in subsector x but who are members of a union in subsector y are included in the subsector y union density rate.) Second, note (from panel C of Table 6.1) that subsectors with high rates of union density and high rates of employment growth have vastly increased their share of total manufacturing union membership, from 22.9 per cent in 1951–5 to 43.7 per cent in 1981–5, while subsectors which had high union density in 1951–5 but slow employment growth experienced a substantial decline in union membership. Note employment growth and union membership growth are highly correlated. Note that during the late 1960s union birth rates (new union members organized per union member) exceeded adjusted union death rates (union members lost per union member) by a considerable margin in all sectors, suggesting that net new union organizing was taking place, but that by the later 1970s there was generally little new net union organizing. For this reason after the later 1970s, in the era of the consensus *Shuntō*, membership growth through enterprise growth has become more important than ever before.

In sum, under enterprise unionism union officials have a strong incentive to encourage employment growth within their affiliated enterprises since this redounds onto the power of the union and its associated national centre. Hence I assume the union's objective is to maximize the product of per union member utility and employment, that is the total welfare associated with the union:

$$\max [u(w, e, a) \times L] \tag{6.1}$$

where u is per worker welfare expressed as a function of wages (w), effort (e) and amenities (a), and L is total union membership.[15] This is a modified version of Dunlop's famous rule of maximizing the wage bill, that is the product of w times L ($w \times L$), and so can readily be dubbed 'welfare bill' collective bargaining. Now, with this in mind, recall my discussion concerning the collective bargaining dynamics in an industry with more-successful and less-successful firms. In that discussion I argued that union officers in high-productivity firms, but necessarily rank-and-file union members, have an incentive to settle for moderate wage increases and bonuses, short of those the firm could 'afford' to pay. The reason is

TABLE 6.1   Union density, indices of employment and union density, and percentage of union membership for groups of subsectors of manufacturing classified by union density (Ud) in 1951–55 and the index of employment (empin) for 1984–5: Japan, 1951–85 (weighted averages)[a]

(A) Union density

Group of subsectors[b]	*1951–55*	*1956–60*	*1961–65*	*1966–70*	*1971–75*	*1976–80*	*1981–85*
Ud ≥ 40 % and empin for 1984–5 ≥ 100	54.7	41.7	46.6	47.9	50.4	49.7	46.5
Ud ≥ 40% and empin < 100	57.7	51.0	53.3	55.3	57.2	56.4	55.5
Ud < 40% and empin ≥ 120	24.4	19.9	19.2	19.1	19.4	19.2	19.5
Ud < 40% and empin < 120	25.1	23.6	25.1	25.4	26.5	26.0	25.9

(B) Employment indices (empin) and relative employment to union membership indices (reui): 1961–62 = 100

	empin				*reui*			
	1951–2	*1961–2*	*1972–3*	*1984–5*	*1951–2*	*1961–2*	*1972–3*	*1984–5*
Ud ≥ 40% and empin ≥ 100	38.8	100.0	154.3	173.8	81.6	100.0	89.4	98.3
Ud ≥ 40% and empin < 100	70.3	100.0	104.1	73.6	91.3	100.0	95.5	104.9
Ud < 40% and empin ≥ 120	45.1	100.0	158.2	149.8	74.4	100.0	107.0	98.8
Ud < 40% and empin < 120	57.1	100.0	126.3	108.3	99.8	100.0	88.4	91.3

TABLE 6.1   (*continued*)

(C) Percentage of manufacturing union membership

	1951–5	1961–65	1971–75	1981–85
$Ud \geq 40\%$ and empin ≥ 100	22.9	30.9	37.8	43.7
$Ud \geq 40\%$ and empin < 100	41.5	34.2	27.0	22.4
$Ud < 40\%$ and empin ≥ 120	16.7	18.4	18.7	18.1
$Ud < 40\%$ and empin < 120	18.2	15.9	15.7	15.0
Total	100	100	100	100

Notes:
(a) Within each of the groups the sub sector figures are averaged by weighting through by the average percentage of union membership over the period 1951–85 in the subsector.
(b) In the group $Ud \geq 40\%$ and empin ≥ 100 are six sub sectors: f27 (petroleum and coal products), f28 (rubber products), f34 (general machinery), f35 (electrical machinery), f36 (transportation equipment), and f37 (precision instruments).

In the group $Ud \geq 40\%$ and empin < 100 are five sub sectors: f20 (textile mill products), f24 (pulp and paper), f26 (chemicals), f31 (iron and steel), and f32 (non-ferrous metals).

In the group $Ud < 40\%$ and empin ≥ 120 are four sub sectors: f21 (apparel), f25 (publishing and printing), f29 (leather) and f33 (fabricated metal products). In the group $Ud < 40\%$ and empin < 120 are five sub sectors: f18 (food and tobacco), f22 (lumber and wood products), f23 (furniture), f30 (ceramic, stone and clay products), and f38–9 (ordinance and miscellaneous).

Sources:
Nihon Rōdō Daijin Kanbō Seisaku Chōsabu (various years: various tables); Japan. Statistical Association (1987: Tables 3–9, pp. 396–97).

simple. If the union officers do negotiate such a settlement, firm profitability per worker increases, and thereby the probability of future firm growth, and hence union membership growth, is enhanced. In this sense union officials are more willing to trade off u gains for L gains in equation (6.1) than are rank-and-file workers. For even if individual workers are politically apathetic the union officers usually are not. But even for the average rank-and-file worker L is an important variable, especially in the conditions of slow economic growth and the consensus *Shuntō*. For the Japanese union does play an important role in monitoring management retrenchment policies, *shukkō* practices and *haichi tenkan* reorganizations of plant and work group assignments.[16] In this sense we can say that the employment stabilization aspect of large firm labour contracts takes precedence over the per-worker welfare aspect within the institutional context of Japanese enterprise unionism.

To summarize the main points considered here and to provide a guide for the subsequent empirical analysis I review three key propositions of the section:

(a) Private-sector Japanese collective bargaining is bargaining over the general terms of the large firm labour contract and centres around the variables in equation (6.1): wages (w), effort (e), amenities (a), and employment stability and internal firm labour force size (L). In particular the union attempts to maximize the product $u(w, e, a) \times L$, and management attempts to minimize its total labour costs per unit of output produced (which involves setting efficiency wages for promoted works and rent sharing with non-promoted senior workers). There is an inherent tilt towards L in this bargaining process which is attributable to the high costs of employment separation for both company and worker.

(b) The large-firm labour contract divides workers within and between firms. It divides the workers within an enterprise into competing interest groups, creating the spectre of a split within the union into two competing unions. Because unions compete against each other for membership through the performance of their firms, and because union leadership is well aware that part of its membership might leave it and set up a rival enterprise-specific union in the event of a protracted and bitter strike or slowdown action, unions are reluctant to commit themselves to a strong, coordinated federation stance directed at their companies as a group. This impairs a union's ability to wage effective strikes.

(c) Wage increases do not match productivity increases in high-productivity firms. As a result of conditions 1 and 2, pressure to increase wages tends to be equalized across firms, and wage hikes tend to be set at the lower end of the distribution across firm productivity gains. For this reason, in high-productivity-growth sectors there is little if any relationship between productivity growth and wage increase, whereas in low-productivity-growth sectors there is a quite close relationship between the two growth rates. Hence high-productivity-growth sectors have a natural tendency to accumulate capital through the wedge opened up between value added per-worker and the per worker average cost of labour.

6.3 THE *SHUNTŌ* SYSTEM

The *Shuntō* system originated in 1954 in the private-sector unions of the left-leaning Sohyo national centre (whose creation had originally been promoted by the SCAP authorities, the Nikkeiren, and the Ministry of Labour as a conservative force which would bring stability to strike-prone labour–management relations) as a mechanism for overcoming the inherent inability of enterprise unions to carry on protracted strikes. During its early phase the *Shuntō* was predicated on using the strike and other confrontational strategies. Hence I describe the *Shuntō* system of the 1954–60 period as radical. But with the defeat of the Miike strike in 1959–60, which was precipitated by a government decision to promote the rapid development of the petroleum industry in Japan at the expense of coal mining, and which followed on the heels of major labour defeats in the early 1950s like the defeat and splitting up of the Nissan union in 1953 through a Nikkeiren-sponsored lock-out campaign, the popularity of the strike and confrontation in general waned. During the second phase, the high-growth-era *Shuntō*, rapid labour productivity growth coupled with rapid output and employment growth in manufacturing guaranteed year after year of substantial wage hikes coupled with employment stability in most sectors other than mining, substantial wage increases were won by the ever-widening number of union members participating in the *Shuntō*. (For instance, in 1961 about 4.4 million workers participated; by 1971 it climbed to 6.03 million and in 1973 it was about 9.7 million; decrease in participation did not set in until the end of the 1970s. The Dōmei national centre, more conservative and pro-business than Sōhyō, stayed out of the *Shuntō* joint struggle committee, but waged its own spring offensive dubbed the *Chintō* wage offensive.) This being the case, and the strike having proven to be an ineffective weapon in the hand of the union movement which could be easily divided and conquered by a determined Nikkeiren working closely with the government, it is not surprising that

there was a move within the labour movement towards a more accommodating stance towards management and a disavowal of confrontation. And
yet this came slowly and not out of the *Shuntō* pioneering Sōhyō itself,
but rather out of International Metalworkers Federation–Japan Council
(IMF–JC) which emerged out of an alliance of metal industries (iron and
steel; shipbuilding; electric appliances; and automobiles). Why? Why was
the political path towards a more integrative *Shuntō* so long and torturous?

To understand why the operation of the *Shuntō* system ultimately promoted a integrative outcome in the economic arena but set up roadblocks
to integrative political solutions which were not won until the third period
(the consensus Shuntō of the 1974–90 era), it is useful to review the main
quantitative features of the *Shuntō*. Consider Table 6.2 which provides
indicators on collective bargaining over the period 1956–1987. Three
points stand out. First, the coefficient of variation between firms in terms
of the wage increase won has narrowed tremendously under the influence
of *Shuntō* collective bargaining. Second, defeat in many of the major
strikes during the radical period affected behaviour in the high-growth era:
strike levels dropped to low levels in the 1960s to pick up again only
briefly in the early 1970s. Since that surge, strike activity has fallen off
dramatically. Under the consensus *Shuntō* strikes are extremely infrequent.
Third, as can be seen from the figures in panel C of Table 6.2 the wage
increase rate for the private railroads (shitetsu roren) is approximately
equal to the increase rate for the private overall average in the 1959–73 era
(that is throughout the high-growth era *Shuntō*). But the shitetsu is not a
pure free market industry because the government sets the ticket prices
for the railroads, and as a result nominal wage increases in the industry
have to coordinated with nominal ticket price increases allowed by the
public authorities. It is apparent that during the course of the high-growth
era the *Shuntō* became a consensus system for settling wage increases, and
that the government was playing a significant role in the process. And yet
a true integrative consensus *Shuntō* which could effectively serve as a
substitute for incomes policy did not emerge until after 1974. Why?

In my opinion a important clue to explaining why economic outcomes
quickly became integrative and yet political outcomes did not lies in the
ambiguous position of the left-leaning Sōhyō national centre which had
created the *Shuntō* to begin with. Consider panel B of Chart 6.1, which
gives data on the laws governing collective bargaining rights for union
members affiliated with the various national centres. In 1945 all employees including those in the public-sector were covered by the Trade Union
Law and were allowed to strike. But after 1947 SCAP converted to a
'reverse course' in the labour field, abandoned some of its initiatives

TABLE 6.2   Selected aspects of collective bargaining in Japan, 1956–87
[A] Wage increase, dispute intensity and supply/demand balance in the labour market

| Year | Wage increase rate demanded (%) | | Wage increase rate agreed to (%) | | | Days lost to strikes and lockouts of over $\frac{1}{2}$ day in duration per 100 employees | Labour market supply/ demand balance | | Increase rate for |
| | Large companies[a] | Small and medium-sized firms[b] | Large companies[a] | | Small and medium-sized firms[b] | | Active opening rate[c] | Sufficiency ratio[d] | Consumer price index[e] |
			Mean	Coefficient of variation					
1956	n.a.	n.a.	6.3	0.29	n.a.	23.9	0.44	38.0	0.5
1957	n.a.	n.a.	8.6	0.20	n.a.	27.5	0.45	36.7	3.1
1958	n.a.	n.a.	5.6	0.29	n.a.	28.3	0.40	38.3	−0.5
1959	n.a.	n.a.	6.5	0.20	n.a.	26.8	0.61	29.7	1.0
1960	13.8	n.a.	8.7	0.17	n.a.	20.7	0.83	23.1	3.9
1961	18.9	n.a.	13.8	0.14	n.a.	24.8	1.04	18.6	5.2
1962	21.2	25.0	10.7	0.13	14.1	20.8	1.15	12.2	6.7
1963	19.5	22.3	9.1	0.16	11.9	10.1	0.73	17.5	7.6
1964	20.8	22.7	12.4	0.10	15.8	11.5	0.79	15.8	3.9
1965	21.0	22.9	10.6	0.16	12.1	19.7	0.61	19.4	6.4
1966	20.6	21.8	10.6	0.12	11.1	9.2	0.81	15.5	5.3
1967	20.1	23.2	12.5	0.07	12.9	6.0	1.05	12.6	3.7
1968	21.4	25.4	13.6	0.07	14.4	9.0	1.14	12.1	5.5

TABLE 6.2 [A] (continued)

Year	Wage increase rate demanded (%)		Wage increase rate agreed to (%)			Days lost to strikes and lockouts of over	Labour market supply/ demand balance		Increase rate for
	Large companies[a]	Small and medium-sized firms[b]	Large companies[a]		Small and medium-sized firms[b]	$\frac{1}{2}$ day in duration per 100 employees	Active opening rate[c]	Sufficiency ratio[d]	Consumer price index[e]
			Mean	Coefficient of variation					
1969	22.7	26.9	15.8	0.07	16.6	11.4	1.37	10.8	5.5
1970	23.8	29.7	18.5	0.06	19.9	11.8	1.35	10.7	7.6
1971	24.3	29.8	16.9	0.07	18.3	17.7	1.06	12.3	6.0
1972	23.3	28.4	15.3	0.08	16.5	14.9	1.30	10.1	4.6
1973	25.0	31.1	20.1	0.05	21.1	12.7	1.74	7.9	11.7
1974	39.9	47.3	32.9	0.07	33.7	26.6	0.98	11.6	24.5
1975	32.1	37.3	13.1	0.16	14.1	22.0	0.59	12.8	11.8
1976	18.1	23.8	8.8	0.10	9.7	8.8	0.64	12.9	9.4
1977	15.5	19.9	8.8	0.17	9.4	4.0	0.54	14.3	8.0
1978	12.5	16.5	5.9	0.20	6.4	3.6	0.59	12.6	3.7
1979	8.8	13.7	6.0	0.10	6.5	2.4	0.74	10.5	3.6
1980	9.3	13.5	6.9	0.06	7.4	2.5	0.73	10.8	8.0
1981	10.7	14.5	7.7	0.06	7.9	1.4	0.67	10.6	4.9

TABLE 6.2 [A] (continued)

Year	Wage increase rate demanded (%)		Wage increase rate agreed to (%)			Days lost to strikes and lockouts of over $\frac{1}{2}$ day in duration per 100 employees	Labour market supply/ demand balance		Increase rate for
	Large companies[a]	Small and medium-sized firms[b]	Large companies[a]		Small and medium-sized firms[b]		Active opening rate[c]	Sufficiency ratio[d]	Consumer price index[e]
			Mean	Coefficient of variation					
1982	9.7	13.4	7.0	0.06	6.9	1.3	0.60	11.0	2.6
1983	7.8	11.3	4.5	0.15	4.5	1.2	0.61	11.0	1.9
1984	7.0	10.1	4.6	0.12	4.5	0.8	0.66	11.0	2.2
1985	7.6	10.3	5.1	0.09	4.8	0.6	0.68	10.9	2.0
1986	7.6	9.8	4.6	0.14	4.2	n.a	0.62	n.a.	0.4
1987	5.8	8.1	3.6	0.18	3.3	n.a.	0.70	n.a.	n.a.

[B] Coefficient of variation by firm size: 1975, 1980, 1985

Year	Total	5,000 and over	1,000–4,999	300–999	100–299
1975	.196	.095	.129	.207	.203
1980	.116	.099	.089	.099	.124
1985	.164	.105	.117	.125	.193

TABLE 6.2   (*continued*)

[C] Wage increase accepted and demanded for selected unions, 1959–73

Year	Tanrō[f]			Tekkō Rōren[g]			Denki Rōren[h]		
	Demand	*Agreed*		*Demand*	*Agreed*		*Demand*	*Agreed*	
	Amount	*Increase rate*		*Amount*	*Increase rate*		*Amount*	*Increase rate*	
1959	2,000	600	3.5%	2,000	1,240	5.5	2,070	1,570	9.5
1960	2,000	395	2.3	2,000	1,840	6.8	2,667	2,140	12.9
1963	5,000	1,375	6.2	5,000	1,492	4.5	3,613	2,178	11.7
1964	n.a.	2,063	8.7	n.a.	3,160	9.4	n.a.	2,898	14.3
1965	n.a.	1,719	6.3	n.a.	2,440	6.5	n.a.	2,741	12.4
1967	10,000	1,879	6.4	6,150	4,166	12.6	n.a.	n.a.	n.a.
1968	n.a.	3,200	10.1	n.a.	4,346	9.2	n.a.	5,683	18.9
1969	n.a.	4,100	11.4	n.a.	5,240	10.0	n.a.	7,084	20.7
1970	9,638	5,050	12.3	10,149	7,420	12.2	10,436	8,652	21.7
1971	n.a.	n.a.	n.a.	11,000	7,513	10.8	12,123	8,688	18.6
1972	n.a.	n.a.	n.a.	12,000	7,600	9.9	13,784	9,489	17.2
1973	n.a.	n.a.	n.a.	18,900	14,624	20.2	17,999	14,494	21.1

Sources:
(i)   Figures on wage increase rates, labour market conditions, the coefficient of variation, and days lost due to strikes from Kume (1988: various tables).

Notes:
(a)   Technically *shuyō kigyō* (leading companies).The sample size varies from year to year but includes about 70–85 companies in the 1950s, around 150 to 250 companies in the 1960s, and from about 250 to 290 companies in the 1970s and 1980s. The coefficient of variation is calculated by taking the difference between the wage increase at the third quartile and that at the first quartile, and dividing this difference through by twice the median value for the wage increase.
(b)   Based on a sample of companies with 300, or less, employees. The sample size varies from year to year but was aroud 6 000 in thelate 1960s, and around 7 000 to 8 000 in the 1970s and 1980s.
(c)   Defined as the ratio of monthly active openings (at employment exchange offices) divided by monthly active applicants (at employment exchange offices).
(d)   The ratio in percentage terms of monthly placements divided by monthly active openings at employment exchange offices.

which had stimulated radical communist activity, and retrenched on the right to strike and encouraged the passage of legislation prohibiting the

TABLE 6.2 [C]   (*continued*)

Year	Shitetsu Rōren [i]			Private average			Kōrokyō [j]		
	Demand	Agreed		Demand	Agreed		Demand	Agreed	
		Amount	Increase rate		Amount	Increase rate		Amount	Increase rate
1959	2,000	1,270	7.2%	2,400	1,500	7.0	n.a.	n.a.	n.a.
1960	3,000	1,624	8.1	2,561	1,691	8.2	n.a.	n.a.	n.a.
1963	5,057	2,228	9.0	4,185	2,237	9.1	n.a.	n.a.	n.a.
1964	n.a.	3,336	12.9	n.a.	3,305	12.4	n.a.	2,209	7.8
1965	n.a.	3,035	10.7	n.a.	3,014	10.3	n.a.	3,038	9.6
1967	7,957	3,949	14.5	n.a.	n.a.	n.a.	n.a.	n.a.	n.a.
1968	n.a.	5,043	13.5	n.a.	5,213	13.5	n.a.	3,374	11.9
1969	n.a.	6,742	16.1	n.a.	6,768	15.8	n.a.	n.a.	n.a.
1970	15,071	8,993	18.7	11,977	8,983	18.3	n.a.	8,626	16.0
1971	15,071	9,743	17.2	14,232	9,522	16.6	n.a.	n.a.	n.a.
1972	18,071	10,243	15.5	15,485	9,907	15.0	n.a.	9,701	13.6
1973	n.a.	n.a.	n.a.	18,897	15,159	20.1	n.a.	n.a.	17.5

Notes: (*continued*)
(e)   Based on a series which excludes imputed rent for owner occupied housing. Comparison during the period when the consumer price index which includes an imputed rent for owner occupied housing of the consumer price index with and without the imputed rent, reveals minute difference in the behavior of the two series.
(f)   Short for Nihon Tanrō Rōdōkumiai (Japan Coal Miners' Union).
(g)   Short for Nihon Tekkōsangyō Rōdōkumiai Rengokai (Japan Federation of Steel Workers Unions).
(h)   Short for Zen-Nihon Denkiki Rōdōkumiai Rengokai (Japanese Federation of Electrical Machine Workers' Unions)
(i)   Short for Nihon Shitetsu Rōdōkumiai Sorengokai (General Federation of Private Railway Workers' Unions of Japan).
(j)   Public Sector Employees Union.
n.a.: not available and/or not estimated.

right to strike by government workers and employees of public-corporations. As implemented by the Diet in 1948 and 1949 the legislation followed classic divide and conquer principles. Not only were government and public-corporation employees removed from the purview of the Trade Union Law and thereby denied the right to strike, they were placed under four separate laws depending on whether they were in national or local government service, or in a national or local public corporation. As a result the government was able to divide up two of the most militant labour unions: the Communication Ministry Workers' Union (Zentei) and the National Railway Workers' Union (Kokutetsu Sōren). This prohibition on the right to strike was bitterly fought by Sōhyō, which appealed to the International Labour Organization for international intervention on its behalf. Thus public-sector employees have been forced to conduct 'demonstrations' instead of strikes and the organizers of these 'demonstrations' are fired on occasion (see Yamaguchi, 1983). Given the breakdown in negotiations implicit in the calling of illegal demonstrations, wage settlement in these cases is settled by mediation under the auspices of the Personnel Authority in lieu of normal negotiations between the unions and the administrative authorities. Koshiro (1983a, 1983b, 1983e) gives convincing evidence that the Personnel Authority which works in the spring under the pressure of the illegal 'demonstrations' takes into account the *Shuntō* settlements reached earlier in the year by the private-sector unions. Thus the public-sector employees benefit from the private-sector settlements, which is important since productivity gain is not easily (if ever) measurable in most public-sector activities, thus precluding any easy criteria for acceptable public-sector wage hikes. Now with this in mind consider the laws governing the Sōhyō unions, Sōhyō being at the core of the *Shuntō*. Note that a mere 30 per cent of Sōhyō union members in 1975 were covered by the Trade Union Law. Thus a very large proportion of Sōhyō's membership was in the public-sector, either in the civil service or in public corporations and public enterprises. Legally denied the right to strike, these unions and the victims of a blatant divide-and-conquer strategy, these unions remained committed to a militant political posture and were naturally reluctant to make integrative overtures towards a pro-business government. But from an economic point of view Sōhyō had to support an integrative wage increase policy since it was clearly in the interests of the public-corporation and government employees it represented. And in the private-sector the logic of collective bargaining was to produce relatively homogeneous wage increases despite significant inter-industry and inter-firm differentials in labour productivity growth and profitability. Therefore a clear trend towards an economically integrative *Shuntō* was achieved in the second period, but an integrative political solution was largely held in abeyance.

However, especially in the private-sector unions, the seeds of an integrative political compromise had been laid in the era of the high-growth *Shuntō*, with the growth in wages itself acting to push union officials towards a more cooperative stance *vis-à-vis* management. For as real wages soared the private-sector unions in Sōhyō and the other rival federations increasingly developed an interest in expanding the scope of labour–management dealings in order to constructively work out solutions to non-wage issues. As per capita income increased, marginal wage gains became less important to the rank and file; of increasing importance became issues involving amenities (e.g. health plans, cleanliness and safety in the workplace, company recreational facilities, etc.) and effort levels (scheduled and non-scheduled hours of work, and overtime pay). To restate this idea in economic terms, with increases in income, the marginal utility of income falls, inducing a substitution on the margin towards non-pecuniary forms of welfare. Thus the IMF-JC spearheaded the drive towards a consensus integrative *Shuntō* which would involve ongoing consultation between labour and management through the agency of Joint Consultation Committees and the like.[17]

The path to the consensus *Shuntō*, then, was blazed by the private-sector unions. The outcome was integrative on three fronts: first, labour–management consultation in the private-sector widened in scope and depth, encourageing a greater flow of information between management and labour, and hence averting the use of the strike; second, beginning in 1970 tripartite commissions involving representatives of labour, business and labour were established; and third, the labour movement moved slowly and steadily towards unification under the Rengō umbrella. While the path to the consensus *Shuntō* was opened up towards the close of the high-growth era, changes in the economic environment, that is the structural shift in the economy experienced during the first half of the 1970s, applied such acceleration to the process that it acquired an irresistible momentum it might otherwise have lacked. The structural changes and the rationale for their impact have already been discussed in Chapters 3 and 5. Here I need merely note that the slowing of the economic growth rate due to a slow-down in labour productivity growth, the ageing of the labour force, and the rising value of the yen relative to the US dollar, worked in tandem to weaken the viability of the no-firing/no lay-off employment security guar-antee under the social efficiency wage system, which in turn shook the confidence of union leaders in the institutional viability of private-sector unionism (see Shimada, 1988 for a discussion of the impact of yen revalua-tion and trade friction on the mood of the labour movement). Or to put it differently the movement towards a consensus integrative *Shuntō* did not occur earlier because the growth rates achieved during the 1960–70 period were so high that the institutional integrity of the typical large firm labour contract under integrated segmentation was not seriously challenged. Once it was challenged, all parties concerned – labour, government and business – developed an incentive to work out a consensual integrative solution to the *Shuntō*.

Political integration occurred along two parallel tracks, the movement in one sphere encourageing movement in the other. First, private-sector unions in the various federations worked to partial unification in the 1970s, establishing thepSeisaku Suishin Rōsōkaigi (Trade Union Council for Policy Promotion) in 1976, which in turn gave birth to the more ambitious Zenmin Rōkyo (All-Japan Council of Private-Sector Labour Organizations) in 1982. (On the detailed politics of the movement towards unification see Inagami, 1988; Nitta, 1988; Taira and Levine, 1985; Yoshimura, 1988). Initially Zenmin Rōkyo had a membership of 4.25 million, drawn from the various unaffiliated unions and from unions within the Sōhyō, Dōmei, and Chūritsurōren national centres. In 1985 Zenmin Rōkyo decided to formally move from a non-affiliated format to federation status in 1987. Thus in 1987 Rengō was officially created. Finally spurred on by a fear of the rationalization policies of the Nakasone government, in particular by the privatization of the National Railways and NTT, the powerful and politically militant public-sector unions who had dominated Sōhyō came to realize that the potential economic costs of their continued resistance to joining the unification campaign, which allowed the government and the business community to more effectively utilize divide-and-conquer tactics in the *Shuntō*, was outweighing the benefits in terms of political and ideological independence. At the end of 1989 the Sōhyō formally dissolved itself and its membership was incorporated into Shin (new) Rengō. Political integration within the labour movement had been achieved, but the protracted holdout of Sōhyō reveals how deep was the division characteristic of labour–management relations, especially in the public-sector, throughout the period of the radical and high-growth-era *Shuntō*.

The second political track along with integration occurred was in the sphere of tripartite consultation. Initiated in 1970 with the Sanrōkon (Industry and Labour Conference) sponsored by the Ministry of Labour, the number of tripartite commissions has markedly increased. The Japan Institute of Labour played a key role in promoting this development (see Taira and Levine, 1985: 259ff.). But the occurrence of extensive consultation between the government, business and labour spheres must be put into perspective, lest we misunderstand the realities of the consensus *Shuntō*. Yes, the network of commissions and consultations allows the consensus *Shuntō* to function as a kind of incomes policy, obviating the need for formal wage and price controls. But make no mistake about it – Labour's position is not on an equal footing with that of business and government. With the exception of 1947–8, when labour was formally included in two Socialist cabinets, labour has never enjoyed the access to government ministries (such as the Ministry of Trade and Industry and the Economic Planning Agency), and has never been as instrumental in bureaucratic-sponsored policy-making as has the business federation, the Nikkeiren, the Keidanren, etc. Second, the potential for a return to a hard-nosed use of the divide-and-conquer approach, the government working hand and glove with the business federations to oppose an easily divided organized labour movement, is always present.

Though sheathed by the velvet glove of consensus Shuntō political rhetoric, the mailed fist of rough-and-tumble, divide-and-conquer tactics can be uncovered by business and government at any moment. The mailed fist is the basic reality of *Shuntō* collective bargaining in all periods: radical, high-growth-era and consensus.

6.4. WAGES, PRICES AND PRODUCTIVITY UNDER THE *SHUNTŌ* SYSTEM

The wage settlement process envisioned in Section 6.2 suggests that wage settlements differ between low- and high-productivity-growth sectors. Specifically it suggests, in so far as *Shuntō* bargaining spills over from one sector into another, that high-productivity-growth sectors will settle for wage increases well short of what enterprises in the sector can 'afford' to pay; but in low-productivity-growth sectors the rate of productivity growth of the least profitable unionized firms in the sector will set a lower bound on the wage increase negotiated and there is a closer association between productivity growth and wage growth. In this section I explore the hypothesis using regressions for the twenty subsectors of manufacturing over the period 1962–87, this being the longest time period for which I could construct a consistent set of time series data files for each of the subsectors. In these regressions the dependent variable is the logarithm of nominal wages (total wages including bonus and *teate* payments, but excluding non-monetized amenities per worker), and the logs of consumer price index and nominal labour productivity are the independent explanatory variables.[18] The advantage of the log–log specification lies in the fact that when we estimate parameter values, we secure elasticities of response, that is the degree of responsiveness of nominal wages to percentage increases in the consumer price index and in nominal labour productivity. In addition, I introduce the active job opening rate (job openings listed at labour exchanges for general labour divided by job applicants). This last variable is a commonly used indicator of supply–demand balance in the active market for hires and it appears in Table 6.2. I report on regressions in Table 6.3 for the high-growth-era *Shuntō*, and in Table 6.4 for the consensus *Shuntō* period. Both of these periods are short, and so I eschew lags because I lack sufficient degrees of freedom for analysis with a lag specification. However, analysis covering the entire period 1956–87 and employing lags yields results similar to those I report here, so I doubt the absence of lags presents much of a problem for the analysis.

In interpreting the results I wish to stress that the price index variable has a number of meanings confounding literal interpretation of its influence. Clearly it stands for the cost of living, and cost-of-living considerations are of importance to the setting of efficiency wage levels and to rent-sharing negotiations. But it is also an indicator for general aggregate economic performance as opposed to industry and subsector of individual enterprise performance. Values of the elasticities for the price index variable in excess of one signal that the real, total-factor productivity growth in the economy as a whole is increasing.

Analysis of data for the entire period 1956–87 (results which are not reported here) yield the following four conclusions. First, the wage bill share has a tendency to decrease in the high-productivity-growth subsectors. Second, there is a rough inverse relationship between the sum of the price index elasticities and the sum of the productivity elasticities. Third, the higher the productivity growth the lower the sensitivity to productivity increase and vice-versa. Fourth, capital accumulation is more rapid in the high-productivity-growth sectors than in the low productivity growth sectors. These are the general tendencies evident from the estimates. But it cannot by any means be said that the ranking yields a perfect correspondence.

Keeping in mind these conclusions for the long period, let us consider the findings for the shorter periods reported in Tables 6.3 and 6.4. There are exceptions in the correspondence between the rank order in productivity growth and the rank order in the price and productivity elasticities, but the general pattern is clear enough. High-productivity-growth sectors are price-sensitive and low-productivity-growth sectors are productivity sensitive. Also, on comparing the 1962–73 elasticities sector by sector with the 1974–87 elasticities it is clear that the price elasticities have declined; and there has been a shift towards increases in the sensitivity to productivity from the first to the second period.

Were firms unable to borrow or were capital markets highly imperfect, they would have to resort to recycling profits in order to invest in new plant and equipment to a greater extent than they might under conditions of perfect financing of investment. If this were the case then the fact that high-productivity-growth sectors appear to have experienced less wage

TABLE 6.3   Nominal Wages, nominal labour productivity, the consumer price index and active labour market conditions in the subsectors of Japanese manufacturing, 1962–73.

Subsector	Growth rates[a]		Investment and capital accumulation[b]		Regression coefficients (coefficients other than the constant term) for log–log regression with nominal average wage as dependent variable[c]		
	Labour productivity	Wage bill share	Investment per worker	Change in capital per worker, 1962 to 1973	Consumer price index	Nominal value per worker	Active job opening rate
[A] Highly unionized							
Petroleum (27)	16.9	−0.4	362	2006	2.27* (6.50)	−.11 (−.89)	.15 (.77)
Iron and steel (31)	15.0	−2.5	112	625	2.07* (5.29)	.01(.04)	.13* (2.14)
Non-ferrous metals (32)	13.4	−1.0	78	358	2.40* (4.00)	−.14 (−.53)	.13*** (1.93)
Textiles (20)	13.2	(−0.2)	23	106	1.52** (2.40)	.36 (1.26)	.03 (.46)
Pulp and paper (24)	13.2	(−.02)	58	270	−1.11** (−2.63)	.62* (4.07)	.21 (1.40)
Rubber prod sets (28)	13.1	.01	32	120	1.62* (3.25)	.37 (1.72)	.04(.72)

TABLE 6.3 [A]   (continued)

Subsector	Growth rates[a]		Investment and capital accumulation[b]		Regression coefficients (coefficients other than the constant term) for log–log regression with nominal average wage as dependent variable[c]		
	Labour productivity	Wage bill share	Investment per worker	Change in capital per worker, 1962 to 1973	Consumer price index	Nominal value per worker	Active job opening rate
Machinery (34)	12.8	(.03)	31	125	1.28*(4.46)	.42(3.07)	.04(.89)
Precision instruments (37)	11.8	.07	21	70	1.61* (5.26)	.28** (1.88)	0.3(.96)
Electrical machinery (35)	11.7	1.1	25	66	1.27* (4.79)	.48* (3.43)	.01 (.27)
Transportation equipment (36)	11.4	0.8	52	148	1.51* (3.73)	.34 (1.56)	–.001 (–.012)
Chemicals (26)	10.8	(1.9)	100	488	2.09*(22.09)	.07(1.15)	.04(.51)

TABLE 6.3   (continued)

Subsector	Growth rates[a]		Investment and capital accumulation[b]		Regression coefficients (coefficients other than the constant term) for log–log regression with nominal average wage as dependent variable[c]		
	Labour productivity	Wage bill share	Investment per worker	Change in capital per worker, 1962 to 1973	Consumer price index	Nominal value per worker	Active job opening rate
[B] Low union density							
Wood products (22)	14.9	–1.2	23	112	2.36* (6.57)	–.004 (–.025)	.09*** (1.97)
Miscellaneous (38–9)	14.2	(–0.4)	32	122	2.14* (3.34)	.10 (.39)	.08*** (2.22)
Furniture (23)	13.5	–0.9	18	84	1.81* (4.47)	.17(.95)	.02 (.48)
Food and drink (18–9)	13.4	(–0.4)	36	150	1.95* (5.09)	.15(.89)	.03(.93)
Fabricated metal products (33)	13.2	(0.3)	30	128	.86 (1.31)	.71** (2.36)	–.11 (–1.37)

[B]   (continued)

Ceramics (30)	13.0	(−0.5)	45	184	2.05* (3.80)	.07(.26)	.04(.73)
Publishing (25)	12.5	(−0.2)	26	128	1.84* (3.50)	.17(.68)	−.02 (−.29)
Leather (29)	11.3	(0.1)	13	55	1.13* (4.26)	.46*(3.34)	001 (.020)
Apparel (21)	9.3	0.8	9	33	1.42* (3.91)	.35***(1.92)	.03 (1.21)

Notes:

(a) Estimated from a regression equation with the log of labour productivity (net value added per worker), or the share of wages in net value added, on time (year) and a constant term.

(b) The underlying investment and capital stock figures are in 10,000 *yen* and the investment data are gross of depreciation.

(c) Estimated from a regression equation with the logarithm of nominal average wages as the dependent variable and the logarithms of the consumer price index, average labor productivity and the active job opening rate (for the same year as the wage data), as independent variables. When the Durbin–Watson statistics did not allow rejection of first-order autocorrelation the regression was re-estimated with the differences in logarithms as the dependent variables. All regressions employed a constant term.

*   Significant at the 1% level (two-tailed test);

**   Significant at the 5% level (two-tailed test);

*** Significant at the 10% level (two-tailed test).

TABLE 6.4 Nominal wages, nominal labour productivity, the consumer price index, and active labour market conditions in the subsectors of Japanese manufacturing, 1974–1987.

Subsector	Growth rates[a]		Investment and capital accumulation[b]		Regression coefficients (coefficients other than the constant term) for log–log regression with nominal average wage as dependent variable[c]		
	Labour productivity	Wage bill share	Investment per worker	Change in capital per worker, 1974–87	Consumer price index	Nominal value per worker	Active job opening rate
[A] Highly unionized[d]							
Chemicals (26)	9.4	−0.4	223	866	1.16* (11.44)	.10* (2.22)	−.01 (−.09)
Petroleum (27)	9.2	− 0.3	702	3633	1.69* (13.06)	−.07 (−1.35)	−.04(9.64)
Iron and steel (31)	8.1	−2.3	242	1330	1.32* (7.18)	.02 (.22)	.07 (.66)
Electrical machinery (35)	7.4	−2.2	89	329	.77* (3.32)	.27*** (2.06)	−.001 (−.009)
Transportation equipment (36)	7.4	−1.5	144	470	.76* (3.61)	.36* (3.02)	−.08 (−1.52)
Machinery (34)	6.7	−0.7	82	350	.81* (5.08)	.38* (3.81)	−.03 (−.76)

TABLE 6.4 [A]   (continued)

Subsector	Growth rates[a]		Investment and capital accumulation[b]		Regression coefficients (coefficients other than the constant term) for log–log regression with nominal average wage as dependent variable[c]		
	Labour productivity	Wage bill share	Investment per worker	Change in capital per worker, 1974–87	Consumer price index	Nominal value per worker	Active job opening rate
Precision instruments (37)	6.6	−1.1	73	259	.77* (6.75)	.33* (4.45)	.004 (.080)
Rubber products (28)	6.5	−1.2	97	314	.72* (3.91)	.34* (2.98)	−.13** (−2.35)
Textiles (20)	6.3	−0.9	49	164	1.00 (1.32)	.19 (1.22)	.13** (2.71)
Non-Ferrous metals (32)	6.2	(−1.1)	173	609	1.28* (5.40)	−.08 (−.53)	.03 (.23)
Pulp and paper (24)	6.1	(0.3)	151	685	.13 (.54)	.73* (3.28)	−.54** (−2.25)

TABLE 6.4 [B] (continued)

[B] Low union density[e]						
Wood products (22	7.1	−1.5	55	249	1.01* (7.52)	.20* (2.63)	.04 (.75)
Ceramics (30)	7.1	−1.3	115	496	.76* (5.48)	.36* (4.42)	−.08 (−1.72)
Apparel (21)	7.0	−0.7	16	61	.61* (2.84)	.20* (2.63)	.04 (.75)
Furniture (23)	6.9	−0.7	42	208	1.06** (2.83)	.25 (1.08)	.06 (.04)
Miscellaneous (38–9)	6.9	−1.6	80	306	.82* (8.50)	.27* (4.57)	−.06 (−1.67)
Fabricated metal products (33)	6.5	−1.2	71	329	.60* (5.06)	.44* (5.83)	−.02 (−.60)
Publishing (25)	6.2	−0.4	75	327	.61 (1.49)	.51*** (1.86)	−.06 (−.92)
Food and drink (18–9)	6.0	−1.0	88	325	.92* (5.07)	.18 (1.41)	−.05 (−1.19)
Leather	6.0	−0.7	25	127	.74* (4.73)	.35* (3.25)	−.06 (−1.50)

Notes:
(a)   See note (a) to Table 6.3.
(b)   See note (b) to Table 6.3.
(c)   See note (c) to Table 6.
(d)   Subsector with this density greater than an equal to 40% in 1951–55.
(e)   Subsector with this density less than 40% in 1951–55.
*   Significant at the 1% level (two-tailed test).
**   Significant at the 5% level (two-tailed test).
*** Significant at the 10% level (two-tailed test).

pressure than low-productivity-growth sectors, especially in the high-growth *Shuntō* era of 1962–73, should have allowed firms in these sectors to accumulate extraordinarily generous per-worker capital accumulation funds, thereby promoting even more rapid labour productivity growth in the ensuing period. Growth feeds on growth – accumulation feeds on accumulation – as it were. This inference is belied by the absence of correspondence between the sectors achieving high rates of labour productivity growth under the high-growth-era *Shuntō*, and those achieving high rates of growth under the consensus *Shuntō*. It is apparent that the demand for capital and/or the pace of technological progress tended to override the potential of accumulation stemming from a declining wage-bill share. The tendency of the *Shuntō* collective bargaining to promote accumulation and growth is independent of the supply/demand balance for investment funds in the individual subsectors. To assess the overall tendency of the system to generate capital accumulation it is useful to consider the bonus component of the wage bill per worker on its own.

Bonus-specific results, with the total of the annual spring and winter bonus payments per worker in each year as the dependent variable, appear in Table 6.5. The specification is log–log. Because junior workers receive lower bonus payments (both in percentage terms as a proportion of the total wage and in absolute terms) I have introduced the growth rate of employment into the regressions as an independent variable. I have also included overtime hours worked in the two years prior to the given year *t* because some of the literature on bonus payments suggests that previous effort levels are rewarded with bonus payment (cf. Koshiro, 1991 for a discussion of various theories of bonus payments).[19] As the reader can glean from the table, at the subsectoral level the bonus is highly responsive to labour productivity. The proxy for effort in previous periods is either not important or takes on both positive and negative signs and hence is inconsistent. However, if one takes into account the average level of overtime hours worked then there appears to be some association between effort and the bonus. I have ranked the subsectors according to overtime hours worked; from this ranking it is evident that there is a tendency, not a strong tendency but a tendency, for the elasticities on the productivity to decline as the level of overtime work effort declines. So higher-effort industries may reward more according to effort, and less according to productivity. In short, the nominal bonus adjusts to productivity but not to prices. By contrast the overall wage bill adjusts more to prices than to productivity, especially in subsectors with high productivity growth. This suggests that firms prefer to pay as much of the wage as possible in the form of bonuses, since by so doing they can link the wage to the actual,

TABLE 6.5 Productivity and the bonus. Log–log regressions of bonus per worker on the consumer price index, average labour productivity, and overtime hours worked in the subsectors of manufacturing, 1964–87 (sub sectors ranked by average overtime hours worked, 1966–70)

				Overtime hours worked						
Subsector	Constant	Year	Consumer price index (previous) year	Previous year	Two years before	Value added per Worker	Change in log of numbers of workers	Time[a] dummy	Adjusted R^2	Durbin–Watson statistic
[A] Highly unionized										
Iron and steel (31)	148.6** (2.1)	–.07** (–1.94)	.63 (1.03)	–.58* (–3.00)	.30*** (1.83)	1.19* (3.02)	–1.23 (–1.17)	–.25 (–1.38)	.97	1.76
Transportation equipment (36)	135.9* (2.7)	–.07** (–2.51)	.08 (.19)	–.14 (–1.34)	.28* (2.46)	1.64* (6.33)	.02 (.05)	.03 (.25)	.99	2.40
Non-ferrous metals (32)	–29.7 (–0.6)	.02 (.78)	–.33 (– .80)	–.36* (–4.00)	.14 (1.66)	1.14* (7.75)	.20 (.56)	–.19 (–1.56)	.99	1.81
Machinery (34)	114.2* (2.3)	–.06** (–2.10)	–.26 (–.70)	.10 (1.07)	–.08 (–.84)	.32 (1.12)	.33 (1.21)	–.07 (–.62)	.99	1.96
Pulp and paper (25)	n.e.	n.e.	n.e.	n.e.	n.e.	n.e.	n.e.	n.e.	n.e.	n.e.

TABLE 6.5 [A]   (continued)

| Subsector | Constant | Year | Consumer price index (previous) year | Overtime hours worked | | | Change in log of numbers of workers | Time[a] dummy | Adjusted R^2 | Durbin–Watson statistic |
				Previous year	Two years before	Value added per Worker				
Petroleum	7.96	−.002	1.60*	.10	.80**	.17	−.03	.03	.98	1.12
(27)	(.12)	(−.065)	(2.16)	(.15)	(1.74)	(.62)	(−.07)	(.85)		
Electrical	183.8*	−.09*	−.53	−.06	.11	2.16*	.32	.12	.99	2.18
machinery (35)	(3.9)	(−3.70)	(−1.42)	(−.68)	(1.23)	(8.84)	(.95)	(1.05)		
Rubber	35.8	−.02	.89**	−.26**	.13	1.82*	−.27	−.16	.99	1.76
products (28)	(.8)	(−.60)	(−2.61)	(−2.64)	(1.26)	(10.35)	(−.52)	(−1.58)		
Precision	106.2	−.05	−.43	.14	−.14	1.81*	.85	−.14	.97	1.21
instruments (37)	(1.1)	(−.97)	(−.81)	(.75)	(−.77)	(3.57)	(1.09)	(−.75)		
Chemicals	171.40*	−.09**	.93**	−.34**	.16	1.31*	−.45	−.16	.99	1.96
(26)	(2.57)	(−2.46)	(2.38)	(−2.50)	(1.12)	(7.26)	(−1.65)	(−1.48)		
Textiles	65.7	−.03	−.97	.08	.08	2.04*	.99	−.15	.98	2.38
	(1.0)	(−.86)	(−1.61)	(.33)	(.35)	(7.54)	(.76)	(−.70)		

TABLE 6.5 [*continued*]

| | | | | Overtime hours worked | | | | | | |
Subsector	Constant	Year	Consumer price index (previous) year	Previous year	Two years before	Value added per Worker	Change in log of numbers of workers	Time[a] dummy	Adjusted R^2	Durbin–Watson statistic
				[B] Low union density						
Publishing	−22.0	.02	−.55	−.28	−.18	1.20*	.52	−.01	.99	1.93
(25)	(−.5)	(.73)	(−1.50)	(−.85)	(−.58)	(5.12)	(.54)	(−.08)		
Fabricated metal	129.8*	−.06*	−.27	−.05	.003	1.85*	.17	−.15	.99	1.83
products (33)	(2.7)	(−2.58)	(−.72)	(−.48)	(.026)	(10.56)	(.37)	(−1.30)		
Ceramics	164.1*	−.08*	.28	.02	.06	1.76*	−.05	−.33**	.99	2.21
(30)	(3.06)	(−2.93)	(.71)	(.17)	(.40)	(9.07)	(−.09)	(−2.63)		
Wood	122.5	−.06	−34	−.61*	.21	1.94*	1.75*	−.48* ·	.98	2.52
products (22)	(1.7)	(−1.56)	(−.59)	(−3.10)	(1.03)	(2.39)	(2.39)	(−3.46)		
Furniture	−38.5	.03	−1.15*	−.19	−.07	.10	.10	.001	.99	1.99
(23)	(−1.1)	(1.27)	(−4.12)	(−1.57)	(−.58)	(.22)	(.22)	(.010)		

TABLE 6.5 [B] [*continued*]

Overtime hours worked

Subsector	Constant	Year	Consumer price index (previous) year	Previous year	Two years before	Value added per Worker	Change in log of numbers of workers	Time (a) dummy	Adjusted R^2	Durbin Watson statistic
Food and drink (18–9)	125.5* (4.5)	–.06* (–4.21)	.01 (.03)	.14 (.58)	–.004 (–.020)	1.61* (11.71)	–.09 (–.20)	–.14* (–2.24)	.996	2.08
Miscellaneous (38–9)	164.1* (3.1)	–.08* (–2.93)	.28 (.71)	.02 (.17)	.06 (.40)	1.76* (9.07)	–.05 (–.09)	–.33** (–2.63)	.99	2.21
Leather (29)	21.9 (.5)	–.01 (–.35)	–1.29* (–2.90)	–.13 (–.71)	.01 (.07)	2.00* (9.31)	.35 (.87)	–.15 (–1.41)	.99	2.82
Apparel (21)	37.3 (.7)	–.02 (–.57)	–.98** (–2.67)	–.40 (–1.39)	–.01 (–.03)	2.06* (5.45)	.42 (.66)	–.04 (–.36)	.99	2.62

Notes:

(a) This variable has the value '0' for years before 1974, and the value '1' for 1974 and all subsequent years.

* Significant at the 1% level (two-tailed test).

** Significant at the 5% level (two-tailed test).

*** Significant at the 10% level (two-tailed test).

already-realized performance in their industries (cf. Koshiro, 1991, which shows that sectoral performance is more important than firm-specific performance in determining the bonus levels in the case of private railways). Bonuses also serve as an effort-enhancing inducement to non-promoted senior workers and hence paying a higher share of the wage in the bonus helps reduce the costs of monitoring senior non-promoted workers. Hence firms with high productivity growth, feeling less regular wage pressure than their less-fortunate rivals, enjoy the opportunity of tilting their wage bill towards effort-enhancing bonuses.

6.5 PROFITS AND WAGES

The hypothesis I have developed concerning collective bargaining has implications for sectors. Nevertheless the direct concern of the theory is with enterprise behaviour as conditioned by the other firms in the industry. Consequently in this section I explore the hypothesis using data on collective bargaining settlements for 147 individual union and their associated enterprises for the year 1985. Specifically I analyse the relationship between the wage increase and the wage increase rate, and indices of profitability and variability in profitability for the individual unions and for the federations to which the unions belong. Since my hypothesis bears on the relationship between the individual union and its associated enterprise as conditioned by the federation within which the union carries out *Shuntō* collective bargaining,my empirical analysis is targeted directly at my hypothesis.[20]

Before reporting on my regression analysis with the 1985 data set, several remarks of a general nature concerning the properties of the data set are in order. First, it contains figures on profitability and its variability within the firm group associated with the federation; the wage settlement demanded; the wage settlement achieved; and the settlements with the most and least profitable firms in the federation. Second, within the entire sample of 147 unions there is great variability in wage demands and wage settlements. Third, there are nine federations in which there is no variation in the wage settlement demanded (of which five had no variation in the wage settlement agreed to). All nine of these federations were in the set of unions whose federations faced groups of firms with low profitability variability. Fourth, there is a rough association between the average wage settlement and the average index of profitability for the firms facing unions in the federation, but the association cannot said to be strong. On the other hand, if we restrict our attention to the settlements with the most-profitable and least-profitable firms within each federation, it is clear that more-profitable firms tend to grant higher wage increases in general, although there are exceptions. Finally, variability in profitability has an unmistakable influence on variability in settlements: the greater the variability in profitability the greater the variability in the federation settlement patterns. In short in the settlements there is a strong regression towards a settlement appropriate for the profitability average for the group of firms facing the unions in the federation; the regression towards the mean is greater the smaller is the variation in profitability; and the least-profitable firms tend to increase wages the least while the most-profitable firms tend to increase them the most.

Regression analysis, reported on in Table 6.6, further confirms these results. In this table I have restricted my attention to federations having at least eight members so as to have enough degrees of freedom to run regressions on the observations *within* each of the federations. The dependent variable is the level (or rate) of the increase actually agreed to; the dependent variables include the increase demanded (which partially reflects information the union has about the firm's actual business situation which is not captured in the index of profitability as well as the union's relative degree of bargaining strength *vis-à-vis* the firm) and the index of profitability. As can be seen, whenever the coefficients are significant (with the exception of the increase rate for Zensendōmei) then the signs are as expected.

In short the data for the 1985 *Shuntō* display patterns which are consistent with the model developed in Section 6.2.

6.6   THE UNION WAGE EFFECT IN MEDIUM-SIZED FIRMS

Is there a union wage effect? Examination of Tables 6.3 and 6.4 reveals little, if any, impact of unionization on manufacturing wage gains over the long run. Are we to conclude from this finding that the Japanese union has no impact on wages? That wage payments negotiated through the union are virtually identical to wage payments offered to employees who are not represented by a union?

The most pressing problem posed in evaluating the impact of private-sector Japanese unions on the wages (more generally the impact on wages, amenities, effort levels and employment security) of the employees they represent is statistically disentangling the influence of the union from the influence of the large-firm labour contract which is more deeply entrenched in the segment of the private-sector where union density is the

TABLE 6.6   Negotiated wage increase, wage demand, and index of profitability, 1985: selected union federations

Data set, federation (number of observations in [ ])	With total average wage bill per worker as dependent variable: linear regressions				With wage bill per worker increase rate as dependent variable: log linear regressions			
	Constant	Increase demanded[a]	Index of profitability	Adjusted R^2	Constant	Increase demanded[a]	Index of profitability	Adjusted R^2
All Unions	4372.5*	.34*	32.86*	.48	−1.18**	.26*	.08**	.14
[147]	(7.2)	(11.14)	(3.75)		(−2.10)	(4.63)	(2.22)	
Denkirōren (electrical	3230.1	.47**	13.74	.34	4.37**	− .29	.04***	.34
machinery) [13]	(1.19)	(2.70)	(1.59)		(2.16)	(−1.41)	(2.05)	
Jidosharōren	4549.4	.37	32.89**	.59	8.77*	−.79**	13**	.47
(automobiles) [9]	(1.2)	(1.29)	(2.02)		(3.43)	(−2.82)	(2.63)	
Zenkokukinzoku	−115.5	.35	146.69	.20	−1.48	.17	.40	.21
(metal manufacturing) [8]	(−.02)	(1.63)	(1.37)		(−.69)	(.95)	(1.91)	
Zenkindōmei	7201.3*	.30	−24.55	.62	−3.99	.44	.36	−.30
(metals) [8]	(2.0)	(1.62)	(−1.01)		(−.27)	(.32)	(.59)	

TABLE 6.6   *(continued)*

Data set, federation (number of observations in [ ])	With total average wage bill per worker as dependent variable: linear regressions				With wage bill per worker increase rate as dependent variable: log linear regressions			
	Constant	Increase demanded[a]	Index of profitability	Adjusted R^2	Constant	Increase demanded[a]	Index of profitability	Adjusted R^2
Gokarōren	9485.8*	.09	19.91	.04	3.73	−.19	−.06	.32
(chemicals)[9]	(4.5)	(.74)	(1.02)		(3.21)	(−1.50)	(−.06)	
Zensendōmei (textiles,	−8359.6*	1.06*	80.85*	.89	12.58*	−1.00**	−.40	.14
garments and allied) [15]	(−4.5)	(10.76)	(4.53)		(2.31)	(−1.94)	(−1.61)	
Shokuhinrōren	3638.5	.52*	−24.13	.90	−3.04	.50*	−.08	.60
(food industries) [10]	(1.35)	(8.49)	(−.31)		(−1.56)	(3.54)	(−0.13)	

Notes:
(a)   Stated in *yen* per worker (not as a rate).
*   Significant at the 1% level (two-tailed test).
**   Significant at the 5% level (two-tailed test).
***   Significant at the 10% level (two-tailed test).

highest. For union density is the highest in the world of giant firms where the large-firm labour contract institutions are the most strongly entrenched.

Knowing this I have elected to focus on the relationship between unionization in medium-sized firms. In the medium-sized-firm sector unionization rates vary tremendously. In the case of small firms unionization rates are low everywhere, effectively precluding meaningful analysis. Hence I restrict my attention to medium-sized firms.[21] However, it should be kept in mind that many medium-sized firms operate with contracts which approximate the stylized large-firm contract in my model.

In measuring the union wage effect in medium-sized firms I have looked at three different types of impact: the impact on wages, the impact on the secular increase in wages; and the impact on the annual (year to year) increase in wages. My results appear in Table 6.7. Panels A and B give results for the cross-section in 1965, 1970, 1975, 1980 and 1985. Panel C gives trend results for the 1965–85 trend period. And finally in panel D I have examined annual increases resulting from the *Shuntō* bargaining rounds in 1970/1 and 1980/1. In the cross-sectional specifications I entertained the possibility that capital intensity and wages can be simultaneously determining each other (i.e. higher wages induce a substitution of capital for labour, and greater capital intensity raises wages by raising labour productivity). In this case one must use two stage least squares in estimating the two equations. For the simultaneous estimation I have:

$$w = a_0 + a_1\,(vapw) + a_2\,(ud) + e \qquad\qquad (6.2a)$$

and

$$K/L = b_0 + b_1\,(w) + b_2\,(ud) + e \qquad\qquad (6.2b)$$

where w = wages per worker, $vapw$ = value added per worker, ud = union density, and K/L = ratio of capital to labour.

From the cross-sectional estimates it is clear that there is a positive union effect on wages but not on capital intensity. This impact on wages is quite stable over time. But there is no discernible impact of the union on the secular increases in wages or on annual increases in wages. Thus the union wage effect in medium-sized firms is 'one-shot'. Unionizing appears to raise the rank of the firm within the industry, but does not seem to affect the wage gain over time once the union is in place.

The union has other positive benefits not captured in these regressions.[22] It works to better the terms of medical and health insurance plans offered by the firm. And its presence increases the communication between workers and management (see the discussion of *kyōgi kikan*, in

TABLE 6.7   The union wage effect in medium-sized firms: log–log regressions[a]
(OLS and two-stage least-squares) on cross-sections of subsectors of
manufacturing, 1965, 1970, 1975, 1980 and 1985

	Average wage as the dependent variable					Capital intensity as the dependent variable			
Year	Constant	Labour productivity	Union density	Capital intensity	Adjusted R^2	Constant wage	Average density	Union	Adjusted R^2
					[A] Ordinary least-squares				
1965	1.05	.20	.34*	.12**	.50	−2.97	2.67*	−.74	.43
	(1.70)	(1.65)	(3.35)	(2.15)		(−1.35)	(4.02)	(−.74)	
1970	1.10*	.41*	.30*	−.01	.88	−5.55*	3.36*	−1.18*	.68
	(3.32)	(4.43)	(4.56)	(−.10)		(−2.64)	(6.26)	(−2.71)	
1975	1.28**	.37*	.33*	.10**	.82	−4.75***	3.01*	−1.47*	.67
	(2.62)	(3.99)	(3.82)	(2.22)		(−1.77)	(6.00)	(−3.50)	
1980	1.89*	.21**	42*	.14**	.78	−6.18*	3.08*	−1.42*	.73
	(3.20)	(2.32)	(4.25)	(2.69)		(−2.37)	(6.92)	(− 3.69)	
1985	2.19*	.41*	.22**	.01	.81	−8.72	2.92*	−.56	.66
	(4.05)	(3.36)	(2.70)	(.15)		(−3.27)	(6.22)	(−1.45)	

TABLE 6.7   *(continued)*

| Year | | *Average wage as the dependent variable* | | | | | *Capital intensity as the dependent variable* | | |
	Constant	*Labour productivity*	*Union density*	*Capital intensity*	*Adjusted R^2*	*Constant wage*	*Average density*	*Union*	*Adjusted R^2*
			[B] Two-stage least-squares[b]						
1965	−.24	.16	.69*	.18*	.25	−9.18	5.44*	−1.89	−.17
	(−.22)	(.81)	(3.38)	(1.74)		(−1.43)	(3.51)	(−.85)	
1970	.58	.37*	.49*	.009	.82	−6.96	5.39*	−3.23**	.61
	(1.25)	(2.79)	(4.67)	(.110)		(−1.68)	(4.19)	(−2.22)	
1975	2.10**	.15	.35*	.17*	.76	−4.37	3.46*	−2.21	.60
	(2.43)	(1.08)	(2.56)	(2.94)		(−1.16)	(4.33)	(−1.48)	
1980	−.04	.31***	.81*	.11	.55	−9.59	3.74*	−1.51	.69
	(−.03)	(1.83)	(3.70)	(1.10)		(−1.16)	(6.38)	(−.86)	
1985	1.53	.14	.61*	.18	.45	−4.10	4.90***	−4.97	−2.00
	(1.42)	(.48)	(2.47)	(1.01)		(−.42)	(1.75)	(−.92)	

TABLE 6.7   (*continued*)

Year	Average wage as the dependent variable					Capital intensity as the dependent variable			
	Constant	Labour productivity	Union density	Capital intensity	Adjusted R^2	Constant wage	Average density	Union	Adjusted R^2
				[C] Trends, 1965–85					
1965–85	1.63*	.11**	–.07	.13	.45	–1.61	1.70*	.10	.32
	(12.98)	(2.08)	(–.99)	(1.56)		(–1.50)	(3.30)	(.43)	
1965–85 (b)	–3.31	–1.39	1.91	4.28	–109.51	3.95	–.96	–.36	–.79
	(–.17)	(–.23)	(.23)	(.11)		(.66)	(–.33)	(–.44)	

TABLE 6.7   (continued)

[D] Annual Increases, 1970/1 and 1980/1

Per cent increase in wage bill	16.59*	.19***	.01	−.01	.05	−2.85	−.59**	.31	.003	.24
	(3.90)	(1.94)	(.06)	(−1.60)		(−.15)	(−2.51)	(.73)	(.664)	

Notes:

(a) Log–log regressions (OLS and two-stage least square regressions) on cross-sections of subsectors of manufacturing in 1965, 1970, 1976, 1980 and 1985.

(b) Instruments for the equations with average wage as dependent variable are as follows: in 1965 they are the log of small firm wages, investment per worker in medium-sized firms, and the log of the wage bill share in medium-sized firms. In 1970, 1975, 1980 and 1985 they are the same as in 1965 only the log of investment per worker is used instead of the level of investment in worker. For the equation with capital intensity as the dependent variable the instruments are the log of the wage bill share in small firms and the log of capital intensity in small firms in all years except 1975 and 1985, when the log of value added per worker in small firms is used in place of small firm capital intensity.

*   Significant at the 1% level (two-tailed test).
**   Significant at the 5% level (two-tailed test).
***   Significant at the 10% level (two-tailed test).

particular the discussion in note 17 of this chapter), thereby raising productivity and productivity growth, decreasing quits, reducing the incidence of labour–management disputes, and internalizing the firm's labour market in the sense that the promotion of lower-ranked employees is given precedence over recruitment from outside the firm.

6.7   NEW UNION ORGANIZING AND THE *SHUNTŌ* SYSTEM

In the original conception of the Shuntō during its radical phase, the first generation of postwar officials in Sōhyō conceived of the *Shuntō* as a vehicle for new union organizing as well as a mechanism for coping with management during wage bill negotiations. How has the *Shuntō* fared in this endeavour? Now new organizing has been on the decline over the last two decades. Can this be attributed to the way the *Shuntō* has operated and/or evolved as it moved from its radical inception in the 1950s, to the high growth-era, to the consensus system it became after the mid-1970s?

Freeman and Rebick (1989) attribute the decline in Japanese new union organizing to increased resistance on the part of management to fresh organizing drives and to legal changes which have bolstered management resistance. They believe that the decline in union density observed for postwar Japan can be attributed to a decline in the union birth rate, which in turn is due to a stiffening of managerial opposition to unions, attributable to a slowing of economic growth after the oil crisis. In the matter of declining unionization, they think the situation in the United States and Japan is similar. In both countries union density is on the decline, and they think the root causes are identical. In both cases a squeeze on business profits raises the costs of unionization to employees and hence employers intensify their efforts to stave off organizing campaigns. Moreover, because the parties with legislative power have been sympathetic to the needs of business, accommodating legislative changes have helped management push up the cost of organizing to potential union members in both countries.

I agree with Freeman and Rebick that a decline in Japanese union organizing has been an important factor in causing a decline in union density. But I think they exaggerate the impact of the decline on the union birth rate. Structural changes in the composition of employment, in particular a shift out of heavy industry towards technology-intensive service production, has played a greater role than they credit. Estimates for mine not reported here demonstrate that at least in some subsectors of manufacturing the falling union birth rate has worked to reduce density.

However, my results also show that the employment growth rate is consistently a more telling variable that the union birth rate. New employment opportunities tend to be in non-unionized firms and/or employment decline has been greater in unionized than in non-unionized companies. Still, the union birth rate has fallen. Why?

In my opinion the answer lies, not in employer resistance but in employee resistance, and the reason for enhanced employee resistance is the economic performance of the *Shuntō* and the evolution of the system towards its current consensus form. First, it should be pointed out that the legal situation in the United States and Japan is different. It is far easier to organize a union in Japan than in the United States because the proportion of yes votes required for certification among the rank-and-file of an enterprise is lower in Japan than in the United States. Second, as I have demonstrated, union wage pressure is less of a problem to employers under *Shuntō* than it is in the United States where industrial and craft unions vie for members by attempting to outdo each other in securing generous wage increases. In Japan unions compete against each other for members through the relative success of their companies.

With this in mind, consider Table 6.8 which treats the union birth rate as a dependent variable and the average *Shuntō* wage increase rate as an independent variable. (I also experimented with the overall manufacturing wage increase rate in place of the *Shuntō* increase rate.). I report on regressions for the twelve subsectors of manufacturing (out of twenty) for which the coefficients on either the *Shuntō* increase rate or the average manufacturing wage increase rate were statistically significant. Union density and the time dummy are introduced as controls, with the time dummy capturing the influence of the structural shift in the *Shuntō* from a radical to a consensus form. Note first that with the exception of Sector 26 (Chemicals) all the subsectors for which *Shuntō* was important initially had low levels of union density. That is they were sectors in which there was tremendous room for new unionization and one of the main attractions of unionization, was formal entry into the *Shuntō* collective-bargaining process. As the reader can see, for these subsectors the greater the *Shuntō* increase rate the greater the union birth rate. Moreover the time trend variable has a negative coefficient. Why do we get these effects?

First consider the influence of wage increases. The ultimate reason for the rapid growth of wages followed by a much slower growth of wages was the rapid rise in labour productivity followed by a slowing productivity rise after the early 1970s. If labour knew this – and there was extensive discussion of the issue in academic circles and the media – then why did the *Shuntō* increase rate serve as an important organizing tool? First of all,

TABLE 6.8   The *Shuntō* wage increase rate, the overall manufacturing wage increase rate, and the adjusted union birth rate, (new union members freshly organized per 1000 union members): sectors in which wage increase is important for organizing 1962–87 [a]

				Regression							
						One year previous					
Sub-sector number	Rate of labor productivity growth	Union density 1965–70	Dependent variable	Constant	Employment growth rate	Union density	Shuntō wage increase rate	Average manufacturing wage increase rate	Time dummy[b]	Adjusted R^2	Durbin–Watson statistic
38	11.3%	12.6	br	−29.43 (−.71)	.28 (.91)	2.51 (.82)	1.45* (4.66)	n.e.	−9.38*** (−2.14)	.63	2.02
38	11.3	12.6	br	−44.04 (−1.11)	.11 (.41)	3.55 (1.21)	n.e.	1.58* (5.19)	−9.58** (−2.33)	.68	2.01
22	11.1	9.9	br	112.47** (2.80)	−.71 (−.80)	−9.42* (−2.30)	1.16* (2.70)	n.e.	−1.70 (−.20)	.41	2.04
22	11.1	9.9	br	100.75* (2.83)	−.80 (−1.01)	−8.58* (−2.40)	n.e.	1.38* (3.49)	−1.81 (−.23)	.51	2.28
23	11.0	8.6	br	97.18*** (1.93)	.61 (.48)	−8.52 (−1.42)	1.27 (1.47)	n.e.	−3.97 (−.24)	.23	2.36
23	11.0	8.6	br	84.03*** (1.77)	.45(.37)	−7.59 (−1.39)	n.e.	1.66*** (2.00)	−4.21 (−.28)	.30	2.47

TABLE 6.8 *(continued)*

						Regression					
							One year previous				
Sub-sector number	Rate of labor productivity growth	Union density 1966–70	Dependent variable	Constant	Employ-ment growth rate	Union density	Shuntō wage increase rate	Average manufac-turing wage increase rate	Time dummy[b]	Adjusted R^2	Durbin–Watson statistic
25	10.7	29.2	br	33.76 (1.35)	.33 (1.04)	−.85 (−.94)	.31 (1.67)	n.e.	−6.27 (−3.11)	.41	1.64
25	10.7	29.2	br	43.95 (1.68)	.40 (1.28)	−1.25 (−1.31)	n.e.	.42*** (2.00)	−6.14* (−3.15)	.45	1.69
18	10.6	21.2	br	109.06** (3.68)	.59 (1.59)	−4.26* (3.68)	.54** (2.30)	n.e.	−1.72 (−.32)	.68	2.27
18	10.6	21.2	br	103.07* (3.76)	.58 (1.67)	−4.05* (−3.12)	n.e.	.66* (2.89)	−1.64 (−.33)	.72	2.29
20	10.6	36.2	br	15.36 (.98)	.12 (.53)	−.07 (−.14)	.19 (1.22)	n.e.	−11.18* (4.38)	.79	1.76
20	10.6	36.2	br	21.13 (1.39)	.18 (.83)	−.26 (−.57)	n.e.	.30*** (1.80)	−11.58* (−4.82)	.81	1.83

TABLE 6.8 (continued)

| | | | | Regression | | One year previous | | | | | |
Sub-sector number	Rate of labor productivity growth	Union density 1966–70	Dependent variable	Constant	Employ-ment growth rate	Union density	Shuntō wage increase rate	Average manufac-turing wage increase rate	Time dummy[b]	Adjusted R^2	Durbin–Watson statistic
33	10.6	19.1	br	65.88* (1.59)	.17 (.30)	−2.24 (−1.00)	.64** (2.60)	n.e.	−14.16 (1.95)	.74	2.05
33	10.6	19.1	br	60.61 (1.57)	.11 (.19)	−2.07 (−.99)	n.e.	.74* (3.06)	−14.18** (−2.08)	.77	2.20
26	10.4	81.5	br	7.10 (.49)	.05 (.15)	−.02 (−.12)	.27* (3.37)	n.e	−3.60 (−2.42)	.68	2.70
26	10.4	81.5	br	6.95 (.49)	01 (.04)	−.02 (−.13)	n.e.	.29 (3.48)	−3.44** (−2.32)	.61	2.47
35	10.4	50.5	br	55.49* (2.78)	.12 (.45)	−.99** (−2.46)	.94 (3.62)	n.e.	−8.14* (−2.81)	.59	2.03
35	10.4	50.5	br	61.26* (3.68)	.16 (.80)	−1.17* (−3.44)	n.e.	1.17* (5.14)	−7.03* (−2.90)	.72	2.43
24	10.3	32.6	br	−13.32 (−.17)	.36 (.23)	.61 (.26)	.52 (1.69)	n.e.	−5.28 (−1.06)	.15	2.22

TABLE 6.8   (continued)

Regression

| Sub-sector number | Rate of labor productivity growth | Union density 1966–70 | Dependent variable | Constant | Employment growth rate | One year previous | | | Time dummy[b] | Adjusted R^2 | Durbin–Watson statistic |
						Union density	Shuntō wage increase rate	Average manufacturing wage increase rate			
24	10.3	32.6	br	−20.14	.48	.75	n.e.	.69**	−4.29	.24	2.37
				(−.27)	(.33)	(.34)		(2.26)	(−.91)		
29	9.8	12.0	br	−15.46*	−1.78**	2.06	1.08***	n.e.	−9.49	.18	1.76
				(−.43)	(−1.85)	(.74)	(1.86)		(−1.08)		
29	9.8	12.0	br	−10.81	−1.78***	1.77	n.e.	1.00	−9.94	.14	1.83
				(−.29)	(−1.76)	(.62)		(1.54)	(−1.09)		
21	9.3	15.4	br	47.57	−.95	−1.36	4.27*	n.e.	−35.84*	.84	2.11
				(.76)	(−.70)	(−.31)	(6.20)		(−2.90)		
21	9.3	15.4	br	50.82	−.18	−2.09	n.e.	4.56*	−28.04*	.88	2.50
				(.94)	(−.16)	(−.56)		(7.58)	(−2.58)		

Notes:

(a) In the regressions using the *Shuntō* wage increase rate the time period is 1965–85.

(b) Defined as DUM = 0 for 1973 and before 1 for 1974 and later.

like everyone (including my economist colleagues and myself), Japanese workers are not fully rational. They may have been victims of a illusion, perhaps perpetrated by labour union leaders. We cannot rule out this possibility. Second, under the regime of rapid wage increases, younger workers tended to do better than older workers because in many years during the high growth *Shuntō* the wage settlement was stated in absolute increases per worker (all getting the same absolute nominal increment), and it was younger workers who were more prone to take up the initiative to defy management (because they are do not yet receive the firm-pecific social efficiency wage benefits accorded their senior colleagues). Under slow-growth conditions the attraction to younger workers in absolute amount diminished significantly, cooling their enthusiasm for unions. Third, union dues in Japan are high because the unions tend to be enterprise, specific and must pay the wages of their officials out of the pockets of their members (see Shirai, 1983). For this reason the larger is the wage increase the greater is the margin out of wages available for paying dues which hitherto, without the union, had not been required (for instance if the wage increase is 10 per cent and union dues are 3 per cent of wages the worker still takes home a net 7 per cent increase). The ability to pay is a factor. When the increase is small it is harder for organizers to talk the employees of an enterprise into forming a union since the marginal cost of the union relative to incremental income is large.

What about the time trend? As the *Shuntō* evolved ideologically, two important changes occurred: the ideological commitment of being associated with a union was degraded; and the distance between the union and the management narrowed. An idealistic young person wishing to reshape his or her society no longer looks to the union movement for a vehicle for mounting a campaign of reform. Surveys show that workers feel the quality of union organizers has declined. The erosion of an ideological edge to the union movement has probably been the main culprit behind this. And as the movement towards labour–management cooperation developed and *kyōgi kikan* proliferated there were two important consequences. First, the union officials became almost identical to management; indeed the accusation that the union's leadership constitutes a second personnel division for the company is actually seriously entertained in Japan. And second, companies without unions found that introducing *kyōgi kikan* helped stave off unionization; once improved communication between rank and file on the shop floor and the managerial echelons was realized the workers were perfectly content to settle for the status quo. In short, the integrative direction travelled by the *Shunto* has undermined one of its original aims, new union organizing.

6.8 CONCLUSIONS

Has the *Shuntō* been a failure, as Ohta, one of its original architects, claimed, writing at the very moment that the *Shuntō* system stood poised on the threshold of becoming a fully integrative system and a substitute for an incomes policy? In the terms in which Ohta thought about the *Shuntō* during its radical phase, the answer is 'yes'. The large-firm labour contract indeed differentiates between entry-level and senior workers, and then again among senior workers between efficiency-wage and non-efficiency-wage workers, divides workers within and between firms, weakening the ability of unions to wage protracted strikes. The original architects of the *Shuntō* attempted to devise a system of common struggle and coordination to remedy the defect. They were not successful in their endeavour. The secular decline in strike activity is a clear sign of this. Nor has the Shuntō fared well as an organizing tool for the labour movement. If we were to use the results of new union organizing campaigns as a gauge, our answer would again be 'yes'. Declining rates of new union organizing and union density attest to this. Japanese workers have voted on the issue. They have expressed themselves in their attitude towards new union organizing drives. Their vote is clear. As a radical rallying cry for the labour movement the *Shuntō* has failed. Thus in Ohta's own terms the *Shuntō* has indeed died, just as he claimed it had.

But the integrative *Shuntō* system is not a failure if we assess it in terms of its significance for aggregate economic policy. Those scholars like Professor Nitta (cf. Nitta, 1988) who reject Ohta's jaundiced view of the demise of the *Shuntō* point to its continuing ability to generate a consensus wage settlement which promotes further economic growth. There is no doubt about the growth-inducing nature of the *Shuntō*. Indeed, many of my statistical arguments in this chapter have been devoted to establishing this point. The *Shuntō* system coupled with other facets of integrated segmentation tends to promote savings and investment, thereby increasing the drive of the engine of Japanese capitalist growth. But in the high-productivity-growth sectors wage gains have been depressed by the *Shuntō* system. Its very egalitarianism, its integrative force, which to many is a positive aspect of the system, works to generate wage increases towards the lower end of productivity growth rates in the private-sector. This works to protect employment stability, but does so at the expense of wage hikes. In this sense, we can say the system is both a failure and a success: a failure because it mutes wage gains in some areas of the economy, a success because it stabilizes employment. In short the *Shuntō* system has performed wonderfully well as a substitute for national incomes policy:

inflationary pressures are kept in check and employment security is protected, suppressing unemployment. Viewed from this vantage point we would have to say that the creation of the integrative *Shuntō* in the closing decades of the twentieth century, in a society no longer bound together by the integrative cement of Imperial Nationalism, is one of the most remarkable achievements of the Japanese policy and economy.

7 Conclusions

The growth of the Japanese economy over the twentieth century is one of the great success stories of our era. In a country beginning at a relatively low level of per-capita income, per-capita product rose at hitherto unheard-of rates over the seven decades 1900–70. During the duration of a single human lifespan, Japan emerged from a condition of relative economic backwardness to being one of the great economic powers. The key to her ability to achieve rapid growth in income per head was the growth in labour productivity, which, in turn, can be attributed to importing and adapting foreign technology (total factor productivity growth); to capital accumulation per worker; and to improvements in the capacity and willingness of the average worker to give effort and to learn the skills required to implement the new technologies. Ohkawa and Rosovsky (1973) advance the concept of the social capability to import and adapt foreign technology; they argue that Japan's capacity rose during the course of the period 1900–70, generating a tendency towards acceleration in the growth rate of total factor productivity. In my opinion one of the chief ingredients of the social capability to import and adapt technology is the emergence and refinement of integrated segmentation in Japan. Under supply-side segmentation the incentives to secure an advanced technical education were strong, and the allocation of potential workers to firms of various sorts was efficient; under demand-side segmentation workers in large firms received contracts which give them a strong incentive to give effort and to flexibly adapt to new production conditions and to new technologies. Economic integration of small companies and large companies through subcontracting and labour transfer arrangements also contributed to efficiency on the demand side, both because of the potential for sharing technology and for the elimination of redundancies in large companies. Moreover, politically inspired integration narrowed differentials in earnings between sectors utilizing foreign technology and sectors using traditional Japanese techniques, defusing potential social conflict between small, family-run firms and employees of large manufacturing concerns. But integrated segmentation contributed more to the engine of Japanese growth than just bolstering the capacity to import and adapt new technology. As we have seen in this volume it has contributed both to savings and capital accumulation rates and to domestic price stability.

The idea of integrated segmentation is not complicated. On the supply side segmentation occurs because the educational system is centralized,

hierarchical, and specialized. As a result, graduating from a certain institution sends a signal to prospective employers which is quite precise in
terms of the prospective worker's expected effort capacity, costs of training, and time horizons. Segmentation on the demand side involves labour
market contracting: the terms under which training and monitoring occurs
and the nature of the incentives associated with effort and productivity. I
distinguish between three types of firms in this book: small, family-run
firms which restrict their hiring to family members whom they train and
whom they do not fire; small commercially operating firms who have zero
monitoring and firing costs and operate without firm-specific skilling; and
large firms who have high monitoring and firing costs and who operate
with firm-specific skilling. Thus segmentation is sharply demarcated on
both the supply and demand sides. But associated market outcomes are
much less highly differentiated than the contracts imply. For integration is
achieved through a variety of market and non-market mechanisms:
through the overlap between supply segmentation which leads to relative
efficient job matches between employers and employees; through interfirm
movement of workers especially involving small firms; through government market intervention policy and regulation; through subcontracting
and labour transfer arrangements within territorial groups; and through centralization of curriculum in the compulsory component of the educational
system. As a result of integration internal social conflict in Japan, which
might otherwise have emerged under the impetus of growing segmentation
following the era of Meiji balanced growth, has been held in check.

Integrated segmentation did not emerge overnight. Decades were
required before it reached fruition. The origins of the labour contracts
which came to characterize the various types of firms can be found in the
Tokugawa period. For instance the origins of an educational system which
sends signals about effort capacity and training costs can be found in fief
schools attended by the samurai élite; and the origins of an internal firm
training system (which ranks individuals according to effort capacity and
training costs) can be found among merchant houses. Thus as segmentation on the supply and demand sides of the labour market became starkly
drawn with the rapid expansion of heavy industry after 1910, firms were
able to draw upon tradition in developing the types of labour contracts
which would meet their new found needs. But although choices were conditioned by the past, the contemporary reality of extreme heterogeneity in
labour market supply was of much greater import in shaping the development within large heavy-industrial firms of a two-track labour recruitment
system in which white-collar-workers were treated as an élite and
accorded contracts building in age-seniority wages, extensive training and

job security and blue-collar workers were treated the way light industry treated its workers, hiring and firing on a regular basis. Gradually during the interwar period secular evolution on the supply side brought on by the programme of Imperial Nationalism – expansion of the educational system; diffusion of the samurai family ideology; and militarization – changed the nature of labour market signalling for blue-collar workers and made maintenance of a two-track recruitment and training system economically less attractive to large firms in heavy industry. But it was not until the political and institutional reforms of the late 1940s and early 1950s that the 'large-firm labour contract' was fully extended down to the shop floor. It was also during this period that educational opportunities were broadened for groups which hitherto, by dint of sex or family income, had been denied the ability to compete for highly valued labour market signals. And it was also during this period that government price supports for rice and other legislation helped narrow market outcomes associated with segmentation. Hence we can say that during the interwar period segmentation became strongly etched both in terms of disparities in labour market contracts and in terms of outcomes. This segmentation set off social discontent both in the countryside, as evidenced by the increase in landlord–tenant disputes and calls for rice price stabilization, and in large heavy-industrial firms, as evidenced by blue-collar worker demands (voiced both through unions and in other ways) for the muting or dismantling of the two-track recruitment and promotional system, that is for the extension of job ladders down to the shop floor. But before the social discontent could be defused through government intervention and a restructuring of contracts at the firm level, the Pacific war ensued. As an occupied Japan emerged out of the ashes of war devastation, the thrust towards integration begun during the interwar period was rapidly brought to fruition.

Thus integrated segmentation was well established by the mid-to-late 1950s. The basic contract type sharply differentiating firms had come into being, as had most of the integrative government policies which worked to equalize earnings for workers across the segmented markets. But the evolution of the precise institutional rules governing contracts; governing labour market signalling; and governing collective bargaining did not cease. As we have see in Chapters 5 and 6, the with changes in the economic environment and particularly changes in the growth rate of production, the *nenkō/shūshin koyō seido* version of the 'large-firm' labour market contract gave way to the *shokunō shikaku seido/shukkō* form; and the *Shuntō* system of collective bargaining has evolved from political divisiveness towards a more integrative negotiating process. These changes are important, and they testify to the flexibility of the institutional constraints under-girding integrated segmentation in Japan. The viability of integrated segmentation under rapidly evolving economic conditions is testimony to its efficiency in allocating and motivating labour. In short, rather than being a paradoxical curiosity, the fact that the postwar Japanese labour market is simultaneously deeply segmented and deeply integrated is one of the key elements underlying Japan's dramatic emergence as a major economic power during the course of the twentieth century.

Notes

1 THE APPROACH

1. Much of debate in the literature concerning Japanese labor–management practices concerning the relative merits of the 'cultural' versus the 'economic efficiency' position could be resolved if the distinction between efficiency and 'meta' efficiency were properly understood. Efficiency subject to cultural and institutional constraints is consistent with the idea that the constraints are gradually transformed under the force of agents seeking to recast institutional rules in order to increase efficiency in the market. This type of interaction between institutional constraints and optimizing behaviour does not imply that the at any given moment in time the set of institutions are selected so that the population maximizes social welfare subject to a technological constraint. I, for one, whether that such 'meta' efficient choice of rules occurs. On the debate between cultural and efficiency based theories of Japanese labor-management relations, cf. Shirai (1983).

2. The specific analytical models for individual sub-sectors developed here are largely based on the work of other scholars, although no one has to my knowledge developed a theory which integrates the various types of models together as I do here. For the presentation of a welfare-maximizing theory of the family run enterprise see Sen (1966). For the idea of an insider–outsider theory and for the particular version of efficiency wage maximization condition presented in the appendix see Lindbeck and Snower (1988). For a general discussion of efficiency wage theories and their empirical relevance see Katz (1986). The specific way efficiency wage considerations and insider–outsider rent sharing are combined in the model of large-firm labor contracts is my own as is the theory of promotion discussed in this chapter. For other analytical approaches to developing an efficiency based theory of promotion see *inter alia* Lazear and Rosen (1981). For a general discussion of social fairness which undergirds the idea of rent sharing in large firms see Fogarty (1961), Hyman and Brough (1975), and Swenson (1989). On the political economy dimensions of market segmentation in the United States see Edwards *et al.* (1973) and De Freitas (1988). For a recent comparison of divisive industrial conflict in Japan and the United States see Brown *et al.* (1993). For the empirical importance of training in Japan the research of K. Koike is exemplary (see, *inter alia*, Koike, 1983).

2 LABOUR SEGMENTING IN INTERWAR JAPAN

1. On contradictions in the imperial programme of the Japanese government, and for a detailed discussion of its political dimensions, see Gordon (1991).

2. For specific applications of the late-developer concept to Meiji Japan see Rosovsky (1991), Dore (1976), and Cole (1979).

3. For the discussion of prewar education I have heavily relied on Amano (1979), Horimatsu (1959, 1985), Japan. Ministry of Education (1963), Japanese Education Association. World Conference Committee (1938), Karasawa (1955), Kikuchi (1984), Kobayashi (1976), Nihon. Monbushō (1962), Ohkawa (1986) and Taga (1956). For an interesting study of the development of educational institutions from earlier Meiji using local data for a district in Hyogo prefecture see Amano (1991). Amano (1991) focuses on the social meaning of education an in particular on the development of 'credentialism' (*gakurekishugi* in Japanese).

4. See Smith (1986) for an interesting discussion of the careful attention to the efficient use of time in rural Japan.

5. For the 1930's it is possible to use farm household budgets drawn from the *Noka keizai chōsa hōkoku* (Reports of the Survey of Agricultura Economy) based on a sample size of approximately 300 households to exactly gauge the change in labour input in terms of hour worked. Mosk (1993) does this and finds that over the course of the 1930's hours worked actually declined in most groups of household (classified by farm size and tenancy status). For some of the farm size/tenancy groups this decline is attributable to a shift towards females and away from males, since females worked less hours than males, but this is not always the case. For a discussion of other aspects of this issue see the ensuing text.

    It is important to keep in mind that by the interwar period most agricultural households were generating a substantial portion of their income from sidelines (between 10 to 20 per cent of total household income depending on the size and tenancy group; large landholders tended to generate relatively little sideline income and small tenants a relatively large amount). In effect by the interwar period farm households were quite diversified in their activities, reducing overall risk in their complete portfolio of income-generating activities by dividing their capital and labour investments (including skill acquisition) between an increasingly diverse set of opportunities. For details including productivity comparisons between sideline and non-sideline activities cf. Mosk (1993).

6. I agree with Minami and Ono that the flow of agricultural workers out of the villages into manufacturing fluctuated with the demand for industrial workers and was not determined by fluctuating demographic supply conditions *per se*. That is, I reject Namaki's thesis that the relative unavailability of land in rural areas automatically forced second and third sons to leave villages and take up factory work (cf. Minami, 1986: 287–90). Basically I feel workers responded to job opportunities and took up urban industrial employment when and only when jobs were available; cf. Ohkawa and Rosovsky (1973) for a well-worked-out 'job opportunity' model of the Japanese labour market.

7. On the stagnation of interwar agricultural growth see Minami (1986: 66–70), and Hayami (1975). For a discussion of some of the controversy surrounding the stagnation issue cf. Brandt (1993) and Mosk (1993).

8. I am grateful to Professor Yasuba Yasukichi for emphasizing this point to me. For his views which are opposed to the surplus labour thesis espoused

by Minami (see *inter alia* Minami, 1986, Minami and Makino, 1986, Minami and Ono, 1978, 1981, and 1986); see Yasuba (197b). Also see Brandt (1993) for a rejection of the labour surplus thesis for prewar Japanese agriculture.

9. The estimates of textile and agricultural wages which I use throughout this chapter are contract money wages, and exclude extra *teate* payments (for instance payments for transportation costs) and non-pecuniary benefits such as free or subsidized boarding services and the like (these non-pecuniary benefits are known as *makanai* in Japanese). Data from which *makanai* estimates can be made are too scanty to yield adjusted time-series figures for light manufacturing and agricultural wages, in my opinion, and therefore I restrict my analysis to wages excluding non-pecuniary amenities. For scattered estimates of *makanai* see Kidd (undated) and Tsurumi (1990). I am grateful to participants in the Economic Development Seminar at Hitotsubashi University's Economic Research Institute and especially to Konosuke Odaka for pointing this out to me.

10. The textile industry experimented with a variety of specific wage schemes depending on the skill levels required. In silk reeling, before technical advances in the 1930's reduced the demands on the dexterity of the girls' fingers, skill differentials were substantial and girls were graded according to their skill level, and this ranking was used in distributing wages. For instance some of the silk-reeling firms employed relative wage classification schemes, which were designed around the measurement of throughput in terms of quality and quantity for each individual worker, with the evaluation used to place workers into relative productivity classes (Tsurumi, 1990: 76–7).

11. Saxonhouse (1976) uses data on data on wages by tenure of employment in his analysis of textile workers. Since most workers left the industry after a few years of work, those who accumulated long years of seniority were relatively rare. It is quite likely that they stayed precisely because they their inherent talents gave them a comparative advantage in acquiring skills which rendered them unusually productive (and were rewarded in accordance with their exceptional productivity). This raises the issue of sample selection bias: those who stayed in firms were unusual by dint of native ability or attitudes towards factory work or because of their social situation (for instance because their marriage prospects were poor).

12. For details concerning the gradual decline in the Tokugawa merchant style system of recruitment and promotion, and the growing dominance of the system based on hiring from higher educational institutions see Daito (1993). On the trend towards increasing promotion of managers to the highest levels of companies, that is onto the ranks of the boards of directors, see Morikawa (1989, 1991). Morikawa is not alone in pointing out there is an important switch after 1900 from the company run largely by owners and stockholders to companies run mainly by salaried managers. In the Japanese literature companies run by salaried managers are usually called *keieisha kigyō* (managerial companies). On the importance of specific American techniques concerning engine maintenance and the production of rolling stock in the railroad industry for productivity growth after nationalization in 1906 see Daito (1989). On labour turnover for managers in a

food-processing company see Fruin (1978). Morikawa (1989) notes that many of the managers who were successfully promoted to high rank had backgrounds in engineering. Nakagawa (1989) argues that Japan's late-developer status necessarily promoted an emphasis on book learning and the capacity to absorb and apply existing technical knowledge from early Meiji on.

13. I am grateful to members of the Economic Development Seminar at Hitotsubashi University's Economic Research Institute, and especially to Professor Minami Ryoshin, for suggesting that I incorporate capital stock growth into my estimates of the growth of demand for engineers and scientists.

14. Odaka (1984) does analyse a detailed data set for Mitsubishi Shipbuilding over most of the prewar period. However it is not clear how typical of heavy industry Mitsubishi Shipbuilding was. After all it was one of the great *zaibatsu* complexes.

3   CONTINUITY AND DISCONTINUITY

1. On the importance of importing foreign technology for growth in Japanese labor and total factor (combined labor and capital) productivity see Kosai (1986), Lincoln (1988), Nakamura (1981) and Ohkawa and Rosovsky (1973). Ohkawa and Rosovsky offer an interesting version of the continuity thesis. Basically they view Japanese economic development from 1900 to 1970 as a continuous process dominated by investment-driven trend acceleration and facilitated by the creation and refinement of the social capability of importing and adapting foreign technology. However, they view the period 1938–52 as an aberration; an abnormal period outside the general historical growth path of the Japanese economy. As should be clear from my account in this chapter I do not share this view of the war and postwar Occupation period.

2. For my account of the SCAP reforms I especially rely on Garon (1987), Kosai (1986), Moore (1983), Nakamura (1981), and Sumiya (1974b).

3. On the prewar proposals for legislation see Garon (1987) and Nishinarita (1987). Many of the bureaucrats who staffed the newly created Ministry of Labour had worked in the Home Ministry before the war. Their detailed and sophisticated knowledge of Western labor legislation went a long way to convince the GII SCAP that they could be trusted to draft the details of the new legislation largely on their own.

4. Of lesser significance were the three laws of 1947 concerning unemployment: the Employment Stability Act, the Unemployment Insurance Act, and the Unemployment Allowance Act. These laws have proven to be less important because unemployment rates have been low throughout the postwar period.

5. On strikes and production control during the 1945–50 period see Farley (1950), Fujita (1974), and Moore (1983). The Japanese Supreme Court outlawed production control in a 1950 decision, although as a practical matter this had little impact since the incidence of production control declined rapidly over the period 1946–7 and virtually disappeared by 1948.

6. For this discussion of the *Densan* settlement I rely on Gordon (1985: 349 ff.) and Fujita (1974: 326 ff.).

7. Ohkawa and Rosovsky (1973) convincingly argue that during the twentieth-century period of catching up with the West, that is during the seven decades between 1900 and 1970, investment demand growth, was the driving force behind income growth, and export demand growth was the passive factor. That is economic growth was not 'export-led' but rather 'investment-driven' during this phase. However after the Oil Crisis of 1973–4 increments to export demand appear to be have been extremely important for generating increments to total national income; cf. Lincoln (1988).

8. It is interesting to speculate whether the terms of the large-firm labour contract promoted a particular type of technological and organizational progress in Japan. For instance, it could be argued that since firing is costly employers are especially eager to reduce the costs of monitoring workers, thereby justifying the firing of low-productivity workers to the workers who are not fired. Along these lines it can be argued that 'just-in-time' inventory practices, as exemplified by the famous *kanban* (flag) system employed by Toyota motors, reduces monitoring costs because if a division produces defects it will almost instantaneously be discovered by the other divisions using the guilty division's output as an input. Part of management's motivation for introducing *kanban* type practices was to raise the incentives of hard work under the rules of the social efficiency wage exchange. This argument suggests that technological progress is not completely independent from the system of labor–management relations. For a general argument along these lines see Lazonik (1990).

9. For the discussion of the oil crisis and the Nixon shocks I rely on Blumenthal (1987), Kosai (1986), Lincoln (1988). Blumenthal (1987) argues that the recession was really a depression and lasted five years, from 1973 until 1977.

4 EDUCATION AND LABOUR SEGMENTATION IN THE ACTIVE LABOUR MARKET

1. Amano (1979: 23ff.) argues that on the eve of the Pacific War there was a consensus among educational reformers that the distinction between the *senmongakkō* and the university (*daigaku*) should be eliminated, and all of the institutions of higher learning integrated into a system of three- and four-year universities that would take graduates from the secondary schools. In light of this it is not surprising that the Japanese educational community promoted a reform of the higher educational system under the Occupation which precisely implemented this plan: the *senmongakkō* were turned into universities, and entrance to universities was opened up to all graduates of the secondary school sector.

2. For the views of a staunch defender of the liberal arts view of eduction for Japan see Nagai (1971). A journalist, Nagai was Minister of Education for a period. Nagai is a critic of the notion that the labor markets and educational markets should be tightly intertwined, at least as the labor markets have

operated throughout the postwar era. Nagai represents an important human-istically oriented community in Japan, which sees the obsession with economic productivity as debasing the meaning and function of education.

3. The annual publication of detailed model wage tables giving wages by educational level, sex, age, seniority and firm size, provides a wealth of information with which individuals can make informed choices (see Chapter 5 for a discussion of model wage tables). Even if individual students are not aware of the detailed tables (or find it conceptually difficult to fully grasp the implications of the numbers), school counsellors are, and they advise students. In this sense the school system as a institutionalized set of organizations directs the student population in a manner which mimics individual rational decision making-behaviour, despite the fact that individual students may be ill-informed about or uninterested in labor market conditions.

One problem with the plausible idea that individuals or their counsellors form expectations of wage profiles, however, involves the practical question of whether these expectations are secured from the cross-sectional model wage table information (or the various annual wage censuses from which the model wage tables are drawn) or from cohort data. Nakata and Mosk (1987) report on experiments which they did in empirically estimating demand functions of higher education in Japan in which they alternately used cross-sectional rates of return or cohort rates of return in specifying demand. They found that specifications employing the cross-sectional rates of return performed far better than those utilizing cohort rates of return. This is plausible since the model wage tables are widely used in Japan and are based on cross-sectional data alone. Of course it is possible that individuals may mix together cross-sectional and cohort data in forming a picture of forgone earnings, although how they would actually achieve this in practice is a matter of pure speculation.

4. As for the benefits conferred by education in the case of women (or of men for that matter) solely concerned about the marriage market and not the labor market it should be noted that pure narrow economic considerations may be as important as social returns. For finding a spouse among the ranks of high-status university students enhances one's chances of enjoying the ample family income which a graduate of a high-status school is likely to reap once he enters the labor market.

That educational attainment has become an important vehicle for social status differentiation in Japan is apparent from a variety of pieces of evidence, but especially from the competitiveness of mothers regarding the academic achievement of their children (the term '*kyōiku mama*' is com-monly applied to these women who go to incredible lengths to see that their charges excel in the schools). All of this is tied up with the social reproduc-tion costs of the household head: Japanese parents are especially concerned about their children performance in the school system and the subsequent career path they manage to negotiate because it reflects on the future of the ie they are associated with. For this reason, as income per-capita has risen parents have found themselves with a greater capacity to expend substantial sums of money for *juku* (cram schools aimed at improving performance on school entrance examinations) which children attend during the hours they are not in regular schools. As the labor market has increasingly become dominated by white-collar workers as opposed to farmers and blue-collar employees, the proportion of parents concerned with ensuring that their offspring perform well in school has expanded and hence so has the per-capita demand for *juku*.

One consequence of the expansion of the *juku* system is a stifling of inter-generational social mobility, for parents in the lower socioeconomic brackets find it difficult to raise the kind of funding for *juku* schooling that the better-off socioeconomic classes can muster. This fact has been widely documented in the literature because Ministry of Education surveys have enquired about the occupational standing of students' parents for some time now. Rohlen (1983: 138) shows a strong drift toward increased concentration of the higher socioeconomic groups in university entrants over the period 1961–74 (also see Yonekawa, 1992). However, Kikuchi (1984) warns that some of the documented drift towards class differentiation may be a byproduct of the type of data used for the analysis. He compares results based on income statistics from the Ministry of Education survey on university and college student life with those based on the Prime Minister's Statistical Office survey of family income and expenditure, and finds significant discrepancies between the two sets of findings.

That Japanese families hope to either reduplicate their social status in the next generation (or see it increase) is intimately tied up with the issue of the planning period over which parents and children develop a strategy for school advancement. In my model, decisions are assumed to be made in the year prior to advancement. But it is likely that in higher socioeconomic groups the decision about sending children on to higher education is made many years before, perhaps when the children are in infancy. How can we reconcile this with the short-term planning model I develop in this chapter? My view is that the short-term model is designed to capture the behaviour of marginal investors, and not that of those committed to a long-term strategy. That marginal investment matters is apparent from the rapidity of change in demand for higher education in postwar Japan, for if average investors committed to a long-term strategy dominated incremental behaviour in the time-series then we would expect change to be slow and steady and to not exhibit year-to-year fluctuations, since the slow shift towards a white-collar labor force would account for most of the change over time. The proof of the cooking is in the taste. The results secured in this chapter strongly support the marginal-investor hypothesis as *an explanation for trends and fluctuations over time.*

5.   For a careful discussion of the rate of return concept and an examination of some of the problems encountered in estimating rates of return (including the differences between rates of return adjusted for hours worked and those unadjusted for hours worked) see Eckaus (1973).

Estimates for private and national universities such as those made by Nakata and Mosk (1987) provide useful information because they show private (as opposed to social) rates of return are generally lower in the private university sector in comparison to the national and public sectors, but must be treated with caution. For one thing they do not take into account *rōnin* periods (see the discussion of *rōnin* in Chapter 2 and below in this chapter) nor do they take into account quality of school environment in so far as it contributes to consumption benefits.

6. Japanese schools use a standard grade distribution curve to grade students. Thus a bright student in a very bright class might only get mediocre grades; but if placed in a less competitive class environment might well perform at the very top of the class. Thus to use class scores only would be perceived of as 'unfair' in the sense that it violates the idea of equal opportunity in competing for scarce slots further up the hierarchy of the school system.

7. As noted in the text the programs in the *teijisei*, and in the industrial and commercial high schools or commercial and industrial tracks of regular high schools having such tracks tend be very practical in orientation, focusing on developing the skills useful for working in a factory or office environment. For example my study of the course offerings in technical industrial schools [data from Nihon Monbushō Daijin Kanbō Tōkeika (1967)] convinced me that the Japanese government provides the basic training for many industrial and office workers at public expense: courses in machine design, machine mechanics, automobile machine operation and design, etc. abound. For examples of more recent (mid to late 1980s) curricula in technical and commercial high schools see Dore and Sako (1989): pp. 37–47.

5 COMPETITION AND COOPERATION: WAGE PROFILES, JOB RETENTION, AND DUALISM

1. This chapter draws heavily on the published work of Yoshi-fumi Nakata, especially upon Nakata (1990), and upon Nakata's unpublished doctoral dissertation (Nakata, 1987). I am grateful to Professor Nakata for his comments upon the material appearing in this chapter.

2. For a model of subsector junior/senior worker and wage ratios derived from different principles but containing some of the features of that given in equations (5.1) and (5.2) see Nakata (1987).

3. Befitting the fact that the analysis is pitched at the aggregate level and is not explicitly linked to issues of seniority, the model developed in Mosk and Nakata (1985) is quite different from the one developed in this chapter. For references to the general literature on Japanese age-wage profiles see Mosk and Nakata (1985) and Shimada (1981).

4   The sample of firms covered by the annual wage census (at present entitled either *Chingin Sensasu* or *Chingin kōzō kihon chōsa* – Basic Survey of Wage Structure) depends on whether the publication is for internal government use and for free distribution or is for sale to the general public. This makes it difficult to estimate retention rates for sub-sectors covered in the census, since the reliability of the estimate is questionable, especially in the case of smaller sub-sectors of manufacturing. For the wage census sample as a whole the retention rate estimated is reasonably reliable and so I employ it here.

5. There are many different possible ways to calculate wage profiles from the Japanese data given in the wage census and in other sources. From the wage census in most years one can get figures on scheduled (monthly) wages

which exclude overtime pay and the biannual bonus payments (see Chapter 6 on the bonus); on total (monthly) contract earnings including overtime pay; and on total hours worked, broken into scheduled and overtime hours. In some years and for some types of data one can also secure figures on bonus payments (although it is not possible to get the bonus data in the detail which would be required to generate the tabulations presented in Tables 5.3 to 5.5 inclusive of the bonus). Thus in principle one can work with profiles either with or without the bonus, with or without overtime, on an hourly or on a total monthly basis, etc. In fact, differences between the age-wage profiles and senior–junior wage ratios according to these various approaches are not very great. In most of what follows I use monthly contract earnings including overtime but excluding the bonus. In Mosk and Nakata (1985) there is discussion of a comparison of the profiles from hourly, wages but the difference between profiles computed from hourly and from monthly figures is not large, and so most of my computations avoid this extra computational step. Consider, for instance, the following 1988 figures on scheduled, overtime and total hours worked for males in the various prime working ages:

Age	Scheduled hours	Overtime hours	Total hours
20–24	180	25	205
25–29	179	24	203
30–34	201	22	201
35–39	179	20	199
40–44	179	18	197
45–49	179	17	196
50-54	180	16	196
55-59	181	15	196

As can be seen, profiles calculated on a hourly basis would be slightly steeper than those calculated on a monthly basis, but the difference would not be substantial. However in comparing wages between company size groups (cf. Table 5.7) it is useful to adjust for hours worked, since workers in small companies tend to work considerably longer hours than those in large companies. As for the bonus, in most companies the bonus is calculated as a multiple of the base wage, the multiple being the same for everyone except the for the fresh inductee who gets a lower multiple. Thus we doubt whether profiles would look significantly different with or without the bonus. However, for comparisons between firm size-groups the bonus rate varies, being higher in larger companies and lower in small companies, and therefore in Table 5.7 I present tabulations from figures inclusive of the bonus.

6. I use figures for 1961 rather than 1960, because the 1960 wage census does not generally differentiate between age and seniority in its published tabulations, making it unusable for our purposes. See Nakata (1987) for details.

7.   For Japan the figures are for 1955–9, 1960–4 and 1965–9.
8.   See Ohkawa and Rosovsky (1973) for a job availability hypothesis which links the degree of dualism to the capacity of the modern-technology-using industrial sector to absorb labour.

6   COLLECTIVE BARGAINING AND CAPITAL ACCUMULATION

1.   Almost all large firms (1000 employees or over) are unionized, although there are prominent exceptions. Taira and Levine (1985: 279) give figures on unionization rates for firms of 500 employees or more in 1972 and 1980: the figures are 63.6 per cent and 62 per cent respectively. Since the larger the firm the higher the probability of unionization, it is widely accepted that the unionization rates for firms with 1,000 workers or over are very high.
2.   Even within the expanded *Rengō* (unified labor front) of the early 1990s (see panel A of Chart 6.1) the former national centres like Sōhyō continue to maintain factions and to continue to press for their ideological interests.
3.   White union shop agreements are common, the 'perfect union' shop agreement which stipulates that the employer dismiss an employee eligible for union membership if he or she quits the union is uncommon in Japan.
4.   Employees at or above the level of section chief (*kachō*) or assistant section chief are usually excluded from membership in the union. This is partly due to Occupation-inspired legislation. During the late 1940s the SCAP general headquarters became extremely concerned about the presence and active participation in union affairs of higher-level management personnel whose commitment to an independent union stance was questionable at best. The Occupation authorities first tried education, and then resorted to legal coercion, working through the Central Labour Relations Commission, in order to get higher-level managers removed from the ranks of the union.
5.   That the *Shuntō* is an ongoing affair with continuous informal discussions between management and the union taking place is indicated by the chronological table giving the timing of various *Shuntō* related activities for the 1981 *Shuntō* in the *Zenkoku Kinzoku* federation. See Tokyo Toritsu rōdō kenkyūjō (1983).
6.   Japanese enterprise union members only possess ownership rights in their unions as long as they are members of the firm to which the union is attached. This state of affairs, in which the concept of an individual's rights in one's company takes precedence over his or her rights in the union, can be usefully contrasted to the situation in North America and England in which an individual can have ownership rights in the union whether or not he or she possesses any employee rights in a firm.
7.   Nihon. Rōdōshō (1974: 16ff.) gives interesting data on the extent to which collective bargaining involves negotiations over minimum wage levels for specific age and sex categories. The surveys carried out in the early 1970s reveal that about three-quarters of the negotiations included discussions on minimum wage levels for younger workers, and about 60 per cent for older workers, but that only a small proportion of the negotiations were sex-blind. In most cases, especially for older workers, the incidence of negotiations

concerning minimum wage levels for *males* was high, but the incidence of negotiations for *females* was low. This accords with my notion that the application of labor market contracting reflects social attitudes about sexual typing in the family system with the locus of financial responsibilities assumed to fall on the shoulders of the male household head.

8. For this reason the battle over introduction of *shokumu* and/or *shokunō shikaku seido* wage systems between Sōhyō and Nikkeiren was bitter, since in principle the weight given to age and seniority declines with the introduction of *shokumu* and/or *shokunō shikaku seido* systems. On the debates cf. Ishida (1990), especially chapter 2.

9. As a founder of the radical, strike-oriented *Shuntō* system, Ohta is a staunch advocate of confrontational tactics. Hence it is not surprising to find him rejecting the consensus integrative *Shuntō* which was emerging under the leadership of accommodating leaders during the early 1970s. His book (Ohta, 1975) is a bitter attack on the integrative strategy adopted by the younger leaders of the labor movement and in particular of the IMF-JC.

10. Professor Y. Ohkusa of the Institute of Social and Economic Research at Osaka University has indicated to me that many unions engage in slow-downs rather than strikes, and that these slowdowns are not included in the official data on work days lost to strike activity. In effect a slow-down or a union decision to 'work to rule' amounts to a reduction in effort levels supplied by the union members.

11. Shirai (1974): 273–4 gives a concrete example of the process I describe here. For other examples of collective bargaining in the private sector, and for an analysis of wage spillover from one industry to another, see Ishida (1976) and Sano *et al.* (1969). For a discussion of information sharing between unions and management and its implications for the incidence of industrial disputes see Morishima (1991).

12. In this section I refer to the bonus as the adjustment mechanism, but in fact there are many more components of the remuneration package which management can and does use to compensate workers above and beyond the wage bill increases negotiated in the *Shuntō* settlements. For instance, firms can and do offer better amenities including more luxurious company housing, more extensive medical care programs, nicer resort facilities, cleaner and safer shop-floor settings. Moreover they can and do offer higher overtime rates and extensive overtime work opportunities. Thus many analysts refer to the officially recorded wage increases (officially recorded in newspaper and media reports and including in the *Rōdō Undōshi* data which I analyze in Section 6.5 of this chapter) as 'made-up' numbers, which do not fully reflect the full benefit package agreed to. I do not dispute this. Indeed I agree that the firms which are more profitable do partially compensate their employees through firm-specific benefits above those enjoyed by other firms in the same industry both in the form of the bonus and in the form of in-kind rewards. But the point is that this compensation is in general incomplete, in the sense that it does not fully dissipate the higher profits per worker that accrue to the owners of the more successful firms. Moreover the existence of ever increasing amounts of extra firm-specific benefits per worker works to enhance future worker effort in the company, and to create greater potential for divisions amongst union members. For discussion of

special secret clauses governing overtime work payments and related issues which go beyond the officially announced settlements in the case of some unions within the steel industry see Koshiro (1983a, 1983e).

13. In reference to the debate between those who argue that unions are fundamentally economic entities and those who argue that the goals of unions are primarily political (as typified by the 1950s debate between J. Dunlop, who favoured a narrow economic interpretation, and A. Ross, who argued for a political model) I take an intermediate position, although I lean more heavily toward Dunlop than the Ross position.

    Shirai (1983b: 220–1) directly links the standing and leverage of a union within the union movement to its ability to retain a cohesive internal structure, a large membership, and a satisfactory record of dealing with management. For instance, he notes that the electrical power union Densan lost its leadership position in the labor movement when it split into two rival factions in 1952; and that Tanrō, the coal miners' union, found its status seriously deflated when the Miike Coal Mine Union, one of its largest affiliates, lost in the 1959–60 strike.

14. It is interesting that the union which has most aggressively organized supermarket workers and other service sector employees is Zensen Dōmei, which is based in textiles, a sector which has suffered from massive declines in employment over the last fifteen years. For details see *inter alia* Nakamura *et al.* (1988).

15. Since the average worker in a unionized large firm expects to stay with the firm until retirement, it is reasonable to suppose that the average worker utility in equation (6.1) is the discounted present value of expected future welfare states taken over a time horizon determined by the age of the presently employed union membership and the compulsory retirement age. If we conceive of equation (6.1) in this way we actually increase the importance of job security as represented by the L variable. I am grateful to Professor Y. Ohkusa for this suggestion.

16. For example the union is active in discussing the contracting terms under which *shukkō* takes place, and in determining who gets transferred and why. See Chapter 5 for a discussion of both *shukkō* and *haichi tenkan* redeployment of forces.

17. A 1977 Ministry of Labor survey (*Rōdō Daijin Kanbō Tōkei Johobu*, 1977) concerning labor–management joint consultation committees (termed *kyogi kikan* in the report) reveals some interesting facts about the committees. First, unionized firms were more likely to have the committees than non-unionized firms; second, larger amongst non-unionized firms smaller firms were generally more likely to have the committees than larger firms in the areas of rationalization and redeployment of forces, but in most other areas large firms were more likely to have the committees than small firms. In that year there were committees set up to deal with the following issues: basic managerial direction of the firm; production–sales planning; company organization and reorganization; rationalization; *haichi tenkan*; temporary release time; personnel adjustment and dismissal; hours of work and vacation time; work-floor safety and hygiene; and the retirement system. It is interesting to note that in the event of worker discontent, younger workers were more likely to report their grievances directly to a supervisor rather

than going through a formal grievance management committee or the union, while older workers were more likely to work through the committee or the union. This suggests younger workers are more willing to be individually associated with their complaints. Whether it also means older workers are more fearful of retaliation is an open question.

18. The wage bill data and productivity data were secured from the *Kōgyō Tōkei Hyō* (Census of Manufactures) of the Ministry of International Trade and Industry. In order to construct a consistent time series I restricted myself to figures for firms with thirty workers or more.

19. Figures on overtime work and bonus payments are taken from M. Kume (1988).

20. I am grateful to Professor T. Tsuru of the Institute of Economic Research at Hitotsubashi University for suggesting to me the idea of using individual wage increase data from the *Rōdō Undō shi* to test my model and to Professor K. Koike of Hosei University for steering me to the *Tōyō keizai Bessatsu* for profitability measures. Finally I wish to thank Professor Y. Sano of Keio University for advising me about some of the pitfalls of using profits-per-worker data to estimate profitability. The problem with the worker data for individual firms is that the figures usually given in the tables reported by the Ministry of Finance are for *seishaiin*, a subclass of the group of regular workers (usually called *jōyō rōdōsha* in official reports). Professor Sano emphasized to me that in some companies *seishaiin* may not constitute much more than 50 per cent of the company's actual employees, since many workers who actually work at company A are listed on the roles of separate dispatching companies B, C,.etc. In short the upshot of my discussion with Professor Sano was my decision to use a simpler measure of profitability other than profits per worker, and that is why I use the *Tōyō Keizai Bessatsu* indices of profitability in this section.

    There are actually more than 147 unions for which there is data in the 1985 *Rōdō Undō Shi*. I had to reject some of the data because I could not find a match for the union data in the *Tōyō keizai Bessatsu*; and in the case of some tiny federations with two unions or less I lacked sufficient number of observations to make a meaningful calculation of the variables I use in Tables 6.6.

21. A number of studies show that wage increases for unionized medium-sized and small firms exceed increases for non-unionized medium-sized and small firms (cf. Nakamura *et al.*, 1988); Nihon Rōdōshō, 1974). But these studies do not control for productivity gain in the firms analyzed. On medium-sized and small firm unions in the Tokyo ares cf. Tokyo Toritsu Rōdō Kenkyūjō (1983, 1984, 1986).

22. See the citations in Note 21 and Nihon. Rōdō Daijin Kanbō Seisaku Chōsabu (1986) for documentation concerning these effects.

Bibliography

Amano, I. (1979) 'Continuity and Change in the Structure of Japanese Higher Education,' in Cummings, Amano, and Kitamura (eds): pp. 10–39.

Amano, I. (1983) '*Senzenki no setsubi ninka gyōsei*' ('The Prewar Administration of Accreditation'), in I. Amagi (ed.), *Daigaku no Setsubi kijun no kenkyū* Research on University Accreditation (Tokyo: Tokyo Daigaku Shuppankai): pp. 79–122.

Amano, I. (1991) *Gakureki shugi no shakaishi: Tanba Sasayama ni miru kindai kyōiku to seikatsu sekai* (Tokyo: Yushinto Kobunsha).

Aoki, M. (1984) *The Co-operative Game Theory of the Firm* (Oxford: Oxford University Press).

Aoki, M. (1988) *Information, Incentives, and Bargaining in the Japanese Economy* (Cambridge: Cambridge University Press).

Blumenthal, T. (1987) 'Depressions in Japan: the 1930s and the 1970s,' in R. Dore and R. Sinha (eds) *Japan and World Depression, Then and Now: Essays in Memory of E. F. Penrose* (Basingstoke: Macmillan).

Bowman, M. (1981) (With the collaboration of H. Ikeda and Y. Tomoda) *Educational Choice and Labor Markets in Japan* (Chicago: Chicago University Press).

Brandt, L. (1993) 'Interwar Japanese Agriculture: Revisionist Views on the Impact of the Colonial Rice Policy and the Labor-Surplus Hypothesis,' *Explorations in Economic History*, vol. 30, no. 3: pp. 259–93.

Brown, C., M. Reich, D. Stern and L. Ulman (1993) 'Conflict and Cooperation in Labor–Management Relations in Japan and the United States,' IRRA 45th Annual Proceedings: 426–36.

Brunello, G. (1988) 'Transfers of Employees between Japanese Manufacturing Enterprises: Some Results from an Enquiry on a Small Sample of Large Firms,' *British Journal of Industrial Relations*, vol. 26, no. 1: pp. 119–32.

Clark, R. (1979) *The Japanese Company* (New Haven: Yale University Press).

Cole, R. (1979) *Work, Mobility and Participation: A Comparative Study of American and Japanese Industry* (Berkeley: University of California Press).

Cook, A. (1966) *Japanese Trade Unionism* (Ithaca: Cornell University School of Industrial and Labor Relations).

Cummings, W. (1980) *Education and Equality in Japan* (Princeton: Princeton University Press).

Cummings, W., I. Amano and K. Kitamura (eds) (1979) *Changes in the Japanese University: A Comparative Perspective* (New York: Praeger).

Cusumano, M. (1985) *The Japanese Automobile Industy: Technology and Management at Nissan and Toyota* (Cambridge, Mass.: Harvard University Press).

Daito, E. (1989) 'Railways and Scientific Management in Japan, 1907–30,' *Business History*, vol. 31, no. 1: pp. 1–28.

Daito, E. (1993) 'Business and Education in Historical Perspective: The Interwar Years in Japan,' in N. Kawabe and E. Daito (eds) *Education and Training in the Development of Modern Corporations* (Tokyo: University of Tokyo Press).

DeFreitas, G. (1988) 'Hispanic Immigration and Labor Market Segmentation,' *Industrial Relations*, vol. 27, no. 2: pp. 195–213.

Dore, R. (1965) *Education in Tokugawa Japan* (Berkeley: University of California Press).

Dore, R. (1976) *The Diploma Disease: Education, Qualification, and Development* (Berkeley: University of California Press).

Dore, R. and M. Sako (1989) *How the Japanese Learn to Work* (Routledge: London and New York).

Dunlop, J. (1950) *Wage Determination Under Trade Unions* (New York: Augustus M. Kelley).

Eckaus, R. (1973) *Estimating the Returns to Education* (Berkeley: Carnegie Foundation for the Advancement of Teaching).

Edwards, R., M. Reich and D. M. Gordon (eds) (1973) *Labor Market Segmentation* (Lexington, Mass.: Heath).

Embree, J. (1939) *Suye Mura: A Japanese Village* (Chicago: University of Chicago Press).

Farley, M. (1950) *Aspects of Japan's Labor Problems* (New York: John Day).

Fogarty, M. (1961) *The Just Wage* (London: Geoffrey Chapman).

Freeman, R. (1971) *The Market for College-Trained Manpower: A Study in the Economics of Career Choice* (Cambridge, Mass.: Harvard University Press).

Freeman, R. and M. E. Rebick (1989) 'Crumbling Pillar? Declining Union Density in Japan,' *Journal of the Japanese and International Economies*, vol. 3, no. 4: pp. 578–605.

Fruin, W. M. (1978) 'The Japanese Company Controversy: Ideology and Organization in a Historical Perspective,' *The Journal of Japanese Studies*, vol. 4, no. 2: 267–300.

Fruin, W. M. (1983) Kikkoman: *Company, Clan and Community* (Cambridge, Mass.: Harvard University Press).

Fujino, S. (1986) *Daigaku kyōiku* to *rōdō kikō* (College Education and the Market Mechanism) (Tokyo: Iwanami Shoten).

Fujino, S., S. Fujino and A. Ono (1979) *Textiles* (Tokyo: Toyo Keizai Shinposha).

Fujita, W. (1974) 'Labor Disputes,' in Okochi, Karsh and Levine (eds): pp. 309–60.

Garon, S. (1987) *The State and Labor in Modern Japan* (Berkeley: University of California Press).

General Headquarters. Supreme Commander for the Allied Powers. Cival Information and Education Section. Education Division (1952) *Postwar Developments in Japanese Education* (Tokyo: General Headquarters).

Gerschenkron, A. (1966) *Economic Backwardness in Historical Perspective: A Book of Essays* (Cambridge, Mass.: Harvard University Press).

Gerschenkron, A. (1968) *Continuity in History and Other Essays* (Cambridge, Mass.: Harvard University Press).

Gluck, C. (1985) *Japan's Modern Myths: Ideology in the Late Meiji Period* (Princeton: Princeton University Press).

Gordon, A. (1985) *The Evolution of Labor Relations in Japan: Heavy Industry, 1853–1955* (Cambridge, Mass.: Harvard University Press).

Gordon, A. (1991) Labor and Imperial Democracy in Prewar Japan (Berkeley: University of California Press).

Hanami, T. (1988) 'Unfair Labor Practices: Law and Practice,' in Japan Institute of Labor (ed.): pp. 127–130.

Harada, S. (1928) *Labor Relations in Japan* (New York: AMS Press 1968 reprint of original 1928 Columbia University Press edition).

Hayami, Y., with M. Akino, M. Shintani and S. Yamada (1975) *A Century of Agricultural Growth in Japan: Its Relevance to Asian Development* (Minneapolis: University of Minnesota Press).

Hirschmeier, J. and T. Yui (1975) *The Development of Japanese Business, 1600–1973* (Cambridge, Mass.: Harvard University Press).

Horimatsu, B. (1959) *Nihon kindai kyōkushi – Meiji no kokka to kyōiku* (Modern Japanese Educational History – Nation and Education in Meiji) (Tokyo: Risosha).

Horimatsu, B. (1985) *Nihon Kyoikushi* (Japanese Educational History) (Tokyo: Kotokusha)

Hyman, R. and I. Brough (1975) *Social Values and Industrial Relations: A Study of Fairness and Equality* (Oxford: Basil Blackwell).

Ichikawa, S. (1979) 'Finance of Higher Education,' in Cummings, Amano and Kitamura (1979): pp. 40–63.

Inagami, T. (1983) 'Extension of Mandatory Retirement Age and Changes in Personnel Management,' in Japan Institute of Labour (1988): pp. 28–32.

Inagami, T. (1988) 'Labor Front Unification and Zenmin Rokyo: the Emergence of Neocorporatism,' in Japan Institute of Labour (1988): pp. 82–5.

International Labour Office (1933) *Industrial Labour in Japan* (Geneva: International Labour Office).

Irokawa, D. (1985) *The Culture of the Meiji Period* (Princeton: Princeton University Press) (translation edited by M. Jansen).

Ishida, H. (1976) *Nihon no rōshi kankei to chingin kettei* (Japanese Labor–Management Relations and Wage Determination) (Tokyo: Toyo Keizai Shinposha).

Ishida, M. (1985) '*Chingin taikei to rōshi kankei – Nihon no jōken*' Wage System and Labor Management Relations – Conditions in Japan' (parts 1 and 2), *Nihon Rōdō Kyōkai Zasshi*: pp. 3–14, 39–49.

Ishida, M. (1990) *Chingin no shakaikagaku – Nihon to Igirisu* (Tokyo: Chuo Keizai Sha).

Japan. Institute of Labour (various years and dates) *Japan Labor Bulletin* (Tokyo: Japan Institute of Labour).

Japan. Institute of Labour (ed) (1983) *Highlights in Japanese Industrial Relations* (Tokyo: Japan Institute of Labour).

Japan. Institute of Labour (ed) (1988) *Highlights in Japanese Industrial Relations*, vol. 2 (Tokyo: Japan Institute of Labour).

Japan. Ministry of Education (1963) *Japan's Growth and Education* (Tokyo: Ministry of Education).

Japan. Ministry of Health and Welfare. Institute of Population Problems (1968) *Standardized Vital Rates by Urban and Rural Areas for All Japan, 1920–1965* (Tokyo: Ministry of Health and Welfare).

Japan. Ministry of International Trade and Industry (various years) *Census of Manufactures* (Tokyo; Ministry of International Trade and Industry).

Japan. Ministry of Labour. Minister's Secretariat (1986) *Yearbook of Labour Statistics, 1985* (Tokyo: Ministry of Labour).

Japan. Prime Minister's Office (various years) *Statistical Yearbook* (Tokyo: Prime Minister's Office).

Japan. Prime Minister's Office. Bureau of Statistics (various years) *Employment Status Survey* (Tokyo: Prime Minister's Office).

Japan. Statistical Association (1987) *Historical Statistics of Japan*, vol. 1 (Tokyo: Japan Statistical Association).

Japan. Statistical Association (1988) *Historical Statistics of Japan*, vol. 5 (Tokyo: Japan Statistical Association).

Japanese Education Association. World Conference Committee (1938) *Education in Japan*, vol. 2 (Tokyo: Japanese Educational Association).

Johnson, C. (1982) *MITI and the Japanese Miracle: The Growth of Industrial Policy, 1925–1975* (Stanford: Stanford University Press).

Kaibara, E. (1905) *The Greater Learning of Women* (London: John Murray).

Karasawa, T. (1955) *Gakusei no rekishi: Gakusei seikatsu no shakaiteki kōsatsu* (History of Students: Sociological Investigation of Student Life) (Tokyo: Sobunsha).

Karsh, B. and S. Levine (1972) 'The Concept of a National Industrial Relations System.' in Okochi, Karsh and Levine (eds): pp. 3–14.

Kato, H. (1984) '*Shūdan shushoku* ("Group Job Search"),' in Economisto, *Shogen: Kōdō seichōki no Nihon* (Attestation: Japan during the High Growth Era) (Tokyo: Mainichi Shinposha).

Katz, L. (1986) 'Efficiency Wage Theories: A Partial Evaluation,' *NBER Macroeconomic Annual, 1986* (Cambridge, Mass.: MIT Press).

Kawada, H. (1972) 'Workers and Their Organizations,' in Okochi, Karsh, and Levine (eds): pp. 217–67.

Kawada, H. and R. Komatsu (1973) 'Post-War Labor Movements in Japan,' in A. Sturmthal and J. B. Scoville (eds) *The International Labor Movement in Transition: Essays on Africa, Asia, Europe, and South America* (Urbana: University of Illinois Press).

Kidd, Y. (undated) 'Women Workers in the Japanese Cotton Mills: 1880–1920,' paper for China–Japan Program, Cornell University, Ithaca, New York.

Kikuchi, J. (1984) 'The Emergence and Development of a National Educational System in Modern Japan,' *Osaka Studies in Sociology of Education*, vol. 5: pp. 1–17.

Kirihara, S. (1960) 'Education Within Industry in Japan,' *Reports of the Institute for Science of Labor*, no. 56: pp. 32–47.

Kitamura, K. (1977) '*Sengo no gakusei kaikaku to secchi ninka gyōsei*' ('Postwar Reform of the Educational System and the Administration of Accreditation') in I. Amagi and T. Keii (eds) *Daigaku secchi kijun no kenkyū* (Research on University Accreditation Standards) (Tokyo: Tokyo Daigaku Shuppankai): pp. 102–22.

Kiyokawa, Y. (1988) '*Gijutsu chishiki o yusuru kantokushaso no keisei to shijo no tekioka – Nihon seishigyō ni oite gakkōde kyofu no hatashita yakuwari*' ('The Creation of a Supervisor Strata Having Technical Knowledge and Adaptation to the Market – The Role Played by School Graduate Female Instructors in the Japanese Silk-Weaving Industry'), *Shakai Keizai Shigaku*, vol. 54, no. 3: pp. 309–341.

Kiyokawa, Y. (1991) 'The Transformation of Young Rural Women into Disciplined Labor Under Competition-Oriented Management: The Experience of the Silk-Reeling Industry in Japan,' *Hitotsubashi Journal of Economics*, vol. 32, no. 2: pp. 49–69.

Koike, K. (1983) 'Workers in Small Firms and Women in Industry,' in Shirai (1983): pp. 89–115.

Kobayashi, T. (1976) *Society, Schools and Progress in Japan* (Oxford: Pergamon).

Kosai, Y. (1986) *The Era of High-Speed Growth* (Translated by J. Kaminski) (Tokyo: University of Tokyo Press).

Koshiro, K. (1983a) 'Development of Collective Bargaining in Postwar Japan,' in Shirai (ed): pp. 205–59.

Koshiro, K. (1983b) 'Labor Relations in Public Enterprises,' in Shirai (ed): pp. 259–94.

Koshiro, K. (1983c) 'Analysis of the 1982 Spring Offensive: More Attention Paid to Stabilization of Industrial Relations,' in Japan Institute of Labour (ed): pp. 36–9.

Koshiro, K. (1983d) 'Political Power of Labor Unions in the Diet: Analysis of Results for Simultaneous Elections for both Upper and Lower Houses Held in June 1980,' in Japan Institute of Labour (ed): pp. 54–6.

Koshiro, K. (1983e) 'The Arbitration and Wage Settlement Process in Japan,' in K. Hancock, Y. Sano, B. Chapman, and P. Fayle (eds), *Japanese and Australian Labour Markets: A Comparative Study* (Canberra and Tokyo: Australia–Japan Research Center).

Koshiro, K. (1991) 'Shitetsu boonasu no hendo bunseki' ('Analysis of Fluctuating Bonuses for Private Railway Workers'), *Nihon Rodo Kenkyu Zasshi*, vol. 33, no. 1 (January): pp. 14–25.

Kume, M. (1988) *Chingin chōki keiretsu 50 Nen* (Long-Term Wages Over 50 Years) (Tokyo: Sangyorodo Chosajo Sangyorodo).

Kuznets, S. (1966) *Modern Economic Growth: Rate, Structure and Spread* (New Haven: Yale University Press).

Kuznets, S. (1971) *Economic Growth of Nations: Total Output and Production Structure* (Cambridge, Mass: Harvard University Press).

Large, S. (1972) *The Rise of Labor in Japan: The Yuaikai, 1912–19* (Tokyo: Sophia University Press).

Large, S. (1981) *Organized Workers and Socialist Politics in Interwar Japan* (Cambridge: Cambridge University Press).

Lazear, E. P. and S. Rosen (1981) 'Rank-order Tournaments as Optimum Labor Contracts,' *Journal of Political Economy*, vol. 89: pp. 841–64.

Lazonik, W. (1990) *Competitive Advantage on the Shop Floor* (Cambridge, Mass.: Harvard University Press).

Leupp, G. (1992) *Servants, Shophands, and Laborers in the Cities of Tokugawa Japan* (Princeton: Princeton University Press).

Lincoln, E. (1988) *Japan: Facing Economic Maturity* (Washington, DC: Brookings Institution).

Lindbeck, A. and D. J. Snower (1988) *The Insider–Outsider Theory of Employment and Unemployment* (Cambridge, Mass.: MIT Press).

Lockwood, W. (1968) *The Economic Development of Japan* (Princeton: Princeton University Press).

Lynn, R. (1988) *Education Achievement in Japan: Lessons for the West* (Princeton: Princeton University Press).

Martin, D. (1990) *An Ownership Theory of the Trade Union* (Berkeley: University of California Press).

Matsuda, Kenji (1985) *Chingin seido jitsureishū* (A Collection of Actual Examples of Wage Systems) (Tokyo: Sangyo Rodo Chosajo).

McMahon, W. and A. Wagner (1981) 'Expected Returns to Investment in Higher Education,' *Journal of Human Resources*, vol. XVI, no. 2: pp. 274–82.

Minami, R. (1965) *Railroads and Public Utilities* (Tokyo: Toyo Keizai Shinposha).

Minami, R. (1980) 'Mechanical Power in the Industrialization of Japan: a Case Study of the Spinning Industry,' *Hitotsubashi Journal of Economics*, vol. 21, no. 1: pp. 15–26.

Minami, R. (1986) *The Economic Development of Japan* (Basingstoke: Macmillan).

Minami, R. (1987) *Power Revolution in the Industrialization of Japan: 1885–1940* (Tokyo: Kinokuniya Co. Ltd).

Minami, R. and F. Makino (1986) 'Choice of Technology: a Case Study of the Japanese Cotton Weaving Industry 1902–1938,' in *Hitotsubashi Journal of Economics*, vol. 27, no. 2: pp. 111–132.

Minami, R. and A. Ono (1978) 'Bunpairitsu no susei to hendo' ('Trends and Change in the Income Distribution Rate'), *Keizai Kenkyu*, vol. 29, no. 3: 230–42.

Minami, R. and A. Ono (1981) 'Behavior of Income Shares in a Labor Surplus Economy: Japan's Experience,' *Economic Development and Cultural Change*, vol. 29, no. 2: 309–24.

Minami, R. and A. Ono (1986) 'Income Distribution of Prewar Japan: a Case Study of Yamaguchi Prefecture,' Hitotsubashi University. The Institute of Economic Research, Discussion Paper Series no. 145.

Mitsufuji, T. (1971) 'Industrial Relations in the Public Sector in Japan,' in A. Cook, S. Levine, and T. Mitsufuji (eds), *Public Employee Labor Relations in Japan: Three Aspects* (Ann Arbor: Institute of Labor and Industrial Relations): pp. 3–28.

Moore, J. (1983) *Japanese Workers and the Struggle for Power 1945–1947* (Madison: University of Wisconsin Press).

Morikawa, H. (1989) 'The Increasing Power of Salaried Managers in Japan's Large Corporations,' in W. Wray (ed), *Managing Industrial Enterprise: Cases from Japan's Prewar Experience* (Cambridge, Mass: Harvard University Press).

Morikawa, H. (1991) 'Naze keieisha *kigyo* ga hatten suru no ka?' ('Why Did the Managerial Enterprise Develop?'), in H. Morikawa (ed), *Keieisha kigyō no jidai* (The Age of Managerial Enterprise) (Kyoto: Yuhaikan).

Morishima, M. (1991) 'Information Sharing and Firm Performance in Japan,' *Industrial Relations*, Vol. 30, no. 1: 37–61.

Mosk, C. (1983) *Patriarchy and Fertility: Japan and Sweden, 1880–1960* (New York: Academic Press).

Mosk, C. (1993) 'Efficiency Wage Productivity Gain: The Japanese Farm Household During the Interwar Period,' Working Paper no. 93–06, Department of Economics, University of Victoria.

Mosk, C. and Y. Nakata (1985) 'The Age-Wage Profile and Structural Change in the Japanese Labor Market for Males, 1964–1982,' *Journal of Human Resources*, vol. 20, no. 1: pp. 100–16.

Nagai, M. (1971) *Higher Education in Japan: Its Take-off and Crash* (Tokyo: University of Tokyo Press).

Nakagawa, K. (1989) 'The "Learning Industrial Revolution" and Business Management,' in T. Yui and K. Nakagawa (eds), *Japanese Management in Historical Perspective* (Tokyo: University of Tokyo Press).

Nakane, C. (1970) *Japanese Society* (Berkeley: University of California Press).

Nakamura, D., H. Sato and T. Kamiya (1988) *Rōdō kumiai wa hontō ni yaku ni tatte iru no ka* (Are Labor Unions Really Meeting Needs?) (Tokyo: Sogo Rodo Kenkyujo).

Nakamura, T. (1981) *The Postwar Japanese Economy: Its Development and Structure* (translated by J. Kaminski) (Tokyo: University of Tokyo Press).

Nakamura, T. (1983) *Economic Growth in Prewar Japan* (New Haven: Yale University Press).

Nakata, Y. (1987) *An Analysis of Age-Seniority Wage Profiles: A Case Study of the Japanese Nenko Wage System* (unpublished doctoral dissertation, University of California at Berkeley)

Nakata, Y. (1990) 'Nichibei shūgyō jōtai no anteisei ni kansuru kōsatsu – kōyokankei no anteisei ni taisuru koyōseido no motsu kōka o chūshin ni –' (Comparative Analysis of Employment Stability: The United States and Japan with Special Attention to the Role of the Employment System in Employment Stability –', *Hyōron Shakaikaguku*, no. 40: pp. 35–81.

Nakata, Y. and C. Mosk (1987) 'The Demand for College Education in Postwar Japan,' *Journal of Human Resources*, vol. 20, no. 3: 377–404.

Napier, R. (1972) *The Labor Market and Structural Change in Postwar Japanese Development* (Harvard College: Unpublished Honors Thesis).

Nichols, T. (1976) *Workers Divided* (Glasgow: Fontana/Collings).

Nihon. Monbushō (Japan: Ministry of Education) (1962) *Nihon no seichō to kyōiku – kyōiku no hakkai to keizai no hattatsu* (Japan's Growth and Education – Development of Education and Economic Progress) (Tokyo: Ministry of Education).

Nihon. Monbushō. *Daijin Kanbō Chōsa Tōkeika Tokeika* (Japan. Ministry of Education. Minister's Secretariat. Statistical Survey Section) (various years) *Gakkō kihon chōsa hōkoku* (Report of the Basic Survey of Education).

Nihon. Monbushō. Daijin Kanbō Tōkeika (Japan. Ministry of Education. Minister's Secretariat. Statistical Section) (1967) *Kōtō gakkō kyōiku katei jicchi jōkyō chōsa hokōkushō* (Report on the Survey of Actual Conditions in the Course Offerings in High School Education) (Tokyo: Ministry of Education.)

Nihon. Monbushō. Daijin Kanbō Tōkeika (Ministry of Education. Minister's Secretariat. Statistical Section (1970a and 1970b) *chūgakkō sotsugyōsha* no *shinro jōkyō ni kansuru chosa hōkokushō – Showa 43 nen* (1970a) (Report of the Survey Concerning the Path Selected by Middle School Graduates – 1968) (Tokyo: Ministry of Education); and *Kōtōgakkō sotsugyō no* shinro *jōkyō ni* kansuru chōsa *hōkokushō – Showa 43 nen* (1970b) (Report of the Survey Concerning the Path Selected by High School Graduates – 1968) (Tokyo: Ministry of Education).

Nihon. Rōdōshō (Japan. Ministry of Labour) (1974) *Shuntō chinginage no jittai* (The Actual Conditions Surrounding Spring Offensive Wage Increases) (Tokyo: *Rōdōshō*).

Nihon. Rōdō Daijin Kanbō Tokeijōhōbu (Japan. Statistical Information Department of the Labour Minister's Secretariat) (various years) *Chingin kōzō kikoh chōsa* (Basic Survey of Wage Structure) (Tokyo: Ministry of Labour).

Nihon. Rōdō Daijin Kanbō Tōkeijōhōbu (Japan. Statistical Information Department of the Labour Minister's Secretariat) (1977) *Rōshi comyunkeeshon chōsa hōkoku* (Report of the Survey on Labour Management Communication) (Tokyo: *Rōdōshō*).

Nihon. Rōdō Daijin Kanbō Seisaku Chōsabu (Japan. Ministry of Labour. Policy and Survey Department of the Minister's Secretariat) (various years) *Rōdō kumiai kihon chōsa* (Basic Survey of Labour Unions) (Tokyo: *Rōdōshō*).

Nihon. Rōdō Daijin Kanbō Seisaku Chōsabu (Japan. Statistical Survey Department of the Ministry of Labour Minister's Secretariat) (1986) *Nihon no Rōdōkumiai no genjō* (II) – *Rōdōkumiai katsudōra jittai chōsa hōkoku* (Conditions of Japanese Labor Unions (II) – Report of the Survey on Actual Labour Union Activities) (Tokyo: *Rōdōsho*).

Nihon. Sōmuchō Tōkeikyoku (Japan. Prime Minister's Secretariat. Statistical Office) 1984 *Kyōiku kara mita Nihon no jinkō, Showa 55 Nen Kokusei Chōsa Monografuseirtsu no. 7* (Japan's Population Seen From an Educational Viewpoint, 1980 Census Monograph no. 7). (Tokyo: Prime Minister's Secretariat).

Nishinarita, Y. (1987) '*Ryodaisenkan rōdōkumiai hōan no shiteki kōsatsu*' (Historical Investigation of Legislative Proposals Concerning Labor Unions During the Interwar Period), *Hitotsubashi Daigaku Kenyū Nenpō, Keizai Kenkyū*, 28: 49–132.

Nitta, M. (1988) 'Birth of *Rengō* and Reformation of Labor Organization,' in Japan Institute of Labour (ed): pp. 86–89.

North, D. (1990) Institutions, Institutional Change and Economic Performance (Cambridge: Cambridge University Press).

Odaka, K. (1984) *Rōdō Shijō Bunseki: Nijū Kōzō no Nihonteki Tenkan* (Labor Market Analysis: Japanese Development of a Dualistic Development Structure) (Tokyo: Iwanami Shoten).

Ogura, T. (1967) *Agricultural Development in Modern Japan* (Tokyo: Fuji Publishing Co.).

Ohkawa, K. (1986) 'School Education in Modern Japan: Economic Evaluation and Possible Relevance to Contemporary Less Developed Countries' (Tokyo: International Development Center of Japan).

Ohkawa, K. and H. Rosovsky (1973) *Japanese Economic Growth: Trend Acceleration in the Twentieth Century* (Stanford: Stanford University Press).

Ohkawa, K. and M. Shinohara (eds) (1979) *Patterns of Japanese Economic Development: A Quantitative Appraisal* (New Haven: Yale University Press).

Ohta, K. (1975) *Shuntō no shuen: Teiseichōka no rōdō undō* (The Demise of the Shunto: the Labor Market Under Slow Economic Growth) (Tokyo: Chuo Keizaisha).

Okochi, K. (1958) *Labor in Modern Japan* (Tokyo: The University of Tokyo. Division of Social Sciences).

Okochi, K., B. Karsh and S. Levine (eds) *Workers and Employers in Japan* (Princeton: Princeton University Press).

Organisation for Economic Co-operation and Development. Directorate for Scientific Affairs (1973) *Educational Policy and Planning* (Paris: OECD).

Pempel, T. (1978) *Patterns of Japanese Policymaking: Experiences from Higher Education* (Boulder, Colo.: Westview).

Reder, M. (1984) 'Strike Cost and Wage Rates: Cross-Industry Differences,' in J.-J. Rosa (ed), *The Economics of Trade Unions: New Directions* (Kluwer: Nijhoff Publishing Co.): pp. 27–37.

Rohlen, T. (1977) 'Is Education Becoming Less Egalitarian? Notes on High School Stratification and Reform,' *Journal of Japanese Studies*, vol. 3, no. 1: pp. 37–70.

Rohlen, T. (1983) *Japan's High Schools* (Berkeley: University of California Press).

Rosovsky, H. (1961) *Capital Formation in Japan, 1868–1940* (New York).

Rumberger, R. (1981) *Overeducation in the US Labor Market* (New York: Praeger Scientific).

Saito, O. (1987) *Shōka no sekai-uradana no sekai – Edo to Osaka no hikaku toshishi* (Merchant World – Slum World – Comparative Urban History of Edo and Osaka) (Tokyo: Libro).

Sangyō Rōdō Chōsajo (various years) *Chingin Jitsumu* (The Practical Business of Wages) (Tokyo: Sangyō Rōdō Chōsajo).

Sano, Y. (1977) '*Sangyōbetsu Shunki chinagegaku no kettei yōin,*' ('Factors Determining the Increase Rate of Spring Offensive Wages'), in S. Ujihara, H. Matsu, and H. Yoshimura (eds), *Kōza: Gendai Nihon no Chingin 1* (Lecture Series: Contemporary Wages 1) (Tokyo: Shakaishishosha): pp. 281–313.

Sano, Y., K. Koike and H. Ishida (1969) *Chingin kōshō no kōdōkagaku no kodokagaku – Chingin hakyu no shikumi* (Behavioral Science of Wage Determination: the Mechanism of Wage Spill-Over) (Tokyo: Toyo Keizai Shinposha).

Saxonhouse, G. (1976) 'Country Girls and Communication Among Competitors in the Japanese Cotton-Spinning Industry,' in H. Patrik (ed) *Japanese Industrialization and Ita Social Consequences* (Berkeley and Los Angeles: University of California Press): pp. 97–125.

Sen, A. (1966) 'Peasants and Dualism With or Without Surplus Labor,' *Journal of Political Economy*, 74: 425–50.

Shimada, H. (1981) *Earnings Structure and Human Investment: a Comparison Between the United States and Japan* (Tokyo: Kogadusha).

Shimada, H. (1988) 'Trade Frictions and Industrial Relations,' in Japan Institute of Labour (1988): pp. 59–62.

Shindo, T. (1961) *Labor in the Japanese Cotton Industry* (Tokyo: Society for the Promotion of Science).

Shinohara, M. (1972) *Mining and Manufacturing* (Tokyo: Toyo Keizai Shinposha).

Shirai, T. (1974) 'Collective Bargaining,' in Okochi, Karsh and Levine (eds): pp. 269–308.

Shirai, T. (ed) (1983a) *Contemporary Industrial Relations in Japan* (Madison: University of Wisconsin Press).

Shirai, T. (1983b) 'A Theory of Enterprise Unionism,' in Shirai (ed): pp. 117–44.

Shirai, T. and H. Shimada (1978) 'Labor in the Twentieth Century,' in J. Dunlop and W. Galenson (eds.), *Labor in the Twentieth Century* (New York: Academic Press).

Smethurst, R. J. (1974) *A Social Basis for Prewar Japanese Militarism* (Berkeley: University of California Press).

Smith, R. (1983) 'Making Village Women into 'Good Wives and Wise Mothers' in Prewar Japan,' *Journal of Family History*, Vol. 8: no. 1: 70–84.

Smith, R. and E. L. Wiswell (1982) *The Women of Suye Mura* (Chicago: University of Chicago Press).

Smith, T. C. (1984) 'The Right to Benevolence: Dignity and Japanese Workers, 1890–1920,' *Comparative Studies in Society and History*, vol. 26, no. 4: 587–613.

Smith, T. C. (1986) 'Peasant Time and Factory Time in Japan,' *Past and Present*, no. 111: 165–97.

Sugeno, K. (1988) 'The Coexistence of Rival Unions in Undertakings and Unfair Labor Practices,' in Japan Institute of Labour (ed): pp. 131–6.

Sugeno, K. (1989) 'Shukko (Transfers to Related Firms): an Aspect of the Changing Labor Market in Japan,' vol. 28, no. 4 (April): 3–8.

Sumiya, M. (1974a) 'The Emergence of Modern Japan,' in Okochi, Karsh, and Levine (eds): pp. 15–48.

Sumiya, M. (1974b) 'Contemporary Arrangements: an Overview,' in Okochi, Karsh, and Levine (eds): pp. 49–88.

Sumiya, M. (1981) 'The Japanese System of Industrial Relations,' in P. Doeringer (ed), *Industrial Relations in International Perspective* (Basingstoke: Macmillan).

Suzuki, Y. (1985) 'The Formation of Management Structure in Japanese Industrials, 1920–40,' *Business History*, vol. 27, no. 3: 259–78.

Swenson, P. (1989) *Fair Shares: Unions, Pay, and Politics in Sweden and West Germany* (Ithaca: Cornell University Press).

Taga, A. (1956) *Kindai Nihon kyōikushi* (Educational History of Modern Japan) (Tokyo: Iwasaki Shoten).

Taira, K. (1970) *Economic Development and the Labor Market in Japan* (New York: Columbia University Press).

Taira, K. (1983) 'Japan's Low Unemployment: Economic Miracle or Statistical Artifact?,' *Monthly Labor Review*, Vol. 106, no. 7: 59–72.

Taira, K. and S. Levine (1985) 'Japan's Industrial Relations: a Social Compact Emerges,' in Industrial Relations Research Association, *Industrial Relations in a Decade of Economic Change* (Madison: Industrial Relations Research Association).

Takahashi, A. (1992) 'Changing the Concept of Employment Policy,' in *Japan Labor Bulletin*, vol. 31, 6 (June): 5–8.

Takahashi, T. (1972) 'Social Security of Workers,' in Okochi, Karsh, and Levine (eds): pp. 441–84.

Takisawa, K. (1981) *Shokunō shikaku seido sekkei no jissai to keii – shikaku seido no tsukurikata to shokaku shiken unyo no jimu* (Actual Practices and Particulars of the Design of a Functional Status System – the Methods of Creating a Status System and the Business of Applying Promotional Examinations) (Tokyo: *Sangyō Rōdō Chōsajo*).

Tokyo Toritsu Rōdō Kenkyujō (Tokyo Prefecture Labor Research Institute) (1983) *Chūshō kigyō bunya ni okeru sangyōbetsu rōdōkumiai – soshiki to katsudō* (Industrial Labor Unions in Medium and Small Sized Enterprises – Organization and Activities) (Tokyo: Tokyo Toritsu *Rōdō Kenkyūjō*).

Tokyo Toritsu Rōdō Kenkyujō (Tokyo Prefecture Labor Research Institute) (1984) *Chūshō kigyō ni okeru rōshi funsho no kenkyū* (Research on Labor Management Disputes Occurring in Medium and Small Sized Companies) (Tokyo: Tokyo Toritsu *Rōdō Kenkyūjō*).

Tokyo Toritsu Rōdō Kenkyūjō (Tokyo Prefecture Labor Research Institute) (1986) *Daisanji sangyō ni okeru rōdōkumiai no kessei* (Organization of Labor Unions in the Tertiary Sector) (Tokyo: Tokyo Toritsu *Rōdō Kenkyūjō*).

Toyo Keizai Shinposha (1991) *Showa Kokusei Sōran* (Showa Censuses Overview) (Tokyo: Toyo Keizai Shinposha).

Tsurumi, E. P. (1990) *Factory Girls: Women in the Thread Mills of Meiji Japan* (Princeton: Princeton University Press).

Uchibara, S. (1968) '*Kyōiku to Rōdōshijo*' ('Education and the Labor Market'), in *Kyōikugaku Zenshū* (Collected Works on the Education Field), vol. 14 (Tokyo: Shogakukan): pp. 158–67.

Umemura, M. (1980) 'The Seniority-Wage System in Japan,' in S. Nishikawa (ed), *The Labor Market in Japan: Selected Readings* (Tokyo: University of Tokyo Press): pp. 177–87.

Umemura, M., K. Akasaka, R. Minami, N. Takamatsu, K. Arai and S. Itoh (1988) *Manpower* (Tokyo: Toyo Keizai Shinposha).

Waswo, A. (1977) *Japanese Landlords: The Decline of a Rural Elite* (Berkeley: University of California Press).

Watanabe, A. (1988) 'Outline of Government and Ministerial Ordinances for Implementing the Employee Dispatching Business Law,' in Japan Institute of Labour (1988): 124–26.

Yamamura, K. (1974) *A Study of Samurai Income and Entrepreneurship: Quantitative Analysis of Economic and Social Aspects of the Samurai in Tokugawa and Meiji Japan* (Cambridge, Mass. Harvard University Press).

Yasuba, Y. (1976) 'The Evolution of Dualistic Wage Structure,' in H. Patrick (ed), *Japanese Industrialization and Its Social Consequences* (Berkeley: University of California Press): 249–98.

Yasuba, Y. (1994) 'Natural Resources in Japanese Economic History, 1800–1940,' paper presented to the Meetings of the Cliometrics Association, Boston, Massachusetts, January.

Yonekawa, H. (1992) 'Educational Expansion and Equality of Educational Opportunity in Japan: Inequalities in Educational Development?', paper presented at the CEDAR International Conference on Accountability and Control in Educational Settings, University of Warwick, April 10–12.

Yoshimura, I. (1988) 'Leading Actors Promoting Labor Front Unification,' in Japan Institute of Labour (1988): pp. 77–81.

Index